INSIDE
SECRETS
TO
VENTURE
CAPITAL

INSIDE SECRETS TO VENTURE CAPITAL

BRIAN E. HILL
and
DEE POWER

JOHN WILEY & SONS, INC.
New York • Chichester • Weinheim • Brisbane • Singapore • Toronto

Library of Congress Cataloging-in-Publication Data:

Hill, Brian E. (Brian Edward), 1955–
    Inside Secrets to venture capital / Brian E. Hill and Dee Power.
      p. cm.
    Includes index.
    ISBN 0-471-41406-9 (alk. paper)
    1. Venture capital. I. Power, Dee. II. Title.
HG4751 .H55 2001
332'.04154—dc21   00-065286

Acknowledgments

The authors wish to thank the more than 250 venture capital firms that participated in our surveys over the last three years. And special thanks to the many members of the venture capital community who have provided their detailed insights through answering our questions by e-mail or taking the time to allow us to interview them. We believe this reflects the sincere desire on the part of the venture capitalists to provide entrepreneurs with the information they need to be successful in raising capital.

We had extremely valuable input from a number of service providers specializing in assisting early-stage ventures. We wish to thank them as well.

And dozens of entrepreneurs contributed their views, experiences, and frustrations, which gave this book a more complete picture of the real world of seeking venture capital than it otherwise could have had.

Contents

x   Contents

Preface

Venture Capital: Make No Mystique About It

Every business needs capital.

Investors need to place their money where it can earn substantial returns.

We would think that these two basic facts would bring entrepreneurs and venture capitalists (VCs) together, but in fact a wide gulf separates the two groups. The entrepreneurial road is a tough one, full of setbacks and unforeseen perils, with substantial likelihood of disappointment. Frequently entrepreneurs go into the process of finding capital completely unprepared for what awaits them. The world of the venture capitalist seems foreign to the entrepreneur, even hostile. The terminology venture capitalists use sometimes doesn't even make sense: burn rate, highly scaleable, domain experience.

How venture capitalists make their investment decisions remains a mystery. It is as if a thick, dark velvet curtain exists between the investor and the entrepreneur; the entrepreneur is left with a definite feeling of being on the outside looking in.

Why is the venture capital raising process such a mystery? There is no shortage of advice for entrepreneurs. Business magazines have begun to cover this subject more and more. But the advice usually addresses one particular aspect of the capital-raising process, such as "Ten Secrets for Finding Investors," or "Fifteen Ways Investors Can Cheat You." Magazines seem to think we all love lists.

We have seen quite a bit of misinformation being given to entrepreneurs by self-styled experts. We have attended numerous meetings of business networking organizations where a speaker got up and said: "I know the VCs and here's what they want." In many instances, this turns out to mean the speaker may have acquaintance with half a dozen or so venture capitalists or have been involved in a few transactions. Out of this type of limited experience can be born a host of incorrect generalizations.

Entrepreneurs have an enormous thirst for information that will guide them toward successfully raising money. For the past 15 years we have owned and operated a consulting firm that assists small and mid-size companies with business planning and with strategies for finding capital. In the course of that work, advising companies ranging from a salsa manufacturer in southern Arizona to a real estate developer in Eastern Europe, we have been asked literally hundreds of questions by entrepreneurs looking for capital. The questions fall into these categories:

- Can I get capital for my company?
- How can I get capital for my company?
- From whom can I get capital?

Entrepreneurs worry that:

- It will take them too long to find capital and their business will suffer as a result.
- They will not receive fair value in the transaction (a polite way of saying they will be ripped off by venture capitalists).
- Their business will be taken over by the venture capitalists.
- They won't get capital at all and their company will not be able to grow and will certainly fall behind competitors who have found the keys to the magic venture capital kingdom.

We believe it is possible to bridge this gulf between entrepreneur and investor. Believing that the best way to find out what venture capitalists really think was to ask them, in early 1998 we initiated, through our consulting company, Profit Dynamics Inc., an annual Venture Capital Survey. We collected key statistics about the activity level of venture capitalists, their deal size, and so on, that would be of interest to entrepreneurs. More than 250 venture capital firms have participated in these surveys over the last three years, including some of the largest in the world, as well as smaller funds with a regional focus. The firms that took part in the survey have made investments in thousands of companies.

The surveys also asked more qualitative questions, about how venture capitalists go about finding companies, making investment decisions, and about the trends or changes in the venture capital industry that have come about because of the Internet or the vast amount of capital formation in the United States during the enormous stock market rallies of the last few years.

And we set out to construct this book so that it would include as much as possible the actual words of the venture capitalists themselves. Some were interviewed, and you will see their names and firm names sprinkled throughout this book; others provided opinions for our surveys on a confidential basis and did not wish to be identified by name. We wanted to get as wide a range of opinions as possible. The candid comments of venture capitalists appear throughout this book.

You will find hundreds of tips, pieces of advice, pitfalls to avoid—even words of encouragement from venture capitalists. Input from hundreds of partners in VC firms are included in these pages, the result of three years of information gathering.

You will also see comments and opinions from hundreds of entrepreneurs who have gone about raising capital and from service providers who assist entrepreneurs. Entrepreneurs feel a definite undercurrent of frustration, even hostility, toward venture capitalists. Entrepreneurs often feel as if the venture capital industry conspires to make the process of finding capital as difficult for them as possible.

We also have presented a series of "Deal Tales," stories from our experience with entrepreneurs looking for capital. All of the anecdotes about entrepreneurs we present in this book really happened, proving once again that truth is stranger than fiction.

For their part, venture capitalists express displeasure with the lack of preparation of entrepreneurs, who often approach VCs before their company, their strategy, or their management team is ready.

We hope that when they finish reading this book, entrepreneurs will have a better understanding of how venture capitalists think, and VCs and angel investors will have a better understanding of the concerns and frustrations—and aspirations—of the entrepreneur.

If there is one theme we seek to emphasize, it would be: There is no such thing as "the VCs" or "the angels," as some sort of homogenous class. Investors are individuals with unique perspectives and business philosophies. A lot of commonly held generalizations about how investors seek out companies and make their investment decisions turn out to be incorrect, as you will see.

Think of this book as a panel discussion between several hundred investors and entrepreneurs, exploring their differences and seeking common ground. Fortunately, everyone doesn't talk at once.

We hope this book remedies to some degree the on-the-outside-looking-in problem entrepreneurs face and simplifies the process of finding funding, showing them that the funding of start-up companies is not so much, a chaotic world after all. This knowledge should help entrepreneurs be more confident when knocking on venture capitalists' doors.

Best of luck.

CHAPTER

1

What Is Venture Capital?

Venture capital investing is all about a willingness to accept a high degree of risk in order to obtain the potential for an extremely high rate of return.

Venture capital investing is also about a desire to build a small company into a large one, to build a company that no one has ever heard of into a company that makes headlines.

And it is about the turbulent world that surrounds a company at its inception—the constantly changing objectives, strategies, dreams, owners, personnel, and results, the peaks and valleys. If you go out to the Pacific Ocean and watch an island being formed from volcanic activity—the very beginning of land being created—what do you observe? A tremendous amount of heat and a tremendous amount of gas. It's a dangerous, unstable place to be, and it is impossible to predict how the whole thing will end up looking when the fires cool and the land is made. The same things happen when a company is being formed.

The venture capitalist's job is to be able to tell what is heat and what is just gas.

What Does an Investor Have?

- Money, and the ability to raise money
- Experience in building companies
- An understanding how wealth is created from start-up to the exit event
- Contacts to help build the company's distribution channels
- Contacts to help put together the management team

What Does an Entrepreneur Have?

- An idea: a process, a product
- Something proprietary
- An insatiable desire to succeed
- Business associates with some of the skills and experience needed

What Each of Them Don't Have

Without entrepreneurs, investors don't have:

- The time or personnel to manage companies on a day-to-day basis
- The possibility of earning returns that are substantially higher than in the public stock markets

Without investors, entrepreneurs don't have:

- The funding to fully exploit the opportunity of their product/service and their market

The venture capital industry fills in these gaps. A venture capital fund is really a mutual fund that invests for a very long term, has a relatively small number of "stocks," and seeks very high returns.

Brief History of the Venture Capital Industry

The idea of investing capital in risky ventures with a tremendous upside is not new. The explorers who sailed the globe in the fifteenth and sixteenth centuries looking for fabulous treasure in exotic lands had to get their financing from somewhere. The lucky ones had access to the king or queen and the royal treasurer. Even if you had a great reputation as a seagoing adventurer, it wasn't easy to get an audience with the crown's money men, unless you had someone on the inside to make the contact for you. The more things change . . .

With the Industrial Revolution, funding technology ventures eventually became an interesting diversion for the very rich. In the late nineteenth century, a prolific inventor sought $30,000 in research and development (R&D) funding for a device he claimed would replace the universally popular gas lamp, although attempts to commercialize other similar devices had failed for several decades—they generated an unsafe amount of heat, and the materials used to manufacture the alternative devices were too expensive. A syndicate of financiers, including J. P. Morgan and the Vanderbilts, decided to go ahead and fund the development of the new technology. Potential financial partners might have been concerned about the inventor's lack of formal scientific training or his weak financial management skills. But the inventor was Thomas Edison, and he produced the incandescent electric light bulb.

This shows us that if you notice J. P. Morgan is the lead investor in a deal, go ahead and jump in.

Prior to the Second World War, companies seeking start-up capital often relied on wealthy individuals or wealthy industrial families as backers—"angels," as we call them today. These were old-money type of investors, and deals were often consummated in the quiet dining rooms of country clubs. These were careful investors who knew how long it took to accumulate wealth.

The first true venture fund, in that it raised institutional capital and invested in early-stage ventures, is said to have begun in 1946. The first letter to an entrepreneur declining investment went out that same year, and the phrase "Sorry, your venture does not fit our investment parameters" was coined.

The first business plan is thought to have been written in 1954, revised throughout 1955, and read by an investor for 12 minutes sometime in early 1956.

The U.S. Government passed the Small Business Investment Act in 1958, which created incentives for the development of Small Business

Investment Companies (SBICs) that would provide financing for small companies that did not have ready access to the capital markets. The country was founded in 1776. Thus it only took the government 182 years to figure out that the small business person needs capital.

Silicon Valley emerged in the 1960s, when a company there, south of San Francisco, became the first to make computer chips completely out of silicon. Developments related to this technological breakthrough required venture capital, and a community of engineers and scientists, investors, and managerial talent sprang up. This pattern would later be repeated in other areas of the United States: Plant a seed of technology, fertilize with management talent, water with abundant amounts of venture money, grow companies, and hope for a bountiful harvest three to seven years later.

Over the next 20 years the number of venture capital companies and investment groups in the United States swelled to several thousand and the amount of venture investment grew steadily to the tens of billions of dollars. The investment concentration of these companies changed with major technological innovation: biotech, computer hardware and software, semiconductors, communications, and the Internet have all had their day in the sun. Entrepreneurs have an innate sense of what investment area is currently "hot" because it's the area completely unrelated to whatever company they are seeking capital for at the time.

In the mid- to late 1990s, a tremendous upsurge in stock prices created thousands of new millionaires in the United States, many of whom began to seek out investments in entrepreneurial ventures. These new "angel" investors are quite different from the angels of old. With nearly unlimited access to information, they have the ability to make much better informed decisions than their predecessors.

After all, it can't be that hard to be a venture capitalist, can it?

Who Are the Venture Capitalists?

They are commonly called "the VCs," as if they are a completely homogenous group with uniform background, experience, attitudes and business philosophy. The popular image of the venture capitalist is a middle-age person with a finance background, probably from one of the nation's premier universities. A kind of pin-stripe suit person. Very focused on rate of return. A "bottom-line" guy.

The truth is very different. Some VCs are quite young. It is not unusual these days for partners in venture capital firms to be in their early 30s. Increasing numbers of women are entering this once very male-dominated profession. They are not all finance gurus, either. If you examine the background of venture capitalists that are posted on their web sites, you will see that many have an engineering or technical background, some are marketing experts, and quite a few have general business experience related to starting and growing small companies into large ones. In medical-oriented venture capital funds, a number of the partners are physicians or scientists. Not all venture capitalists are even from the United States. Because business is increasingly conducted on a global basis, you will see partners in venture capital firms from Europe, Asia, and other parts of the world.

ADVICE FROM A VENTURE CAPITALIST

Christie Hart, Director of Entrepreneur Services, Draper Atlantic, www.draperatlantic.com

What is the profile of a typical partner in a venture capital firm?
"Often you see that they have earned an MBA from a top school. They may have professional investment management experience. Some are ex-CEOs, particularly those who ran a technology company before. Generally the partners are around 40 years old."

Their wardrobe is more varied than you might think. We've seen venture capitalists wearing jeans. Even shorts and sandals. It wasn't a pretty sight, but we've seen it.

They do tend to be highly educated, having attained multiple advanced degrees. And rather proud of that fact. Finance/Law and Engineering/Finance are popular combos. Some are stuffy and "old school" enough to seem as if they would be quite comfortable living in an F. Scott Fitzgerald novel. Others are much more down to earth, even genial. They don't all belong to country clubs, but of course they all could if they wanted to.

ADVICE FROM A VENTURE CAPITALIST

Dennis Spice, Managing Partner, Open Prairie Ventures,
www.opven.com

Where do the partners of venture capital firms come from? What is their background? "Our firm may be a little bit different than the typical venture fund. One partner has always worked in the area of funding companies. He has been a merchant banker putting his own money in deals. From the time he was still in school he was training to do this type of work. He went to law school never planning to practice law, but to use this background to help in negotiating deals. He got an MBA for the same reason. Few people know so early on that venture capital is what they want to do.

"I came out of the public investment sector, having managed pension funds. The $6 billion fund I managed had a percentage allocated to venture capital. I found I enjoyed the venture capital part of my work more than the stock and bond part.

"One partner has a background working in portfolio companies. He has a Ph.D. in Physics and Math and has helped young technology companies come out of universities and acted as their COO. He has been on the other side of our business.

"The background of venture capitalists is fairly varied, not just Wall Street people, as is somewhat true with firms that specialize in later stage deals. Early-stage and seed investors typically have assorted backgrounds. Analysts we are hiring today to be future partners have degrees in engineering. This allows us to help entrepreneurs more. If we all had finance backgrounds, it might not be as rich an environment. I enjoy working with the technical people on our team, who bring a totally different perspective, adding value to our business."

WHERE DO VENTURE CAPITAL FIRMS RECRUIT THEIR PARTNERS AND EMPLOYEES?

"VCs are just businesspeople," one entrepreneur said matter-of-factly after going through the process of bringing venture capital into his company.

They work extremely long hours, never getting fully "caught up" with the vast amount of business plans and companies they have to review and process, the numerous board meetings of portfolio companies they have to attend.

ADVICE FROM A VENTURE CAPITALIST

Christie Hart, Director of Entrepreneur Services, Draper Atlantic,
www.draperatlantic.com

How do VC firms recruit their partners and employees? What qualities do they look for in new partners? "They must be super smart and creative. Engineers with top school MBAs are very much in demand."

WHY DO VENTURE CAPITALISTS SEEM SO FOCUSED ON CERTAIN GEOGRAPHICAL AREAS?

A significant number of venture capital firms will consider investing in companies throughout the United States. Many others, however, limit their interest to certain regions, or even certain states.

The main reason for this is simply that it is easier to visit companies and attend meetings with management after funding if the company is within driving distance or at most a short plane trip away from the venture capitalist's office. Another reason is that the venture capital firms tend to locate their offices in areas that are particularly fertile regarding the number of good companies to invest in. They don't see a need to spend time looking outside this area. The reverse is also true: Entrepreneurs are attracted to areas with an infrastructure of venture capital firms and professional service providers that work with start-up or emerging companies.

And then the best managerial talent is attracted to these same areas because there are many challenging job opportunities with the potential for lucrative stock options. So you end up with pockets of the country that have all the ingredients—investors, the hottest technologies, the best management talent, a complete service infrastructure. It's almost as if "It takes a village to build a company." Hmmm. Kind of a catchy phrase.

Entrepreneurs puzzle over venture capitalists who say, "We invest primarily in Southern California but are willing to look at excellent opportunities in other parts of the country." "Should I contact that venture capital firm or not?" asks the entrepreneur in the Midwest, who of course believes that his company represents an excellent opportunity.

In this case the answer is: ???????

Why Is Finding Capital So Difficult for Entrepreneurs?

There are a number of reasons why entrepreneurs have so much trouble finding capital.

- Entrepreneurs don't understand how the process works and do not understand the thought processes of investors. Investors end up seeming more elusive than they really are.

- Entrepreneurs don't know where to look for capital, and do not have the contacts necessary to be introduced to investors.

- Different capital sources fit different stages of investment and type of companies.

- Raising money takes a certain flair for salesmanship that not everyone has. Some individuals are better at doing than talking.

- Entrepreneurs underestimate how long it will take to find investors.

- Raising money is a time-intensive process that takes time away from what the entrepreneur really wants to do: build a successful enterprise.

- And the most important reason: The funding of private enterprises is not an efficient market. It is getting more efficient, but it has a long way to go. It's certainly not an efficient market when willing buyers and willing sellers of a commodity (equity in emerging enterprises) have such an incredibly difficult time finding each other. You would never say the market is efficient when the pricing for the commodity is established by guesswork and the opinions of a handful of potential buyers. And it is not an efficient market when the seller is allowed to meet the buyer only if the seller has met the good friend of a good friend of the buyer at some cocktail party sometime, somewhere.

Fortunately, we will see in later chapters that the Internet is bringing down some of these barriers that keep the entrepreneurs from having access to the investors. But the market inefficiencies show why entrepreneurs should not be too hard on themselves when it takes more time to find capital than they imagined it would. A free and open marketplace would be the ideal; it's not here yet.

What Entrepreneurs Don't Know About Venture Capitalists

Venture capitalists have to go out and raise money, too. Wealthy individuals, or angels, may use their own funds to invest, but professionally managed venture capital firms get the majority of their funds from outside the partners in the firm. They raise the money from corporate pension funds, corporations, public pension funds, foundations, endowment funds, wealthy individuals, and insurance companies. Venture capitalists have people watching them, too. The funds are often organized as limited partnerships, with the venture capital firm serving as a general partner. The other institutional investors are the limited partners.

They may talk like financiers, but they are actually employees of a financial institution—much like your local commercial banker. Venture capitalists will tell you they are much smarter than most commercial bankers, however. Venture capitalists are under a certain amount of pressure to find good investments for the fund within a reasonable length of time, just as commercial loan officers in banks are charged with going out and finding companies that will make good loan prospects.

Venture capitalists have to go out periodically and raise money themselves. This is why they have a keen understanding of what the entrepreneur goes through trying to find money. Venture capitalists will meet with the managers of the large pension funds and the other funding sources mentioned above and describe what the investment focus of the new venture fund is planned to be, and why the venture capitalists believe the partners of their firm are uniquely qualified to find great investments and build portfolio companies. This is why we see venture funds that are extremely focused on a narrow range of investments—some won't do "seed" stage ventures, for example; some only invest in telecommunications, or medical technology. They have secured funding for the venture fund based on the understanding that they will stick close to these criteria. That is why, as a general rule, no amount of discussion or sales effort on the part of an entrepreneur, no matter how persuasive, will get a venture capitalist to deviate very far from the established investment focus of the firm.

The institutions that place money in venture capital funds do so because of the historically superior investment returns venture capital funds have been able to achieve relative to other classes of equity investment. Let's say that in the long run you are able to achieve a return of 10 percent by investing in publicly traded securities. The historical returns venture capital funds have been able to achieve have been closer to 25 percent—a substantially better performance—and even higher in recent years. Some top-performing funds achieve average annual returns of 100 percent or more. Institutional investors typically allocate only a very small percentage of their total investment capital in venture capital funds because there is a great deal of risk in this type of investment.

The 25 percent rate of return just mentioned comes about by averaging the widely varying performance of the individual investments, or companies funded, in the venture capitalist's portfolio. It is often said that venture capitalists seek an annual return of 30 to 40 percent or higher on each investment. The 25 percent average return comes about because some companies are complete busts and the investment has to be written off.

Table 1.1 shows a possible scenario of the results of ten investments.

Some companies fail and the investment has to be written off.

Others will not reach growth expectations but are still viable enterprises.

There will be solid companies that perform as expected in their business plans.

It is hoped that there will be superstars that become phenomenal initial public offerings (IPOs) or will be acquired by other companies for large multiples on revenues or earnings.

Table 1.1   Possible Results of Venture Capital Investments

	Number of Companies Out of 10 Investments	Annual Rate of Return for Venture Capitalist
Failure	4	0%
Viable	3	15%
Solid	2	50%
Superstars	1	100%
Blended average		24.5%

In venture capital investing, you can have seven out of 10, or 70 percent of your investments be disappointing and still end up with an excellent total return for your investors. The key to the whole thing is finding that one superstar. If we move that company into the "Viable" column, the total return drops to 16 percent. At that rate we might as well stay invested in our small-cap public stocks, and avoid all the trouble of finding, funding, and guiding these early-stage enterprises.

This is why venture capital investing is so much more exciting than managing a fund of publicly trade stocks: How often can you earn a 100 percent return each year on a stock you pick? Even the high-flying IPOs we have seen on Wall Street the last several years often run back down just as fast as they run up.

LOOKING BEYOND THE FUNDING

Money is only part of the contribution venture capitalists make to growing businesses. They offer knowledge about how to grow companies, the challenges all entrepreneurial companies face, how to build a distribution network, and how to attract top-flight management. They understand the entire life cycle of a company, from getting started to going public or being acquired.

Venture capitalists manage a portfolio of investments, much as mutual fund managers do with public companies. They consider diversification by stage of company and industry. They hold onto investments longer than mutual fund managers. An entrepreneur may get turned down by a venture capitalist not because the company does not have investment merit, but because the company does not fit into the overall strategy of the fund. Perhaps the fund already has several other investments in similar companies.

Capital availability is not distributed evenly across the United States. Northern California and the Northeast states dominate in terms of the number of companies being funded and the total capital committed to companies there. The pace of investment is picking up significantly in the Midwest and Southeast, however. Companies located in places outside the venture capital hotbeds have a more difficult time finding investors.

Entrepreneurs still think venture capital is available only to high-technology companies. The majority of companies funded have a technology component, yes, but it's not the whole picture. Many entrepreneurs are surprised to find out there are venture capital funds that focus solely on retail enterprises, for example.

ADVICE FROM A VENTURE CAPITALIST

Patrick Sheehan, Partner, 3i Group, www.3i.com

How does a VC firm determine its investment focus? "This varies hugely by firm, based most often from the experience profile of partners in the firm, which largely comes from the deals they've done before. The focus evolves naturally, and rationally. If you're looking for better areas to invest, for us they tend to be areas undergoing rapid change. Why has the Internet been a great area? Because it's actually a catalyst for rapid change. We look first at change rather than technology. Technology is the engine of change, eventually."

How often would partners get together and evaluate the investment focus? "This again depends on the firm. We move tactically on a regular basis. Continual discussion takes place. Certainly, quarterly a more deliberate debate takes place, and then an annual debate. We see that the investment focus of a venture capital firm is not set in stone. It is subject to fairly frequent review and possible change."

OTHER THINGS ENTREPRENEURS WONDER ABOUT VENTURE CAPITALISTS

If all the venture capital is going into Internet companies, who is going to finance the companies that make the products to sell in the e-commerce sites?

If they do too much due diligence on a deal, does it become undue due diligence?

Venture capitalists tell you they have to have exactly 60 percent of your company, a calculation they make based on your projected earnings, but then tell you they have no confidence in your projections.

Venture capitalists say that evaluating the competence of the management team is a critical part of investing, but it is almost impossible for you to get one of the partners on the phone to introduce yourself, so the partner can get to know you.

The months drag on while you wait for them to make a decision, but they want to hold you to a precise timetable for reaching the milestones in the business plan.

ADVICE FROM A VENTURE CAPITALIST

Patrick Sheehan, Partner, 3i Group, www.3i.com

What is it that entrepreneurs don't understand about raising capital? What surprises them about the process? "Entrepreneurs are a diverse group to try and generalize about. For some, there are no surprises in the process at all. For others, a surprise arises out of the failure of entrepreneurs to put themselves in the shoes of the investor. That is the thing most often lacking."

Larry Kubal, Managing Director, Labrador Ventures, www.labrador.com

"I think the biggest misunderstanding entrepreneurs have in the fundraising process is that their venture is (or should be) as important to the people they are pitching as it is to themselves. To me, any given deal is one of thousands that comes through our offices every year. If it is really good, it is one of hundreds in which we may develop a sincere interest. At the very best, it could be one of the 10 or so we fund every year. An entrepreneur's venture is his or her dream, something to which they are dedicating their lives to make happen. Entrepreneurs must understand that their unique jewel is but one in a constant flow to a VC with many gems before and after it. At Labrador, we are aware of, and empathetic with, this fundamental difference in perspective. I believe it is much tougher to recognize clearly from the entrepreneur's side.

"Entrepreneurs also miss the sometimes subtle differentiations between venture funds. The venture business is quite fragmented and segmented along multiple dimensions. At Labrador, for example, we invest relatively early in a company's life cycle. When we are deploying $2M per company, it is unlikely that our heads will be turned by a $100M financing opportunity. Understanding these specialties improves an entrepreneur's chances of success."

What Venture Capitalists Don't Know About Entrepreneurs

Venture capitalists know everything about entrepreneurs. They've seen it all before. That's why entrepreneurs feel as though they are at a distinct disadvantage during negotiations.

THE CONFLICT BETWEEN THE ENTREPRENEUR AND THE INVESTORS

How would you characterize the relationship between an investor and an entrepreneur—as predator/prey? As father/offspring? As partner/partner? As boss/employee? Or as benefactor/beggar?

If you ask investors how the relationship is *supposed* to work, they would uniformly respond that it should be partner/partner. Does it work that way in real life? It can, but not necessarily. And it's not all the investors' fault.

POINTS OF CONFLICT

Many Entrepreneurs Don't Really Want Partners, They Want Money. At the heart of the entrepreneurial desire is the need to be in control, in command. Many talk a good game about wanting to have the investor involved, but they don't really want to. Forming a partnership with an investor inherently creates the potential conflict over who is in control, but there's no way around doing it that way. It can be far too expensive for a small company to go public on its own. And small companies need expertise investors have to offer.

The partnership with the investor results in the entrepreneur's strategies or decisions being questioned, not an easy thing for some people to take. Entrepreneurs can get excessively "stuck on" certain ideas and resent input from investors. They can have a kind of arrogance regarding the benefits or what they perceive as the true perfection of their products or services.

Wow, How Long Does It Take to Grow an Ego That Large? The meeting between the investor and the entrepreneur amounts to the clash of two (or more) tremendous egos. Anyone who has met a venture capitalist at a trade show, a venture capital conference, or any other event can attest that many of them can't wait to tell you how much they know about every aspect of every industry and every enterprise. They always know more than you do—even if you have worked in the industry for a number of years—and they will gladly tell you so. The more successful they are and the more money they have made, the larger the ego grows.

It is an interesting facet of capitalism in general that the people who reach the top and acquire the most wealth eventually, conveniently, forget the sheer luck, the being-in-the-right-place-at-the-right-time phenomena, that was greatly responsible for their success, and recall only the strokes of individual genius that led to their (inevitable) victory.

When dealing with venture capitalists, there's no getting around this ego factor. It is a state of nature with them.

Ah, but the entrepreneur is not so innocent in this regard, either. Several years ago we arranged a meeting for an entrepreneur with a venture capital group that specializes in expansion capital for industry consolidation deals, putting several companies together to create a larger, more competitive entity. The partner of this group is a very pleasant, fair, easy-going individual, whose firm has done extremely well; and his family had done well for generations. The entrepreneur was, at best, a guy with a spotty track record and a tiny company with big dreams. The entrepreneur shook hands with the venture capitalist, sat down in the man's office, and the first thing out of his mouth was "I'm here to see if you're good enough to be my venture capital partner." You probably already can guess this meeting only lasted about two minutes longer.

Back in the 1960s there was a wonderful episode of a science fiction TV series about an older, vastly wealthy businessman who grew tired of not having any challenges any more and longed to go back to the beginning of his career and do it all again. He visited a rather sinister travel agency that accommodated his dream of going back in time. He returned to the small town where he started, a young man again. But this time he missed some of the key connections, the seemingly small incidents of good fortune, that actually caused him to succeed in such a big way. This time things went sour for him, and he learned an important lesson: Business is a team sport.

Class Distinction, or Entrepreneurs Are from Steerage; Venture Capitalists Are Strictly First Class. Entrepreneurs fret over whether they really belong at the negotiating table with these financial wizards, these venture capitalists. Entrepreneurs feel like the ultimate "outsider." It's sort of like, in the film *Titanic*: Rose, the young, rich girl, explains to Jack, the young vagabond, that the rich men in first class leave the table after dinner and retire to a private room—strictly guys only—to smoke big cigars and congratulate themselves on being masters of the universe. Meanwhile, we see that the fun party is actually in steerage, where they are drinking beer and dancing, planning all the adventures they will have when they reach America. These would be the entrepreneurs. When you see the Statue of Liberty for the first time, it is a thrill akin to seeing your company go IPO.

Jack gets to go to a venture capital meeting (dinner in first class). He sees that indeed the VCs do retire to the smoking room (board meeting). Rose represents capital (what Jack desires). The VCs look down on Jack because he doesn't have the money but kind of envy him because of his freedom (entrepreneurial spirit). The VCs aren't sure Jack should have the capital; they put obstacles in his path. Jack doesn't think he can do without it. The boat sinks and takes the VCs and the young entrepreneur with it. Rose's heart goes on to be the subject of an annoying pop ballad. Some would argue that a lot of VCs are about to get their come-uppance as the investors in the *Titanic* did. Of course, nowadays it would be called WhiteStarLine.com.

The Indelicate Subject of Greed. Greed seems to be one of those topics no one wants to discuss. Journalists who were critical of the merger mania and some of the perceived opulent excesses of the Reagan administration referred to the 1980s as the Decade of Greed. After the wild ride we have seen in the equity markets of the last several years, the 1980s seem like a quiet evening in a monastery by comparison.

One venture capitalist explained it to us this way:

> "We hope the market dip takes the dumb money out of the [Silicon] valley. New York investment bankers who have never 'built' companies from the ground up have come here thinking they can become venture capitalists. In reality they're doing it because of the greed factor. In Silicon Valley past, it was always about working together, building the best product and the best companies. Now it's about money. Don't get me wrong: That's a great goal, but when it's the only thing it tends to destroy. I'm concerned what this trend may mean for the traditional Silicon Valley culture."

Investors are not alone in their enjoyment of money for its own sake. Some entrepreneurs are skilled at playing the game of greed as well, as we see.

DEAL TALES: LIFESTYLES OF THE RICH AND FATUOUS

A young, energetic, upwardly mobile young woman decided to establish a company around a product that had lots going for it: strong niche, huge market, little competition, and great operating margins. As we were completing her new company's business plan, she decided to make a few changes in the financial forecast. She tripled her projected salary, added a Lexus as her company car, and included her membership dues at the local country club as part of the company's expenses. As she explained it, she had a lifestyle to maintain and just because she was starting a new company didn't mean she was sacrificing any personal comforts or security. An investor would just have to realize that when committing funds to her business. Needless to say, she's still looking for that special someone. The lesson she had never learned was that investors are not in the business of supporting lavish lifestyles. While a reasonable salary for an entrepreneur is expected and should be included, don't give yourself a raise before the company hits break-even.

Entrepreneurs Feel Intimidated by Venture Capitalists. The whole process of raising capital from venture funds at times appears designed to make the entrepreneur feel small. It seems a little out of whack that the entrepreneur is made to feel grateful for the opportunity to talk with the venture capitalist. Venture capitalists have a commodity, money, that they have to sell in order to satisfy the limited partners of the fund who have put up the money.

Commercial lenders in banks are practically flogged to go out into the marketplace and bring in loan deals. Bankers welcome you at first; they get around to treating you badly much later, when the deal is closer to closing.

Some venture capitalists act as if they are doing you a favor by reading your business plan. This pattern, once set, continues through the transaction. Some entrepreneurs can get seriously psyched out.

We knew one entrepreneur who could talk eloquently for hours about the great things he was going to accomplish with his venture after it was funded. He was dedicated, experienced, enthusiastic—and terrified of venture capitalists. The night before a meeting at a VC's office, he kept us enthralled in the hotel lobby bar as he unfolded his vision for growing the business. Next morning, we sat around a highly polished black lacquer table at the venture capitalist's office in Boston. The first question the VC posed to the entrepreneur was "So tell me, Bill, why do you want to be CEO of this company?" Before his throat completely tightened up, all the entrepreneur could utter was "Ahhhhhh."

If we were really talking about a partnership, why is the purpose of the first meeting to have the company present its merits to the venture capital firm? Why isn't half the meeting spent with the company presenting to the venture capitalists and half the meeting the venture capitalists presenting why they make such great partners?

That Sound You're Hearing Is the High-Pitched Whine of the Entrepreneur. Children on a long, cross-country automobile trip can often be heard to say, in a whiny tone of voice, "Are we there yet?" These children grow up and inevitably want to start their own business. Twenty-five years later, they are still asking the same question. They think investors take far too long analyzing the situation before investing in their company. They think service providers, including attorneys, should work for them for free, just for the sheer honor of being there when their company was started. They blame everyone else, even become bitter, when the task of starting a company proves more difficult than they bargained for. They are never appreciative of others' efforts, because they still aren't "there yet"—they aren't rich. They have an inability to enjoy the journey. Is it possible that selfishness is one of the traits that characterizes the entrepreneurial temperament? And how does an investor even begin to form a successful partnership with an entrepreneur who lets this selfishness take over the transaction?

Investors and Entrepreneurs Don't Speak the Same Language

DEAL TALES: BAD AURA, BAD DEAL

The owner of a high-tech manufacturing company asked us to help him find expansion capital for his business and introduce him to some venture capitalists. He was a New Age type of person who insisted on playing sitar music on his office stereo during meetings and had a large collection of crystals displayed all over his home; they helped him focus his energy, he said. We don't even need to bother mentioning that this company was in California. A venture capitalist in San Diego got really excited about investing in the company. We gave the venture capitalist's brochure to the CEO to study before the first meeting, so he could ask some good questions and the two of them could bond. A few minutes after getting the brochure in the mail, the CEO called us and said he was canceling the meeting because when he held the brochure in his hands, it gave off a negative aura.

If the Object Is to Confuse, Buzz Words Are the Best to Use. Venture capitalists spend a lot of time talking with other venture capitalists. They congregate together, as well, clustering their offices in places such as the famous Sand Hill Road in Menlo Park, California. And there are areas of the San Francisco business district that, if you drop a business plan out a window, you have a 50/50 chance of hitting a venture capitalist walking on the street below. Using that method, at least you wouldn't have to worry about getting the investor's attention.

As with any group that develops such a close community, venture capitalists generate their own jargon.

One of the first buzz words we learned occurred 15 years ago while being quizzed by a venture capitalist about the projections in a company's plan. "Just let me know the burn rate," he said gruffly. "Burn rate?" we mused, wondering if he had some process whereby he turned all the business plans he received into clean-burning firewood. All he meant was "How fast will the company use the capital?" He could have just said so. But buzz words are used to allow others to ascertain if you are a member of their club.

They also talk about the investment being done in "tranches." What could this possibly mean? We're working "down in the tranches"? Could it be as simple as meaning the total amount of investment required will be broken into segments?

One of the best recent buzz terms is "know your space" or your "market space." This doesn't refer to finding out the exact square footage of your apartment. This term sprang from the Internet and the concept of cyberspace. It means, if the market you operate in could be measured in physical dimensions, how large would it be? Your company's market space therefore is how large a share of the market you project that you can obtain. At least that's our best guess for right now.

Just when we caught on to what "market space" meant, they invented a new term, "domain experience." When we figure this one out, we'll get back to you. Maybe they borrowed this term from that famous episode of *Seinfeld*.

Clearly, investors and entrepreneurs don't speak the same language.

What the investor says: "Your business model is interesting."
What the entrepreneur hears: "How much should I write the check for?"

What the entrepreneur says: "We don't quite have our management team in place yet."
What the investor hears: "We have no experience, no track record, and I'm not exactly sure what a CEO does."

What the investor says: "Thank you, but we'll have to decline this opportunity. It doesn't fit our investment parameters."
What the entrepreneur hears: "Just keep talking and I'll eventually cave in and invest."

What the entrepreneur says: "We've been approached by several people who are very interested, our first round of financing is almost oversubscribed, but we'd like to give you the opportunity to invest."
What the investor hears: "Please, please, please invest, you're our only hope."

What the investor says: "How much capital were you looking for?"
What the entrepreneur hears: "To whom should I make out my check, and how much do you need?"

What the entrepreneur says: "To reach the revenue goals in our business plan, we only need to reach 1 percent of a $10 billion market."
What the investor hears: "We haven't got a clue as to who our market is or how we're going to reach it."

What the investor says: "Your management team certainly has an unusual background."
What the investor means: "Where did you find these guys? Leftovers from the Chronically Unemployed convention?"

What the entrepreneur says: "We would welcome suggestions and input by you extremely experienced investors in setting the strategic direction of our company."
What the entrepreneur means: "There's no living way these old fuds are going to mess with my idea."

Where Is the Industry Going?

Money, Money, Everywhere

Entrepreneurs certainly don't have to be concerned with a shortage of venture capital developing over the next few years. According to information from Venture Economics and the National Venture Capital Association (NVCA), venture capital funds are raising more capital than ever before, which means more capital will be available for entrepreneurs than ever before. (See Table 2.1.)

In just the second quarter of 2000 alone, 80 funds in the United States raised $17.1 billion, or an average of more than $200 million per fund. This was more than twice as much as was raised in the second quarter of 1999. The majority of the funds were raised by 33 venture capital firms in Northern California, which brought in $9.9 billion of new capital. Twenty-one funds in the Northeast raised $6.3 billion.

Why is the supply of venture capital growing so much? Because a number of venture funds have achieved excellent—even spectacular—

Table 2.1   Capital Raising Is
Rising

Funds Raised	$ Billions
First Half of 2000	30.3
1999	51.2
1998	27.2
1997	15.4
1996	10.7

returns in their portfolios. The more successful the funds are, the more institutional investors want to place money in these funds. The venture capitalists raise this money, and then they have to place it. Institutional investors are expecting a high rate of return, based on the success the industry has had. That is why the fluctuations of the stock market and the rise and fall of IPOs do not cut off the flow of investment into venture capital. Short-term blips are not as important as the long-range outlook.

We have seen the advent of venture funds with more than $1 billion in them. In fact, New Enterprise Associates' latest fund is said to have raised more than $2 billion.

ADVICE FROM A VENTURE CAPITALIST

Dennis Spice, Managing Partner, Open Prairie Ventures, www.opven.com

Venture funds seem to be getting larger and the size of deals is increasing. Why is that? "Funds are becoming larger because if you are successful with a young fund, it is just natural to make the second one bigger. The problem that occurs is, as the funds become larger, the less interested they become in smaller deals. Why? Because the limited partners who have invested in the fund require an IRR (internal rate of return) sooner, requiring larger amounts of money to be put in individual deals. Also, the amount of capital required for start-ups has increased dramatically. Valuations have gone through the roof, in our opinion, in some of these. We find it interesting that so many companies come in having just incorporated and say they think they need $10 million to get started.

"We encourage companies who say they need $10 million; if we take the lead we will help them raise whatever capital they need. We try to analyze to see if they really need $10 million and perhaps look at it in tranches instead. Maybe in the first year they need $2 million, second year $3 or $4 million. We can increase the value of the company in the short term and extend the time capital is raised. We will find other funds to co-invest at the appropriate time. We think this adds more value than just going out of the box saying they need $10 million today."

VENTURE CAPITAL INVESTMENT REACHES NEW HEIGHTS

Venture capital investment was $24.5 billion in the second quarter of 2000, compared to $12.5 billion over the same period the previous year. During this three-month period, 1,695 companies received investment. There has been a shift away from e-commerce companies, but still toward Internet-related technologies and service companies. The capital flowing into communications infrastructure technologies has grown tremendously. (See Table 2.2.)

Table 2.2   Where the Money Goes

Industry	Total for 2000, 2nd Quarter
Online Specific	800
Computer software and services	346
Communications	165
Medical/health & Biotechnology	141
Semiconductors/electronics	69
Other products	76
Consumer Related	42
Computer hardware	38
Industrial/energy	18
Total	1,695
Regional	
Northern California	511
Northeast	377
Southern California	136
Midwest	139
Mid-Atlantic	137
Southeast	136
Rocky Mountain	65
Southwest	112
Northwest	82
Total	1,695

(*Sources:* Venture Economics and NVCA)

These statistics, although showing the clear dominance of Northern California, do indicate that venture capital investment is taking place in all regions of the United States. It is interesting to note that if you combine the Rocky Mountain Region with the Southeast, that part of the country had the third most activity. Another way to look at these figures is to say that outside of California and the Northeast, fewer than 700 companies were funded by venture capital firms.

Only 1,695 companies were funded by traditional venture capital firms in the entire United States for one-quarter of the year—not that many companies, really. This is a small fraction of the number of companies seeking capital, as we shall see in a later chapter.

Both the number of companies obtaining investment and the average amount invested per company is soaring. From the first quarter of 1999 to the second quarter of 2000, the number of companies receiving investment went up 93 percent, from 877 to 1,695. The average amount per company grew from $7.68 million to $14.50 million.

ADVICE FROM A VENTURE CAPITALIST ON TRENDS IN THE INDUSTRY

Jeff Allen, Managing Director, Rocket Ventures,
www.rocketventures.com

Why do some types of investments seem to be popular and others are not? "In the venture capital industry, it's been referred to as a herd mentality. There are reasons for this, and it tends to create different things being in favor amongst firms at a given time. We're a pretty small firm— we have $80 million under management—and we tend to invest fairly early in a company. We might invest $2 to $3 million into a first round. The company is obviously going to need money for the next round, so we have to be conscious that at the next stage we can get the attention of larger venture firms to provide the larger amount of capital that will be needed, the $10 to $15 million. Naturally this puts us in a position where we really have to understand trends. Our investment of $2 to $3 million may last the company nine months to a year. We have to think about what people are likely to be interested in investing in nine months from now."

To some extent you are in the same shoes as the entrepreneur, trying to understand if the company will be of interest to venture firms. "It's a little different: An entrepreneur knows what he knows about a particular domain, has a certain expertise. We're investing in that expertise. His company may be the best in the world in a particular field. If we don't think that field is going really take off in the next 2 to 3 years, then it's probably not a great investment for us. But it may be a great business he's going to build. So there's a little bit of a distinction.

"Right now, in the current environment, there are really two camps: the business-as-usual camp that looks at fundamentals, uses all the tools the venture capital industry has built up over the last 40 to 50 years and applies them to companies that come in the door. Am I convinced it is going to make money? How much money will it take to get the company to the point where it is a profitable business? Will this company be able to go public? What is the likely exit scenario? How am I going to get my money out? It's interesting that this camp doesn't follow too many trends, relying on the business' fundamentals to take it forward. Their investments may fall into trendy areas, they may not.

"Then there's the other camp, chasing trendy market spaces areas. They tend to be larger firms. Companies they invest in may need $20 million in venture funding. Companies in certain spaces may get $50 to $100 million in venture funding before they go public."

Are these the ones that turned off B2C [business to consumer] and focused on B2B [business to business]? "Yes, and they've been chasing wireless for the last three to six months, and optical networking. Some of the Internet infrastructure companies are having a tougher time. A lot of venture funds are even waiting it out on B2B front, instead looking at what we call 'second derivative' companies—things that are going to make a real impact, trying to find the next Netscapes of the world, a core technology that can make a big difference or business processes, or technology that can get widespread acceptance. It tends to take longer to develop these companies. Some firms are just now beginning to become involved with semiconductor ideas and processes— these are core technologies—and leaning away from Internet software in some respects. That's still a current trend, and a lot of investment is being made there, but new trends are emerging.

"There's been a lot of investment in B2C when public markets are hot, and liquidity is available. Those were straight-line businesses where people look at growing them rapidly and then taking the money out. Second-derivative companies produce some sort of technology that other companies become relied on; it gets this multiplier effect when you get partners and channels developing on a widespread scale."

Why did the short-term Nasdaq pullback in the spring of 2000 seem to have an impact on venture capital investors, who are long-term investors? "Toward the end of last year and the first three months of 2000 there was tendency to put a lot of money into companies whose business fundamentals hadn't yet developed, whose revenue streams hadn't yet developed to the point you could justify high valuations. The Nasdaq was so high flying, companies were easy to sell in public markets, with IPOs.

Venture capitalists were putting money in with the expectation they could get liquidity soon. With the pullback, and companies not being able to go public so easily anymore, venture funds were having to put more money into companies to keep them alive so they can build out the business fundamentals so it becomes a viable company in the public market.

"I don't really think we've seen the full fallout. There have clearly been some companies ready to have the plug pulled. With others, the jury is still out. Venture funds are willing and able to put more money in and some of those companies will fall, if they can't develop the right revenue streams."

What investment trends are exciting to you right now? " I don't get into too many trends except for very macro trends. Everyone in our firm believes that someday the promise of broadband, large amounts of bandwidth, will be available. This will take awhile to deploy. We're beginning to invest on the assumption that large amounts of bandwidth will be available. That opens up a few interesting areas. I don't necessary want to call it the entertainment space, but content delivery and multimedia, applications that use multiple forms of media within them.

"There are enough large VC firms who also believe this, so it becomes an interesting trend. We are in the early stage of it from an investment standpoint. The promise is there, with a lot of firms on the sidelines waiting to see if it will take off in the next one to four years. You're going to see considerable investment in content delivery and core multimedia space.

"If you're a good venture capital firm you're investing right at a time just before there's a take-off point. Some companies take a long time to develop a product before it is ready to market on a mass scale. We as firms want to invest as close as possible to the point where sales are ready to take off. The product needs to be developed, sales need to be ramped up. There is a fear that you'll invest too late to get into these hot deals. So one of the questions we look at is how long is it going to take for this company to develop the product and generate sales. We don't want it to be long, but we don't want to get in too late so the valuation is so high. There's a trade-off."

With the Internet, Finally We Can All Play: a New Era of Entrepreneurship

The Internet has spawned an incredible number of business ideas—new technologies, new products, new services, and new ways of marketing existing products and services. Barriers to entry—both capital and infrastructure—have been lowered in many market areas, allowing more and more people to realize their dream of being an entrepreneur. It's only fitting that this same Internet is making it easier for entrepreneurs to find the capital they need to bring their dream to fruition.

It is becoming easier for entrepreneurs to contact venture capital firms, using the venture capitalist firms' web sites.

New Internet-based services have arisen to match up entrepreneurs with angel investors.

The ranks of angel investors, in turn, have grown as it becomes easier for them to find companies, using the Internet.

This increased speed of contact has begun to compress the time to funding for entrepreneurs, allowing them to launch their companies more quickly and take advantage of emerging markets.

The Internet has made it much easier, and faster, for entrepreneurs to find market research information, and obtain assistance from service professionals.

What the Venture Capitalists Say About Their Industry

GOOD NEWS FOR ENTREPRENEURS SEEKING CAPITAL

"It booms!"

"There's a lot of money chasing a few good deals."

"There is a lot of money chasing deals. It is a great time to be an entrepreneur."

"It's frothy."

A FEW WORDS OF CAUTION

"Too many entrepreneurs have plans and concepts that are not well thought out or executable, and too many VCs are investing very quickly with minimal diligence and lack of capability to provide ongoing support."

"We see a lot of plans, but not a lot of good plans."

"The business is becoming more competitive every day and as funds get larger, entrepreneurs will find it harder to get start-up money unless they have access to terrific 'angels.' It will get even harder to get funded in places like Arizona as VCs do not have the time to travel outside their areas, as they have too much money to invest."

THE IMPACT OF THE NASDAQ SLUMP

In the spring and summer of 2000, there was a significant pullback in the technology-heavy Nasdaq market, where many of the venture capitalists' investments had gone public. This pullback was accompanied by a decline in speculative activity in initial public offerings that had just begun trading. In fact, several IPOs were pulled back due to a perceived lack of investor interest. Comments by venture capitalists included:

> *"It's a jungle and the strong survive."*
>
> *"We're getting tougher on valuations, given recent market conditions."*
>
> *"Despite the April pullback in the public market's valuations of Internet stocks, there is a tremendous amount of venture capital available for companies with sound business models, teams with a will to win, and some demonstration of the ability to execute against a plan."*
>
> *"Competition is getting better—crazies are losing their cash."*
>
> *"The recent Nasdaq slump is a good thing—it should put some rationality back in this business."*
>
> *"Public market appetite for IPOs is declining. So goes the IPO, as goes the IRR."*
>
> *"It is an interesting time to invest. There will likely be a VC bloodbath in the Internet space at some point—the question is when."*

A SIMPLE EXPLANATION OF WHAT HAPPENS

Entrepreneurs in the Internet economy are very much like the explorers of the New World 500 years ago. Rumors of fabulous riches caused these explorers to undertake journeys in waters that were often uncharted. The treasure turned out to be real in many cases, but quite a few of the ships sank before they got back to Spain and Portugal. When the ships didn't come back, many would-be financial backers of expeditions reconsidered for a while, until that wonderful, natural human quality—greed—took over again. With the Internet economy, everyone has discovered that a significant number of the ships are sinking. It doesn't mean the treasure isn't there. It means, just as in 1520, you need a stout ship (e-commerce infrastructure), a crew you can trust (management team), and the best navigation tools available (an extremely refined business model). As you are in the next wave of these explorers, you have the added advantage of knowing where some of the rocky shoals are, having seen where your predecessors crashed. If each new person shopping on the Net were a gold doubloon, think of how the potential riches are growing each year.

But the potential riches have spawned some rather skewed perceptions of how high the returns on venture capital investments should be, leaving some entrepreneurs feeling as if they don't belong in this new, high-flying era of venture capital.

DEAL TALES: IS THAT ALL YOU'VE GOT?

Before he picked up the phone and dialed, Gary H., president of a company in the Southwest that has developed a new consumer technology for the education market, sat at his desk for more than half an hour going over what he planned to say to the venture capitalist. He had been allotted 15 minutes to give the "pitch"—the high points of what was attractive about his company from an investment standpoint. Gary not only knew what ideas he wanted to convey, he had chosen exactly what words to use, how to pace the conversation, even how to build to a powerful close. Gary was ready for anything the VC had to throw at him.

He dialed the number of the senior partner of a San Francisco-based venture capital firm. He waited patiently for five minutes to be put through, his heart rate starting to increase, his confidence level bouncing around like technology stocks on the Nasdaq Exchange.

"Good afternoon, Gary," he heard from a voice that somehow managed to convey a sense that the man was extremely busy, and Gary better get on with it right away. No small talk about the Bay area weather. Don't even bother to bring up the '49ers and their prospects for the upcoming season. Just do the pitch.

So Gary began. He explained that his company was attacking a large, growing market that consensus estimates said would reach $3 billion by 2003. He told the venture capitalist about the unique features of his product—how they were clearly superior in meeting the needs of the customer. About the patent protection that had already been secured. About the management team that included himself, a man who had successfully grown two companies and taken them public, a marketing expert who had run major brand campaigns at several Fortune 500 consumer product companies, a VP of production whose credentials spanned 20 years in the industry, and a finance person who had been with three high-growth enterprises. Gary brought up the fact that the founders had already put $500,000 into the company—always a positive sign for investors.

He then proceeded to play his trump card: the phenomenal margins his company was capable of producing. He told the venture capitalist that his team had projected that by the third year after funding, his company would reach $30 million in sales with a pretax profit of $10 million—an excellent 33 percent of revenues. Gary said they needed an investment of $8 million, and that the company would probably make an excellent acquisition target for a large consumer product company by Year 5.

The pitch completed, Gary finally took a breath, satisfied that he covered all the high points.

He knew his company was the very essence of what venture capitalists look for. He waited for the response.

"Is that all you've got?" asked the venture capitalist.

"I'm not sure I understand," Gary said.

"We get 20 business plans in here each week with roughly the same potential as your company, based on what you have told me. Your numbers aren't good enough. Two of the last four Internet companies we funded went public within 18 months and our return was ten times our investment. You're asking us to stay in for three to five years for a possible return of a fraction of that amount. You say you'll reach $30 million. We see deals with the potential to reach $500 million over that time. Why would we want to fund yours?"

Gary had no answer.

"Thanks for contacting us. Good luck with your venture."

A click and a buzz were the next things Gary heard.

He sat at his desk for another 30 minutes, stunned, unable to process what he had just heard—that a large market, proprietary products, and a management team with a great track record were no longer good enough to obtain venture capital from a large, national fund. Gary half expected Rod Serling to walk into his office and inform him that he had left the business world as he knows it and entered some kind of financial *Twilight Zone* where only imaginary companies with imaginary products and projections based on hallucinatory assumptions received funding. A world where the story you can tell to Wall Street is more important than the products you can offer to your customers.

Had the world gone mad? Gary seriously wondered.

Fortunately, Gary's disorientation lasted only a day or so. He got back to the difficult and often frustrating task of finding investors. The process was slow going, but within three months an "angel" investor put $1 million in his company. It turned out that that funding, combined with some good luck in arranging joint ventures with distribution partners, were enough to get the company rolling.

So, what is going on here? Has the world of venture capital changed that much, or does the financial press just dwell on the high-flying Internet IPOs with little revenues but astounding stock performance, and the venture capitalists who funded them? Was Gary's experience typical, or did he just dial the phone number of the wrong venture capitalist that day?

Entrepreneurs used to think the rewards would come after they had built a great company, three to five to seven years later. This has begun to change, for better or worse. Some entrepreneurs have decided they are in the business of selling bright ideas to investors for enormous sums of money.

DEAL TALES: WHY BOTHER HIRING EMPLOYEES, LET'S JUST GO IPO

We met an entrepreneur named Steve B. through his attorney. Steve was a young man of about 30. He had developed a concept for a unique telecommunications service and needed advice as to where to look for investors. On the surface, the concept was terrific. Therein lies the problem. All Steve had was surface. His "business plan" contained little or no information about how the service could be marketed, what kind of equipment was needed and how much it would cost, and he had exactly one person in the management team—himself. He said he was really only looking for $5 million in bridge financing for no more than six months. Then he planned to take the company public. What will your revenues be at that time? we asked. "About $100,000," he replied. "But that's no problem, 'cause my competitor just went public at a market cap of $750 million and they hardly had any revenues at all." Why do you think the market would be receptive to your IPO, given you will have very few customers at that time? He said, "Well, 'cause I am going to patent my *business model*. Then no one can touch it. That model is worth a fortune." No customers, no market share, no employees. No equipment as far as we could tell. But his *business model* is worth a fortune.

ADVICE FROM A VENTURE CAPITALIST

Bill McAleer, Partner, Voyager Capital, www.voyagercap.com

Entrepreneurs lament the fact that it is so difficult to get their ideas in front of a venture capitalist. What can they do to improve their chances? "First, they need to understand the current environment, the huge number of opportunities being presented to venture capitalists right now. We are being inundated with contacts by mail, e-mail, telephone, fax. The level is really mind-boggling. I receive approximately 40 to 60 e-mails per day, among them five to 10 new companies. It is becoming almost impossible to respond to everyone who sends a summary or a business plan to us. The best way to reach us is to have someone with a connection to our firm—a business associate, accountant, attorney—refer the company to us. But even the level of referral volume has risen tremendously, too.

"A strong idea, articulated clearly, gets our attention. The entrepreneur needs to know the VC firm's 'sweet spot,' the areas of primary investment focus. Stage is important, too. A number of firms do not invest in seed-stage companies, preferring to get involved when the company is further along. The person seeking capital needs to be highly targeted in which firms they contact. For example, our firm is very focused on B2B Internet companies rather than those that offer products or services to the consumer."

The chief reason for this volume increase you are talking about is a result of the large number of Internet companies being formed. Why are Internet companies so attractive to venture capitalists right now? "Part of the answer is that these companies are fairly simple to start: There are not a lot of barriers to entry. But the fundamental reason is that we are seeing a major paradigm shift in how people communicate, and the Internet is causing it. New devices, network computing, broadband applications, increased connectivity—all of these technologies create new opportunities for investment. We still must look underneath to see if there is a strong business proposition within a company. For example, we look at: Have they created another way of marketing in their space? What is the nature of the opportunity? We try to identify the underlying value, the uniqueness of the business. There has to be more than just using the Internet as a new delivery channel. It is also important to be the first mover in a space that is momentum oriented."

Do you think e-commerce and the Internet are going to cool off any time soon? "The business-to-consumer space has cooled off somewhat. A lot of the interest has moved to B2B. Biotech investments seem to be making a comeback, as well. Increased scrutiny is being applied to these Internet business models, at both the public company and venture capital level. That is why there has been some fallout on the consumer side. Lower-margin vehicles do not seem to be working. The venture has to have a model that fundamentally changes the way goods and services are exchanged in their particular market."

Other than the advent of the Internet, what trend has had the most impact on your firm in the last several years? "There is a lot more capital available than ever before. Capital is more readily available than ever before. These trends change how the VC firm has to operate. We need to have a business plan of our own and need to really think about the unique advantages our firm gives our portfolio companies. We have to have more customer focus, if you want to look at it that way. We need to think of ourselves as a company that provides unique services. And we have to organize our resources in order to do a superior job of building these B2B companies we are concentrating on at the present time."

What Entrepreneurs Are Saying About the Venture Capital Industry

"Not surprisingly, VCs are now being more realistic in their decisions regarding Internet start-ups. I think that there is still excitement in the industry, but now the ability to show a profit is still top priority."

"Dot.com businesses are taking money away from traditional start-ups."

"I see the greatest need in the venture capital world is for true seed-stage investors. Angel investors are too diffused. Incubators are too concentrated in a small number of VC epicenters such as Silicon Valley, Boston, Silicon Alley. Many VCs say they are willing to invest in seed-stage companies but rarely deliver."

"The projects and management that I have seen funded are beyond belief. VCs have taken worthless projects and, with 'hoopla' and greed in mind, have funded them at the expense eventually of small [public] investors. The type of company I look to build is one that will be valued and of value for a long haul, not one that will run-up an IPO and all the initial investors bail as soon as possible. VCs and other competitive funding organizations are stressed to the limit on resources to evaluate real opportunities vs. dot.com tangents while feeling incredible pressure to place enormous funds that they have acquired into high-yielding investments. This conflicting process, in my opinion, has caused the recent falling off of investment interest in start-up dot.coms that had no real business chance."

"I think the state of the venture capital industry is in a flux right now due to the number of failures in Internet-based companies. I also believe the industry will make a rapid turn-around in the next six months as the investors realize the potential of other firms: non–Internet-based ventures."

Your Search for Venture Capital

Are You Sure You Want Venture Capital?

Obtaining capital from a venture capital firm has many advantages, the most important being that these firms know how to form partnerships with entrepreneurs and convert ideas or concepts into large, valuable enterprises. They bring a wealth of contacts that can be converted into customers, distribution channels, and strategic alliances. But there are drawbacks to the relationship as well.

Your ability to select the members of the management team will be diluted. Entrepreneurs in early-stage companies face the very real possibility of having someone brought in to replace them as chief executive. The venture capital firm is under pressure to achieve high returns for its investors, and so the pressure to grow is passed on to the management of the portfolio company. The money comes with very high performance expectations. You have to have the fire in your belly to build a large enterprise. It's like the transition a college football player faces when he goes to the professional level: The game seems so much faster. And the venture capitalist doesn't allow you an "exhibition season."

The types of companies that are good candidates for funding from VCs include:

- Those that are or will be offering products and services in large markets, not small but lucrative "niches." A large market is in the billions of dollars.

- Those that will require a relatively large amount of capital over the life of the business. If your company requires only $500,000, there probably is a ceiling on the growth potential of the business. It doesn't mean you can't build a wonderful company, but it may not grow large enough to earn venture capitalists the return they are seeking when they exit.

- Those that will require several rounds of financing. VC firms have the contacts and expertise to make the process of finding these additional rounds much easier for the entrepreneur, who can then concentrate more on the operation of the business itself.

WHAT ABOUT HAVING BOTH VENTURE CAPITAL AND ANGEL INVESTORS?

Many start-up companies find preseed investment from friends and family. The founders may put some of their own capital in as well. Angel investors provide the seed-stage funding, allowing the company to progress in product research and development (R&D), or perhaps even to introduce the product/service to the marketplace. With the value of the company now more firmly established, and with the company having some accomplishments to talk about, the founders go out and seek a larger amount of capital from venture capital firms.

There are questions to ask yourself before seeking investors.

ADVICE FROM VENTURE
CAPITALISTS ON GETTING STARTED

David Cowan, Managing Partner, Bessemer Venture Partners,
www.bessemervp.com

"1. Am I doing this because I want to start a company (power and riches), or because I have experienced a problem in the marketplace firsthand that, damn it, I know I can solve? If it's the former, get a job until you develop the passion and domain expertise to tackle a real market.

"2. I know this is a good business, but is it really an opportunity to build shareholder equity, or it just a good living for me and my team?

"3. Is my team comprised of the absolute best people for the jobs, or are they friends and acquaintances who happened to be interested?"

A partner with Mellon Ventures, Inc., www.mellonventures.com

"Are there any other creative ways to fund your business?

"Do you feel you can ultimately form a true partnership with outside investors for the growth of your business?

"If you do need the outside capital, what do you expect to get from a firm in addition to the money?"

Mike Carusi, General Partner, Advanced Technology Ventures,
www.atvcapital.com

"1. Are the founders thinking big? All too often founders want venture money, but their vision is more often that of a bootstrapped organization which provides a nice lifestyle.

"2. Are they willing to accept the responsibility of bringing in outside investors? By taking in venture money or for that matter any outside dollars, founders have an obligation to build shareholder value. They are beholden to these investors and must do what is in the best interest of the shareholders. Sometimes this is not always in the best interest of the founders/management (i.e., changing a CEO, etc.).

"3. Are they looking for money or partners? Most venture capitalists, for good or for bad, become actively involved in the companies in which they invest. They take board seats, they provide advice, offer up their networks, etc. ATV, for example, works with its companies in a collaborative style. That means in turn that the founders must want to collaborate. If all they want is money (not advice, guidance, etc.), then they should go elsewhere."

Mark Stevens, General Partner, Sequoia Capital,
www.sequoiacap.com

"1. How much $$ do they need to get to cash-flow breakeven and why (use of proceeds analysis)?
"2. What are they looking for besides $$ (help in building a management team, introductions to potential partners, etc.)?
"3. Do I want to build a nice little business or a big corporation someday?"

How Much Capital Do You Need?

This is a question that entrepreneurs have a great deal of difficulty with, often revising their projections half a dozen or more times before they are ready to talk with investors. The problem is that there are no hard and fast rules about how much capital it will take to build a given enterprise. And entrepreneurs must deal with this axiom as well:

If you increase the amount of capital you are seeking, you must either increase the amount of equity you give investors or convince the investors that a higher valuation for your company is appropriate. The first alternative is abhorrent to entrepreneurs; the latter is very difficult for them to accomplish. Their own valuation of their companies is often too high, anyway.

ADVICE FROM A VENTURE CAPITALIST

Dennis J. Dougherty, General Partner,
Intersouth Partners
www.intersouth.com

"You must choose a venture capital firm that aligns with your company's goals and objectives. It's not just about money—it's about creating a long-term, collaborative relationship. Venture capitalists have more than just money to put on the table—they should not only commit dollars, but commit to supporting the company and management team in good times and bad. You should trust your investors and welcome their participation. They can be used as valuable resources for recruiting key management, refining strategies and tactics, and assisting in the formation of strategic partnerships. The money will only get you so far.

"Many entrepreneurs find that their relationships with investors carry long beyond the investment cycle of a single company. Venture capitalists love to back those that they have backed before. Some entrepreneurs join the funds down the road or serve as close and valuable consulting resources to venture investors. Pick a firm whose people are those with whom you would like to have such a continuing relationship."

Most entrepreneurs have a good handle on the cost of equipment, facilities, and personnel but have a very limited ability to forecast marketing expenses. Entrepreneurs either underestimate the cost of reaching millions of potential customers and building a brand name, or they insert a plug figure of X millions of dollars in the plan.

One trend we have seen lately is that Internet entrepreneurs are looking over the shoulder of other Internet companies to see how much capital they have obtained. If they read that one telecom company got $17.5 million capital, they believe they need that much too and set about to "prove" this with a capital budget that usually contains some nebulous figure for marketing expense.

One exasperated entrepreneur who had endured six months of self-inflicted spreadsheet torture told us, "I could do this company with $3 million or $30 million. I've been at this half a year and still have no idea what I need."

Entrepreneurs seem to think that they have to come up with an exact figure in the capital budget, such as $9.65 million. What's the matter with saying that you need $9 to $11 million—a base amount of $9 million with up to $2 million for unforeseen contingencies?

The worst mistake to make is to greatly underestimate how much capital you need and then have to go back and ask for more from your existing investors, or try to bring in additional ones, diluting the investors you already had in place. Your investors tend to get seriously displeased.

Entrepreneurs can use a variety of techniques to surprise investors with an unanticipated request for additional funding. The choice of the right method, depending on the temperament of the investor, may enable the entrepreneur to continue as CEO. It could also be a good time to contact outplacement services. In situations like this, entrepreneurs end up playing a number of roles:

The Flatterer: "You said when you gave us the initial funding that we probably needed more than $7.5 million to enter this market and compete. You were absolutely correct, and it shows why I am lucky to be backed by such a wise venture capitalist."

Search for the Scapegoat (with indignation in your voice): "I just found out that controller of ours forgot some key expense items in our forecast. Luckily, I discovered the problem in time. These financial people. . . ."

The Victim of Dark Forces: "Our market space has been invaded by a virtual armada of well-capitalized competitors."

Disaster Is All Relative: "Isn't it interesting how some companies have spent $25 million or more to get to the point we are—and we've only spent $7.5."

The Murky Explanation: "The incremental functionality appended to our system post-beta test, based on the accretion of credible market data, inevitably caused deployment of resources originally slated for Phase III rollout."

The Comedian: "Hey, you've heard of 'burn rate'? Well, I guess we've got a regular bonfire going!"

The Refreshingly Honest CEO: "Dot.com it, I just messed up."

What Stage Is the Company At?

Companies go through life cycles, from just being a gleam in the eye of the entrepreneur, to being put out to pasture or, as some would prefer, led to the slaughterhouse. These different stages—seed, start-up, first stage, second stage, established, and turnaround—can reflect the degree of risk involved.

SEED STAGE

The idea for a product or company is in the mind of the founder, but there is still substantial research and development necessary to determine whether the idea is viable. There is no business plan and no management team.

START-UP

The company has a business plan, a defined product, and basic structure, but little or no revenues are being generated. The product may still be just a prototype. There may be gaps in the management team.

FIRST STAGE

The product is either ready for market or is generating some revenues. The infrastructure of the company is in place, with a full management team.

SECOND STAGE

Full-scale production is under way. The company's product has been selling and accepted by the marketplace. The company is ready for a major national introduction of the product or introduction of a second product.

ESTABLISHED

The company has been operating successfully for at least three years.

TURNAROUND

The company has been operating for several years but is seriously underperforming and is generating a loss. A company that has undergone a hard turnaround is not only underperforming, but has been in a cash-deficit position with little hope of returning to a positive position without major restructuring.

Venture capital is available for companies at all of these stages. Most VC firms specialize in either early stage or later stage. Some venture capital firms even prefer turnaround situations.

ADVICE FROM AN ENTREPRENEUR

David Mathison, CEO, Kinecta Corporation, www.kinecta.com

What's your relationship with the venture capitalists been like? "Excellent."

Has it changed? "Yes. Most people are under the mistaken impression that things are different over the last six months. Quite the opposite is true—since April 2000 things have gotten back to normal (revenues and profits). I am very comfortable in this era."

What do the VCs contribute to your company? "Insight, advice, contacts, experience, and, of course, capital."

What surprised you about working with VCs? "The ecosystem of the VC community and where each particular VC fits into that ecosystem is something that entrepreneurs should be familiar with before meeting with a potential VC. It will save you lots of time and energy. (It's not enough to know that you fit into their investment portfolio criteria; you also need to know what stage of company they invest in and the percentage stake they want to have at the liquidation event.)"

How much does the VC get involved on a day-to-day basis? "Depends on the day."

How Much of the Company Will You Have to Give Up?

Ten years ago, entrepreneurs were absolutely convinced they would have to give up majority control—more than 50 percent of their equity—in order to obtain capital for their start-up. They used to ask, "What's normal? Giving the investor 70 to 80 percent?"

In this new world of Internet start-ups—and, some would argue, puffed-up valuations—entrepreneurs are just as convinced that they will only have to give up a small minority share, sometimes as little as 20 percent. In both of these extremes the entrepreneurs never tied together the amount of capital requested, the valuation of the business, and the amount of equity they would be giving up. The equity amount was a kind of abstraction, an expression of what is the absolute minimum they will have to give investors and still get the deal done.

Companies often have a number of rounds of financing during the cycle from seed to IPO or merger. As the rounds progress, and the company grows and, it is hoped, succeeds, the original founders normally have a shrinking portion of the total equity. But the value of that equity soars.

CAN YOU LIVE WITH A PARTNER?

More important than the ownership that has to be given up is the management control that is given up. The entrepreneur may be the founder of the company but may not be qualified to be the CEO of a fast-track entity. Venture capitalists insist on quality management, more about this later on. Will the entrepreneur be willing to step aside for a new CEO?

Accepting venture capital funds also means accepting new reporting requirements and establishing an ongoing relationship with the principals of the VC firm.

ADVICE FROM AN ENTREPRENEUR

What surprised you about working with venture capitalists? "The broad spectrum of understanding. Some got what we were doing right away, others didn't get it all, and others ranged somewhere in the middle. Once they thought they understood your business, they could analyze the business model amazingly quickly. All in all, I'd say they are a pretty smart group of people with lots of experience entrepreneurs can learn from."

How much does the VC get involved on a day-to-day basis? "I see him at least once a week and talk to him on the phone or via e-mail about once a day. He's been extremely active in our business from strategy, tactical, and organization decisions."

Was the valuation you received for your company close to your expectations? Why or why not? "It was extremely fair and what we expected."

How Involved Does a Venture Capitalist Prefer to Be in the Management of the Company?

Of course the answer depends on several variables, but in general VCs do not want to run the company; 71 percent of the VCs we surveyed said they would prefer to be on the board of directors or to just provide strategic direction for the company. Only 2 percent would prefer to be involved in the day-to-day management.

ADVICE FROM A VENTURE CAPITALIST

*Dennis Spice, Managing Partner, Open Prairie Ventures,
www.opven.com*

How involved do you become with your portfolio companies?
"Pretty involved in short answer. If we're not at the company physically
each week, we are certainly on the phone with various people in the
company. A recent example is we are helping one of our companies organize an 'open house.' We helped develop the invitation, even arrange
the catering. We're pretty detailed in our involvement. The reason is, our
companies are very high tech. We have a lot of brilliant people running
companies. Technically they know exactly what they are doing but they
need our business expertise. We don't just provide the money and attend
board meetings once a month."

---

*Christie Hart, Director of Entrepreneur Services, Draper Atlantic,
www.draperatlantic.com*

How do VC firms differ in their operating philosophies? "They
do vary by firm. We believe that we offer more 'services' to our portfolio companies and they all feel we help them more than other firms
might."

Getting Started Raising Capital

Entrepreneurs who are successful at money raising have mastered these
three factors:

1. Preparation
2. Positioning
3. Perseverance

Preparation means getting your company ready to be "shown off" to a potential investor or lender, preparing the business plan and other materials that are needed to introduce your company in a professional manner,
and preparing for the negotiations themselves.

ADVICE FROM A VENTURE CAPITALIST

Gerry Langeler, OVP Partners, www.ovp.com

How can entrepreneurs best prepare themselves to begin raising capital? In your experience, what don't entrepreneurs understand about the capital-raising process? "Talk to other entrepreneurs who have successfully raised capital. You will be amazed how many will give you at least a few minutes on the phone—even if they don't know you from Adam. Also, check out the best-run, best-funded start-ups in your area. Get the names of their accountants and attorneys. Then hire them! They will help work your plan and can introduce you to high-quality investors.

"Really do your homework about your potential business, including calling and talking to a number of prospective customers firsthand. Secondhand, grandiose market research is for the birds. Give me 25 people in your target market segment ready to buy. If I can place 10 phone calls and talk to more prospects than you have, I'll know more about your business than you do. That is not good!

"The biggest thing entrepreneurs don't understand is that when competing for capital they are competing against our total deal flow—thousands of other interesting teams and ideas—with about a one-in-200 chance of getting our money and our time. If you want to be funded by us, you need to have a very powerful story and a killer team, not just good ideas and some willing hands. Before you approach us, look at what we've funded before—not just by industry segment, but also by stage and team power. Call those companies and talk to their founders. You can probably either save yourself a lot of wasted energy, or learn the few remaining things you need to do to get your chances up."

Larry Kubal, Managing Director, Labrador Ventures, www.labrador.com

"At Labrador Ventures, we have seen that the best preparation an entrepreneur can have in raising capital is to have raised capital before. Absent that, the next best thing is to talk to people who have and glean what you can from their experience, advice, and possibly even receive referrals to other experienced entrepreneurs, angels, and VCs. Gathering information and expanding your network are fundamental in the capital raising process.

"Another key element in preparing to raise capital is being fully committed to the venture. If you are thinking 'well, I'll just try it and see what happens,' don't bother. You will fail.

"Getting to the point of self-commitment, and then team commitment, involves coming to grips with a multitude of issues on two levels: the rational and the emotional.

"Rationally, you must resolve that your business plan has a good chance for success, that there is a market, and that the business model makes sense. Beat up your plan. Take nothing for granted. No idea is sacred. Do this individually and as a team, and in the end commit and believe in your plan. There is no question that it will evolve through input from funding sources and ultimately the marketplace. But if your business plan is still evolving—or perhaps worse, swirling in uncertainty—when you fund raise, you will fail.

"Emotionally, you must be committed and centered on the venture. This goes much deeper than merely thinking you want to do it. Ask yourself the hard questions: Do I have what it takes? Can I handle the rejection, frustration, and disappointment? Can I lead? What will this do to my relationships with friends, family, spouse, or significant others? Who am I if I fail? If I succeed? Why am I doing this? Money? Something to prove? To whom? The actual answers to these questions are less important than the process of this introspection.

"From my perspective as an early-stage VC investor at Labrador Ventures, all the good analytics of markets, business models, and competitive advantages are necessary but not sufficient reasons to invest. It is our intuitive, subjective, positive assessment of the character of the founding team that convinces us to write a check. The entrepreneur's character assessment is enhanced, and thereby the probability that a given venture will be funded is increased, by the preparatory commitment process described above."

Positioning means understanding that there are thousands of sources of capital in the United States today, sources that run the gamut in terms of amount they are capable of investing, what types of companies they are interested in, what criteria they use to evaluate deals, and what form of investment they prefer to make (debt or equity, minority or majority share). A successful capital search requires determining which subgroup out of this vast universe of investors best fits the type of company you have and concentrating your efforts on this group.

ADVICE FROM A VENTURE CAPITALIST

Dennis Spice, Managing Partner, Open Prairie Ventures,
www.opven.com

What happens when an entrepreneur contacts you? "The process begins with getting an executive summary of the company's business plan.

Once this is received, typically a partner in our firm looks at the summary to determine if it fits within our portfolio dynamic, and if it does, and we see something in the summary interests us, then we ask for a copy of the full plan to be sent to us. And then we would invite the entrepreneur and his team in for an interview. Our investment committee, which is made up of all the partners in the firm, would then review the due diligence we have conducted to that point and make a decision whether or not to make an offer to put a term sheet on the table. Once that occurs, we would begin our full due diligence on the company. And somewhere 30 to 90 days later we would make an investment."

ADVICE FROM AN ENTREPRENEUR

Martin K. Elliott, Ph.D, President and CEO, Caduceus-TeleMedicine Solutions, Inc.

How can entrepreneurs prepare in their search for venture capital?
"First, be certain your family supports your entrepreneurship. Many spouses have a difficult time with no regular paychecks and postponing the annual vacation, etc.

"Second: Test your business concept before leaving your day job. Can you get four to five customers to buy into your product/service at the price you believe you must charge to be profitable?

"Third: The investors will want a clean slate personnel wise. They will require that you hire super-bowl star players for each position. The VCs look for people, people, people.

"Fourth: Know the threshold parameters for your industry—VCs do *not* invest in small outfits. They want a $500 million company in four to five years or less so they can go IPO (initial public offering) or M&S (merger & sale) and cash out. (You have no problem cashing out, do you?)

"Finally develop that 90-second elevator pitch: In 90 seconds, you must tell the investor what huge problem your economically simple but elegant solution will solve, and why/how you and your team will dominate the industry (30 percent) in four to five years with just $n megabucks of his money."

Perseverance simply means a willingness to invest the time and energy to get the job done. Entrepreneurs invariably think the process of finding capital will take substantially less time than it turns out to. They underestimate how much time they need to devote to all the steps in the process, from preparing a business plan to present to investors, to closing the deal and depositing the check(s). Part of the frustration entrepreneurs feel when they are seeking capital comes from their own underestimation, or lack of awareness, of all that is entailed in closing a transaction.

Acquisition of capital is as much a part of the management of a company as producing or selling products and services. It is an ongoing function throughout the life of the business, and the sources of capital that are most suitable, and cost effective, for a business change as the business grows and evolves.

ADVICE FROM A VENTURE CAPITALIST

Dennis E. Murphree, Managing Partner, Murphree Venture Partners, www.murphreeventures.com

"Any entrepreneur seeking funding from a venture capital firm should keep six things in mind:

"1. VCs have a short attention span. Keep your executive summary and the pitch concise, simple to understand, and compelling as a focused story.

"2. Study the potential VC investors as hard as they'll study you and your plan. Each firm and each partner is different from one another, so study your VC candidates and pick wisely.

"3. Within reason, don't worry too much about valuation. Get the money and start executing on the plan and valuations will increase accordingly.

"4. Get a good lawyer who understands VC deals intimately and everything will go more smoothly throughout the negotiation and financing process.

"5. When asked what role you want to play in the enterprise, simply answer 'I'll do whatever is best for the company' and your VC will breathe a sigh of relief . . . and you will have jumped one of the biggest hurdles.

"6. Remember the words of Winston Churchill: 'Never, never, never give up' and keep believing in both yourself and your dream. Most VCs will turn you down, so keep going until you find the right one to buy into the dream as well."

Tom Hiatt, Managing Director, MWV Capital Partners, www.mwvcapital.com

"1. Make the business plan as professional as possible. Venture capitalists are busy people, and you need to approach them with a strong business proposition that is well thought out. Often you will only get one shot, so make it your best.

"2. Be persistent. Venture capitalists are inundated with many opportunities. If you don't promote your own deal, no one else will.

"3. Be wary of intermediaries. If at all possible, spearhead the money-raising initiative yourself. No one likes to raise money, but the CEO or CFO is usually the best person to speak knowledgeably and passionately about the company. Intermediaries can rarely communicate the same level of knowledge and enthusiasm for an investment opportunity.

"4. Be focused. Approach venture capitalists whom you have researched and whom you know will be interested in a transaction like the one you are presenting.

"5. Be prepared for the process to take three to six months or more, from start to finish. Some deals are cut quickly; in my experience, many are not. VCs want to get to know you and your company well before they commit to a long-term relationship."

What Entrepreneurs Say About Raising Capital— Feel the Pain

For several years we have published an Internet newsletter on the subject of planning and financing ventures. To subscribe to the *Capital Connection Newsletter*, just send this message, "subscribe cc-newsletter" (no quotes of course) in the body of an e-mail to: listar@capital-connection.com. We asked the subscribers, mostly entrepreneurs, for their opinions on raising capital. They were not shy about sharing their views, and what comes through loud and clear is that raising capital is difficult for everyone—and many entrepreneurs believe we live in a strange new world.

"I'm an unproven entrepreneur that has a great product in the best position but I don't know anyone so I am struggling to raise capital. It's crazy to see companies in my industry waste millions of dollars on stupid marketing campaigns or ideas when we only need $1 million to take over our market. We've proven it on a small scale and only need money to prove it on a large scale. We have already built the infrastructure and only need a push. What is a guy to do?"

"I think most of these venture capitalists are full of b-s. It isn't as black and white as your newsletter tends to make it seem."

"Most of the true VCs I have met in the last year are egotistical anuses who have suspended all rules of courtesy. I will be glad to rub some noses in our success in the near future. Kinda like Austin Ventures declining to invest in Michael Dell a few years back. Now he gigs them every chance he gets. I await my chance."

"Business planning and proposal writing is very difficult and can break any

person, if he or she is not ready for the downfalls. The venture capital industry can be a blessing for some entrepreneur who has a great idea or plan, but [the VC] may also pull the rug from under them, leaving them penniless."

"A very good management team is more important than the idea, but a great idea is wonderful, just hard to sell if you have no business experience and you are not a current Stanford student."

"We don't live in Silicon Valley, and it is too difficult to meet VCs elsewhere in the world."

"The entrepreneur has the idea—that doesn't mean he has the means to write a great business plan, get a great management team, research the market in depth—all in a short time before somebody else comes up with a similar idea and gets it to market because they get access to the cash first."

"I am personally aware of large amounts of funding going to ventures with little more than a good idea, while developed products with seemingly promising markets are ignored. An example recently appeared in the Washington Post business section about a guy on the block who had raised $30 million. . . . The guy did not seem to have much more than an idea, without technology, market experience, or customers. I understand some of the reasons that this phenomena exists but am puzzled by the frequency with which it occurs."

"We have not contacted any [venture capital companies] because we are not ready and too busy with new growth and a careful approach to marketing. I believe our next step would be to speak to someone who would advise us as to the best way to seek investment in our company. It is difficult if you have never done it, because you don't know what to anticipate and who or what the best investor vehicle would be for us."

"Venture capitalists are greedy and callous—yet necessary."

"I would like to have a real experience with an investor of venture capital, where it can be possible for them to study my project, to analyze its possibilities, to look at the market of it, and discuss its future growth. And then discuss the funds to be invested and the terms and conditions of them. It looks like a dream but this is what I would like: an event between an entrepreneur with a solid project and a venture capitalist. In my case, this has not yet happened."

"From my experience, venture capital is something like a UFO: Everyone talks about seeing it but only one in a million has an encounter."

4

Presenting a Business Plan to Investors

Do You Really Need a Business Plan?

Entrepreneurs often find writing a business plan to be an extremely difficult task. They can agonize for months and months trying to articulate on paper the vision for their company they see so clearly when they close their eyes at night.

Those who are struggling through the process often ask whether they really need a full-blown business plan in order to get capital for their business. A growing body of bad advice out there tells entrepreneurs that all they need is a 10- to 15-page summary business plan, or even just a 3- to 5-page executive summary, because that's all investors have time to read now.

The opportunity to take a shortcut around an arduous task is always beguiling, but in this case there are several flaws in this logic.

Let's look at what the word "summary" means. According to the dictionary, summary is "a condensation of the substance of a larger work."

In order to construct a summary, we need to have a larger work available to us. If you don't have a business plan, how can you summarize it?

The larger issue, though, is what value does the business plan have, anyway. The process of writing is intended to help the entrepreneur and the management team of a company create a blueprint for success, with two main areas of focus: (1) why the company represents a great investment opportunity, and (2) what the specific steps will be to build an enterprise to take advantage of the opportunity. Along the sometimes torturous path from writing page 1 of the plan to page 40 or so, the founders of the company will clarify their strategies, identify holes in the management team that need to be filled, and gain a much better understanding of the financial and personnel resources that will be needed.

It would be very difficult to be able to answer an experienced investor's questions about your company without having the benefit of going through the analytical process of constructing the business plan. Investors do not enjoy hearing a question answered with "Um, I'm not sure. I'll have to get back to you on that one."

The business plan writing process can enhance the entrepreneur's confidence when going into meetings with investors. Projecting confidence is part of making a favorable impression on the investor.

In addition, the planning function will be central to the company's success in the future. If you are successful raising the capital, this will be just the first in many annual plans, with quarterly updates and reforecasts, that you will do.

ADVICE FROM A VENTURE CAPITALIST

Bill McAleer, Partner, Voyager Capital, www.voyagercap.com

Some people tell entrepreneurs to not spend time completing a full business plan, just come up with a punchy Power Point presentation to sell the idea. Do you agree or disagree? "I agree that a Power Point presentation can help them focus. It is a good place to start, to help them outline their ideas. But I like to see a crisply written, concise plan that discusses the key assumptions in more detail than you can do in a Power Point format."

Entrepreneurs who are struggling to write the plan themselves and want to make the business plan writing process easier have three main avenues to take. They can:

1. Hire a consultant or advisor to assist with the preparation of the plan.
2. Enlist trusted business associates to review the plan and make constructive criticism.
3. Purchase business planning software or read books on the subject.

If you choose Option 1, it is important that you work with the consultant in writing the plan. A professional plan writer can be of great help in taking your ideas and putting them in acceptable business planning format, relieving you of the difficulty of organizing the information—but you have to have the ideas ready to go for the project to work out well. It is very difficult for, and you should not expect, a third party to have the degree of understanding about your industry that you do, for example. The plan must reflect you and your management team. It's a good idea to at least try to put some of your ideas down on paper, if at all possible, and then seek out assistance.

It is always a good idea to have people whose business judgment you trust to review your plan from the standpoint of a potential investor and make recommendations about sections that need to be clarified or point out areas you may have missed. Because entrepreneurs are so close to the plan, it is difficult for them to have an objective viewpoint about whether the plan is ready for a prime-time presentation to investors.

Some business planning software programs are very reasonably priced and fairly sophisticated. They organize the plan and are especially useful in helping you construct your financial projections. They do not really plan your company, however. You still have to do the thinking and the strategic design of your business. Software can be useful to help get you started, but you may still need options 1 and 2 as you go along. Most entrepreneurs find it difficult to read a book or two on the subject of business planning and then sit down and write a complete plan. One idea is to read several business plans from other companies and get a feel for the organization and logic of the presentation.

HOW LONG DOES IT TAKE TO WRITE A BUSINESS PLAN?

This depends on the complexity of the company and how much research into the market or the industry is necessary. An entrepreneur who has the key points of the plan pretty well thought out should be able to translate the ideas to paper within four to six weeks. It is a mistake to rush the process; doing so is a good way to omit important ideas or make errors in the financial projections.

What Does a Business Plan Look Like?

Business plans need to be customized to the type of company being started and to the industry the company is in. And entrepreneurs must think of the ultimate audience as well. The degree of detail that is gone into regarding the technical aspects of the company depends on how much understanding the investors have of the specific technology and your industry. One size does not fit all. Certain themes must be emphasized for certain companies. For example, you would not expect the business plan for a motion picture distribution company to even remotely resemble the plan for a medical technology enterprise.

A business plan usually includes these major sections; depending on what you want to emphasize, you may wish to have some of the sections in a different order than that presented here.

Executive Summary

Company Overview

Products and/or Services

Industry or Market Analysis

Competitive Profile

Customer Profile and Marketing Plan

Management Team

Operations and Facilities

Licensing and Regulatory Issues

Risk Factors

Capital Requirements and Proposed Transaction Structure

Financial Projections

Appendix

With this in mind, here is a sample format for a business plan. It is helpful to view writing a plan as a process of answering a series of questions.

EXECUTIVE SUMMARY

The executive summary is extracted from the other parts of the plan when completed, *with a focus on these themes*:

- The great opportunity that exists
- The large market that is not being served adequately by existing competitors
- Your unique capabilities to serve this market
- The compelling competitive advantage that will result

COMPANY OVERVIEW

The company overview is a brief description of what the company does or will do (one to two sentences).

Business Purpose

Why did you decide to enter this business? What is the opportunity you saw? Why was the market not being served adequately? What was attractive about the opportunity? What was your original vision for the company? What market need did you see that you want to exploit? How did the management team come together? Why were you in the right place at the right time, with the required background and experience to build a business out of this opportunity?

Company History and Current Status

This is a description of current operations, product line, revenue streams, operations, and accomplishments. What have you accomplished so far? Include information on:

Product research & development

Web site development

Strategic alliances

Building content

Building a management team

Company Mission

What kind of company do you want to build? What brand image are you seeking to establish, or reputation in the marketplace? How do you want people to think of your company?

Summary of Objectives
What is the long-range objective (for example: to build a $50 million company within five years)?

Business Model
Explain the financial opportunity your company represents. Where do (will) your revenues come from? What cost factors are favorable that can lead to high profitability? Will you have multiple revenue streams? Is the business model highly scalable (once the company begins generating revenues can these revenues grow rapidly, even exponentially)?

PRODUCTS AND/OR SERVICES

You have already given the reader a brief description about your products and services in both the Executive Summary and the Company Overview. Here, you go into much greater detail so the reader can gain a thorough understanding of the technology and benefits of your products or services.

Specific Products/Services
Describe your products/services, their development status, when they will be ready for introduction.

Features and User Benefits
Why do the end users need your product and service? What benefits do your products/services provide that are clearly superior to the competition?

Proprietary Aspects
(These are trademarks, special skills, proprietary processes, distribution channels, and patents.) What are the proprietary aspects of your products/services? What is your sustainable competitive advantage?

System Design Challenges
   Technical difficulty
   Status of design currently
   Vendors

Next Generation of Products/Services or Upgrades

Product Summary Statement (Unique Selling Proposition)
Close this section with a concise statement of why your product/service is the best solution for the customer's need or problem. You cannot emphasize this enough!

INDUSTRY OR MARKET ANALYSIS

In this section you want to focus on explaining what excites you about the industry your company is part of. Why is your industry the best place for investors to put their money?

History of the Industry
Go over the important developments in your industry during the recent past, perhaps the last five years.

Market Description
Size of the market and anticipated growth. Market history and trends. How is the market evolving? What is the driving force behind the growth in the market?

COMPETITIVE PROFILE

Who are your competitors? How are their products/services positioned? How much market share do they have? What are their strengths and weaknesses? What new competitors could possibly emerge?

Key Success Factors
What factors must a company in your industry possess in order to compete effectively?

Barriers to Entry
Are there any barriers to entry? How can you protect your competitive position once it is established? How do you think the competitive environment will change over the next three to five years?

Unique Capabilities/Creating Competitive Advantage
What makes you different and give you a special advantage? What do you have that competitors don't? How will you create an "unfair" competitive advantage?

CUSTOMER PROFILE AND MARKETING PLAN

This section is critical to investors in deciding whether you really understand who your customers are and how to sell to them.

Customer Profile

Describe the markets you have targeted. Who will your customers be? Why did you select these targets?

Marketing Strategies

How are you going to reach the markets? Summarize your strategies: distribution channels, promotion, pricing. Specifically, how will you distribute and promote the products/services? How much will it cost to reach these markets? What will be your expenditures on marketing? (Demonstrate that the cost of entering the market and acquiring customers is not prohibitive.)

Advertising, Promotion, Public Relations

Details of which mediums you want to use, why you chose them. How many prospects do you forecast obtaining? Conversion rate into customers?

Sales Organization

How many people will be required to market your products or services? How will this part of the company be organized? What skill level will you need in prospective employees?

Pricing Strategy

How will you price-position your product or service in the market versus your key competition? Explain the logic behind your pricing strategy.

Service and Support

Superior customer service builds loyalty and repeat business, and therefore ongoing revenue for your company. How will your company outperform the competition in this area?

Strategic Alliances Undertaken or Proposed

Alliances with larger organizations are becoming increasingly important for early-stage companies to establish themselves in their market. Showing the reader your company has alliances in place gives it added value.

Marketing Volume Goals in Units

Providing an easy-to-understand chart of these goals can help the reader see you have put considerable thought into your revenue projections and have a clear understanding of how many prospects you need to reach and how to convert these prospects into sales.

MANAGEMENT TEAM

You will see that a key theme of this book is how important the quality of the management team is to prospective investors. This chapter needs to be much more than a dry summation of resume-type material. You must make a case that you have a special team assembled that is clearly capable of achieving the growth and profitability results you have forecast.

Key Individuals
Background. Role in the company. Value they add (not just technical skill, but skill in all the aspects of building a company).

Accomplishments and Strengths of Team
What prior experience does the management team have that will lead to success in this venture?

Current Ownership of Company
Who owns the stock of your company now? Management or outsiders? What is each person's percentage ownership?

Personnel to Be Added in Order to Build a Successful Team
Few early-stage companies have totally complete management teams. Show the reader/investor that you know what elements are missing and have planned how to add the right people to the team after the company is funded.

Organizational Structure
Chart showing staff levels by category, by quarter.

OPERATIONS AND FACILITIES

How will the product be manufactured? Or, what facilities and equipment are needed to produce this service you offer? Where will your office(s) be located? Space/equipment requirements as you grow.

Key Vendors/Suppliers
Discuss relationships you have in place with these companies, and why you chose them over other potential vendors/suppliers.

LICENSING AND REGULATORY ISSUES

These are more relevant in some industries than others. For example, with companies involved in the financial services industry, the regulatory issues need to be discussed thoroughly in the business plan.

RISK FACTORS

What factors could keep you from achieving the forecast results?

Response from competitors

Technical difficulties

Scarcity of resources (including people and capital)

Changes in technology

Economic factors

Not getting marketing ramped up before "me-too" competitors arise

Contingency Plans
Alternate plans to deal with these risks.

CAPITAL REQUIREMENTS AND PROPOSED TRANSACTION STRUCTURE

Amount of capital being sought, proposed terms of investment

Proposed uses of funds and benchmarks or milestones with timetable for completion and cost

Stages of investment (if applicable)

Possible exit strategies for investors

Forecast return on investment

FINANCIAL PROJECTIONS

Financial History (if applicable)
Profit and Loss Statement Forecasts (3 to 5 years)

Monthly year 1

Monthly or quarterly year 2

Annually years 3 to 5

Balance Sheet Forecasts (3 to 5 years)
Cash-Flow Forecasts (3 to 5 years)
Assumptions Behind the Numbers (Very important!)

APPENDIX

Letters of Intent
Customer Agreements
Strategic Alliances
Market Research

Venture Capitalists Recommendations About What to Emphasize in Your Business Plan

Clarity
"Be clear about what the company does and how that fits into the value chain. Who are the customers, who are the suppliers, and why are they willing to work with you and let you make a profit?"

Brevity
"Send a presentation that is brief and succinct, hitting the top points first of why it's compelling, and recognizing strengths and weaknesses honestly. Brevity is key. If you're seeing 10 business plans per day, as we are, you would want to know in a few minutes why it's worth our while to dig into details."

An Exciting Idea
"A great idea, well-presented in brief form."

Industry Contacts in Place
"Relationships you have in place with industry players, such as potential customers."

Your Market
"Be sure you understand the market and the competition."

Competitive Advantage
"Crystal-clear description of the company's competitive advantage."

You Have Already Received Capital from Some Source
"Tell us that you have your seed financing in place."

Large Market
"Assemble the best team possible and go after a big market."

"A big market, high-quality management."

Partnerships
"Significant, synergistic partnership agreements."

Sales Already Achieved
"Evidence of product validation/acceptance in the marketplace."

Management Team
"Have a management team with outstanding resumes and accomplishments."

"A management team with direct industry experience."

"Assemble a great team with relevant industry experience."

Product/Service Demonstration
"A compelling demo of your product/service/web site that is available for us to see."

Avoid Anonymous Business Plans
"Finally, please make sure a contact person with a phone number and address is included. I am always surprised how many entrepreneurs leave this off the executive summary."

What Do Venture Capitalists Think of the Business Plans They Receive?

Truth Can Be Painful

The business plan and the executive summary of the plan are important tools to get the investor's attention, make a favorable first impression, and prompt the venture capitalist to seek further discussion with the entrepreneur.

With that in mind, who better to evaluate the quality of, and make suggested improvements in, the business plans than venture capitalists themselves—people who see hundreds of these documents each year.

Nearly 250 venture capital firms across the United States were surveyed and asked three questions:

1. What is the worst mistake entrepreneurs can make when completing their company's business plan?

2. What is the most common mistake entrepreneurs make when completing their business plan?

3. What are the most critical mistakes entrepreneurs make in their executive summaries?

QUESTION 1: WORST MISTAKE IN BUSINESS PLAN

According to the respondents to the survey, there are eight major mistakes entrepreneurs can make when completing their company's business plan.

The mistake most frequently mentioned (by 17 percent) was that entrepreneurs were *not clear in explaining the opportunity*—why the business made sense, why it would make a good investment. Some VCs said this was because the plan was incomplete, but others said it was because the plan had too much detail, was not concise or focused.

This lack of clarity kept the venture capital firm from proceeding to the next stage. The business plan was the first chance to sell the investor on the deal, by telling the company's story in a clear fashion—and more than one in seven entrepreneurs wasted their first chance.

Another critical error that is very difficult for entrepreneurs to avoid: *unrealistic projections* (13 percent of respondents); 8 percent said they see "*simplistic assumptions*" in the business plans they read. One respondent complained about the tendency for entrepreneurs to claim their projections are conservative, when this is simply not true. In the many years this venture capital firm has been in business, it has had many "winners" in their investment portfolio, but not once has a company achieved the projections of its original business plan—*not once*. One respondent expressed this mistake as "entrepreneurs believing whatever they write is factual."

The *analysis of competition* in business plans is another area where venture capitalists believe entrepreneurs are weak (10 percent). Many entrepreneurs do not make the effort, or find it too difficult, to gather data in a systematic way about competitors. Entrepreneurs either say there is no competition or underestimate the strength of competitors.

Mistakes and errors appear frequently in the plans, according to more than 10 percent of the respondents, who also said that entrepreneurs sometimes try to mislead them with the information in the plan or do not trust venture capitalists sufficiently to give them key pieces of sensitive information in the plan.

Another response occurring regularly was that *management strengths were overstated* in the plan (8 percent). One respondent went so far to say that entrepreneurs "lie" about their credentials. This is indeed an unfortunate mistake because venture capitalists *always* thoroughly check out the background of people involved in a company they are contemplating investing in.

Incompleteness, including leaving sections out of the plan or not including sufficient financial data, was cited by 8 percent.

Failure to describe a sustainable competitive advantage was also noted by 8 percent. The plan does not describe a competitive advantage the company may have or how to achieve a competitive advantage.

Other respondents felt the plans:

- Were not focused enough on the management team's experience.
- Do not demonstrate an ability to reach the customers and sell the product.
- Indicate that the entrepreneurs do not understand their own plan.
- Have too much detail and are not concise.
- Indicate that the entrepreneurs believe that an IPO is the only possible exit strategy.

QUESTION 2: MOST COMMON MISTAKE IN BUSINESS PLAN

By far the most frequently mentioned mistake entrepreneurs make when completing their business plan is saying that the *company has no competition or underestimating the strength of competitors* (32 percent). Nine percent of respondents mentioned *the failure to describe a sustainable competitive advantage. Not clearly explaining the opportunity* was the next most frequently mentioned mistake, by 27 percent. Following that was the related mistake of having a *disorganized, unfocused, or even poor presentation* (12 percent).

Miscalculation of market share and market size (9 percent) were also regarded as common mistakes, with several respondents saying that they still receive business plans that say, "The total market is $1 billion, if we only get 10 percent of it, we will be a $100 million company"—without ever explaining how they are going to sell $100 million worth of their product.

Respondents also said they commonly see business plans that do not address the risks of a venture, and contain *no contingency plans* for coping with the risks (also 9 percent).

Other less frequently mentioned responses included:

- Entrepreneurs do not explain how they are going to sell the product.
- Entrepreneurs don't understand the venture capital process and send the plan to the wrong audience.
- They overstate management's strengths.
- They make unrealistic projections.
- The information is incomplete; sections are missing; the financials are inadequate.
- Entrepreneurs underestimate the amount of capital required and assume the business will develop easily.
- They refuse to cede control and insist on being CEO.
- The discussion of management is weak.
- Entrepreneurs assume an IPO can be their exit strategy.
- They overestimate the value of their enterprise.

ADVICE FROM A VENTURE CAPITALIST

Dennis Spice, Managing Partner, Open Prairie Ventures, www.opven.com

Many venture capitalists are critical of the job entrepreneurs do on their business plans. What do you think of the plans that come in? "We deal with technical people, so it is easy to be critical of their business plans. To be fair, we have to ask, 'Where did they learn to write a business plan?' There were no such classes in engineering school. We are trying to create one at the University of Illinois, so young entrepreneurs with an engineering background can learn these skills early on."

_____

QUESTION 3: CRITICAL MISTAKES IN EXECUTIVE SUMMARIES

Entrepreneurs are advised to pay extra attention to the plan's executive summary. The venture capitalist often sees the summary first, before reading the full plan. How good a job are entrepreneurs doing on their summaries? According to venture capitalists, the following are the most critical mistakes entrepreneurs make in the executive summaries of their business plan.

Unclear: 24 percent

Too long, not concise: 22 percent

Unfocused: 10 percent

Unrealistic valuation of the company: 10 percent

Not enough information on the management team: 8 percent

Too much emphasis on the product rather than the market: 6 percent

And we thought it must be an easy job to be a venture capitalist! It's no fun having to spend the day trying to read an unclear, verbose, unfocused plan with a ridiculous valuation number that doesn't tell you who the people are or how big the market is. No wonder investors sometimes seem cranky when you get them on the phone.

Let's compare what entrepreneurs think are the most critical mistakes made versus the observations of the venture capitalists.

Entrepreneurs

Unclear: 14 percent

Too long: 11 percent

I don't know: 11 percent

Unrealistic projections: 9 percent

Poorly written: 7 percent

Management discussion weak: 6 percent

Venture Capitalists

Unclear: 24 percent

Too long, not concise: 22 percent

Unfocused: 10 percent

Valuation of the company is unrealistic: 10 percent

Not enough information on the management team: 8 percent

Too much emphasis on the product rather than the market: 6 percent

There is surprising uniformity of opinion about what is lacking. Both investors and entrepreneurs say that executive summaries tend to be unclear and too long. They also both see that unrealistic numbers and lack of adequate discussion of management are problems. For entrepreneurs, "I don't know" was the second most popular response, illustrating that business plan writing is mystifying to a significant number of them.

Venture Capitalists' Criticisms of Business Plans

Completeness
"They forget basic information such as how much capital they are seeking."

"Incomplete evaluation of competition and marketing approach."

Clarity
"No clear understanding of the opportunity."

"Failure to concisely state their opportunity."

"Not enough information on what they really do."

"Not succinctly articulating what the company does in one sentence."

"The basic proposition is not adequately articulated, but is overwrapped in excitement. The reason why we would want to back the people is not sufficiently clear. The precise reasons why the company will be valuable, and to whom, are not made clear."

"The message is unclear. I should know what the company is about within the first two paragraphs."

"They don't get to the point quickly enough."

"Not being clear about what they do."

"Not being precise, lucid—written in a way everyone understands."

An Opposing View
"Entrepreneurs don't think big picture."

(Wait, I thought we were supposed to be precise and lucid.)

VCs Subscribe to Wired
"They spend too much time telling me how the Internet is going to change the world—we already know that."

Credibility
"Too short [low] on cash needs, too high on expectations."

"Overstating revenues/understating competition."

"Unrealistic expectations about the difficulty of getting in the market and the associated costs."

"Making unsupportable claims."

"Unrealistic, unfocused representation of market size and opportunity."

"Overstating their case without an adequate appreciation of the hurdles, which comes off looking like it is from a novice."

"Outlandish claims about the size of the market and their ability to dominate it. A big market is important, and most VCs want to invest in market leaders, but nobody will believe that you have identified an untapped $10 billion market and will be able to gain significant market share while protecting huge profit margins."

"They make a lot of invalidated assumptions about their business."

"They don't do proper research, they aren't compact and to the point, and their projections are unbelievable."

"Unrealistic projections on the potential revenue generation of the business. No one just turns a crank and automatically becomes profitable simply because money is put behind an idea. Presence of other competitors and their effect on the potential of the business being proposed. (There are very few cases of anyone being the first one in with something that no one else has ever done before.) Commitment to actually wanting to see the business succeed, versus just wanting to make money and run."

Organization and Writing Style
"Entrepreneurs don't realize that the executive summary is the marketing tool. The key points need to be clear, concise, short, and simple. Don't forget to mention management team!"

"Too long."

"They forget to include their name and telephone number—it happens 10 to 15 times a week here."

"Entrepreneurs forget to use examples or analogies to explain complex subjects."

"Forgetting to include real-life examples of how the product of process works. Remember, the person reading needs to get this idea quick or he or she will disregard it."

"Not addressing all aspects of running a business—fully addressing industry, marketing plan, financing plan, etc."

Too much *"blue sky."*

"Sloppy writing."

"The inability to find information easily hinders the business plans from getting a thorough review."

"Hyperbole and poor writing."

"Not including a summary of each section of the business plan."

"Generic language."

Must Have Been a Former English Teacher
"Using an apostrophe with the conjunction its in the possessive form."

Business Model
"Not including at least an outline of the business model."

"Don't actually describe the business model and value proposition, or give an estimate of the financing required."

"Product and business model are not presented clearly."

Product
"Focusing more on the concept rather than the team and the concept."

"Being too technically detailed and not describing how what they are doing will benefit the customer."

Market
"No understanding of how to get to the market or what it will cost."

"Have a good product/technology but have no concept of its market."

"Not explaining what the company does and why it is important. Too much market opportunity nonsense."

"Describing a product without describing the customer who might use it."

"Failing to demonstrate a nuanced understanding of the market and its segmentation."

"Inaccurate or poor assessment of the market, or poor description of product/ technology. I need to see how this company is going to get me a return on my investment, so I need to completely understand what the potential of this company is."

"Don't talk enough about the problem they're solving, the value proposition, or how they will sell the product/service."

"Defining target market too broadly."

"Describe the value proposition. Whose pain are you solving?"

"They don't present the market size and market growth potential."

"Listing meaningless industry market size and growth data."

"Failure to show the size and growth in the market."

"They are too focused on the finances and not enough on the product. The general tenor from all the entrepreneurs is that given enough money, the product details can be worked out. This is backward logic. One needs to have a sound product, a defined market, and a pathway to get the product into the market. The last two are generally covered pretty well, but the first one is typically lacking."

Competition and Competitive Advantage

"Failure to identify what in the entrepreneur's eyes makes up their unique competency."

"Naïve view of competitors and competitive challenges."

"They miss the key point—why they are really different."

"Not including a competitive matrix."

Management

"They don't stress the background of the people and the previous investors, both of which are very important."

"Not emphasizing or playing up the past experience/past success of the management team."

"They don't explain why their team would execute well. Most people spend too much time describing their plan rather than the people who will tackle it. So much of the business plan changes in the first few months that it becomes almost irrelevant—VCs really care the most about the people they are backing."

"Failing to talk enough about management."

"Not including management backgrounds."

"Too sure of existing management."

"Poor presentation of the management team."

"Background of management team (just the facts, please: I'll do the interpretation)."

"False statements in management bios."

"They don't show how they had any prior experience in this particular industry."

"They need to clearly show their qualifications."

"Lack of qualified management team or the ability to put one together quickly once financing is found."

"Lack of management information."

"Listing names and title of key players, but nothing about their backgrounds to indicate this is a special team."

Financial Section

"How quickly the investment will be profitable."

"Lack of clear explanations of assumptions."

"Not including amount of money sought and where that gets the company in terms of time and milestones."

"Typically in the start-up area, entrepreneurs underestimate the amount of capital they will require to make the business successful."

"Plans are too long and not focused enough on what the business will do to create a positive cash flow and how soon they can make this happen."

"Projecting a $60 million loss in one year!"

"Unrealistic revenue assumptions."

"Too aggressive on financial plan."

"No financial data is included in the executive summary."

"Omission of current financials."

"They don't provide a quarterly financial summary to show historical unit and revenue ramp."

"Give me more than just one year of projections, please."

"How much money you intend to raise and what you intend to do with it."

"Too much detail on minor balance sheet items, when even revenues are in question."

"Projected revenues way beyond reason."

Valuation

"Trying to calculate their own valuation. Mismatching use of proceeds with cash flow and capital requests."

"The biggest mistake is telling me what price to pay for the equity and how I should calculate my return."

Setting their own valuation: *"I'll sell you x% of the company for $3 million."*

"Incorrect valuation."

"Company valuation way too high."

"They often don't discuss how much is being raised and what the valuation is."

Note that the VCs disagree whether an entrepreneur should include a valuation of their company in the plan. And of course, when the valuation is included, it is often wrong, according to these VCs.

One Venture Capitalist Summed It up This Way
"Too many to list."

At least none of the venture capitalists said they don't like the color of the covers entrepreneurs put on the plans, or the type of binding used.

To Make a Good First Impression on the Investors

From the preceding responses, entrepreneurs should consider the following when constructing their business plan documents:

- The business opportunity is presented in a clear, exciting manner.
- The entrepreneur understands that projections are, at best, hopeful guesses and tries to base the projections on realistic assumptions.
- The entrepreneur makes as full disclosure as possible of the pitfalls of the business as well as its strengths.
- The plan is carefully proofread and edited until it does not contain any errors in grammar or math.
- The plan shows why the company and its products are different from and significantly better than what is out there in the marketplace.
- The company has taken the time to study and understand its competitors and can address their strengths and possible weaknesses.
- The plan contains enough information to tell a complete story about the company but is presented in a concise, tight writing style.
- The plan does not make exaggerated claims about the product or the management.
- The entrepreneur knows the plan by heart before making a presentation to the venture capitalist.

CHAPTER
6

The Capital Crapshoot

The Internet has created both a tremendous opportunity for entrepreneurs and a hurdle for them to overcome in financing their start-up ventures. It is now possible to market your products and services globally with a relatively modest infrastructure—even with a reasonable marketing budget if the company is planned wisely. By lowering the barrier to entry, the Internet has allowed thousands of entrepreneurs to put their ideas into action. But all of these entrepreneurs are competing for a limited quantity of time and attention that investors have to offer. The supply in good ideas is rising quickly; the supply of decision makers at venture capital funds is lagging behind.

Entrepreneurs are frustrated by, and in some cases downright resent, the difficulty they have getting through to the investors, getting them to review their plans, getting them on the phone.

ADVICE FROM VENTURE CAPITALISTS

*Dennis Spice, Managing Partner, Open Prairie Ventures,
www.opven.com*

The number of plans VCs receive is soaring. Given a fixed amount of resources, how do you keep up? "We sit outside of the metropolitan area, in east-central Illinois, out in the middle of the prairie. We are seeing more plans than we ever imagined. We are seeing unbelievable deal flow from all over the Midwest.

"How do we keep up? We have a process that we log every deal in and look at every executive summary. Candidly, we look more closely at deals that have been referred. If Joe the Accountant or Pete the Attorney has referred them, they have somewhat put their reputation on the line, saying 'This looks interesting to me; you're the expert, you take a look.' Those sent in by e-mail, we get a lot of, of course we read them. In those cases, I look at the team and see how strong they are. It's the people at this level that makes the difference.

"It is a challenge to filter through all the information we receive. I tell young entrepreneurs one of the things that frustrates me with executive summaries is how many don't include any mention of the amount of capital they are seeking. Like it's a mystery. Or that they are going to have me call and find out. We don't call, we'll just reject it. State the capital request early in the summary."

Patrick Sheehan, Partner, 3i Group, www.3i.com

"The volume of business plans and opportunities continues to rise. People are struggling to cope in a variety of ways. Some by only looking at deals that come from trusted contacts. Some focus on narrow technology. Some have grown their in-house resources a lot. At 3i, we have a large staff in many international locations, but we still have to cope with a tidal wave of plans. We try to use our network to have a clear idea of what areas of investment are likely to be interesting."

Will this tidal wave of deals continue? "We're still in one of those rare, big, discontinuous changes—created by the Internet, and globalization of world trade is filtering down. The Internet itself is fueling a lot of that. Great ideas ricochet around the world in minutes instead of years. There is an acceleration of the pace of things. Perhaps another factor is that global flows of money have become more of an everyday feature. Capital markets have become more efficient, bringing about a growth of the supply of money into private companies rather than just into publicly traded stocks. So, we have a number of factors conspiring to produce a bigger long-term wave."

Chances of Successfully Obtaining Venture Capital

Playing the roulette wheel in Las Vegas has better odds than winning the game of venture capital. And it's getting harder to win.

Venture capitalists were asked whether the number of new companies that have contacted them over the last 12 months has changed, on a scale from 1 (greatly decreased) to 5 (greatly increased). The average response was just over 4, with two-thirds of those polled saying either 4 or 5.

The results reflect the large number of Internet-based start-up companies that have been organized in the last year and have rushed to obtain funding in order to achieve the first-to-market advantage over competitors.

How Much Do Venture Capital Companies Invest?

While the level of venture capital funding has reached an all-time high so far in 2000 (see Table 6.1), the number of companies receiving funds has not increased by that same accelerated rate. The total dollars increased 397.4 percent the first quarter of 2000 over the first quarter of 1999; the number of companies being funded only increased 93.2 percent, while the size of the average transaction increased 105.8 percent.

This holds true for the second quarter of 2000 as well. The total amount of funds invested increased 255.9 percent over the second quarter of 1999; the average amount invested per company increased by 58 percent, from $7.65 million to $12.12 million, but the number of companies funded increased only 43.3 percent.

Another way to look at this is to hold the average investment amount constant. If the average investment per company remained at the first-quarter 1999 level of $5.89 million, the $17.14 billion invested in the first quarter of 2000 would have funded 2,910 companies rather than 1,414.

Table 6.1   Level of Venture Capital Funding

Quarter	1Q 96	1Q 97	1Q 98	1Q 99	1Q 00
$s billions invested	$1.692	$2.250	$3.032	$4.313	$17.140
# of companies invested	472	575	671	732	1414
$s millions per company	$3.58	$3.91	$4.51	$5.89	$12.12
% change in total $s	n/a	33%	34.5%	42.2%	397.4%
% change in $s per company	n/a	9.2%	15.3%	30.6%	105.8%
% change # companies	n/a	21.8%	16.7%	9.1%	93.2%

Information from the PricewaterhouseCoopers Venture Capital Survey, Second Quarter, 2000

ADVICE FROM AN ANGEL INVESTOR/ENTREPRENEUR

Neil Senturia, CEO, Mohomine, Inc., San Diego, CA

What would you advise young entrepreneurs about raising capital?
"I teach a university class on venture financing. My first message: It's harder than it looks. The second, it's really hard. Third, it's really, really hard.

"I went to a lecture by a panel of several VCs and an Internet expert, about how to get your Internet company started. They each give the same speech: You need a plan, a solid revenue model. The audience that came to listen was mainly young people thinking about launching their first venture. I thought it was a very good lecture, but not really the truth. Yes, the formula is you get a plan together, the first round of investment comes from angels, and you need to get an experienced CEO. Well, there are currently 2,000 open searches for CEOs in the Internet space. Then they said find a CTO (Chief Technical Officer), you need to find technical excellence. Very true, but nobody wanted to say how hard it is to do that."

Competition Is on the Increase

The entrepreneur's hope is that, as the number of deals being reviewed has soared, the number of investments made would be going up as well, so chances of getting funded are at least as good as they were in the past.

The number of business plans the average venture capitalist receives in a year has increased nearly 70 percent from 1998, from about 1,000 to 1,700. The least number of business plans reported was two per week, or 100 per year; the greatest, 200 per week, or 10,000 per year.

Another way to look at this is to say that the average venture capital firm has to review eight business plans per working day.

While on the average venture capitalists are making two more invest-ments per year than they did in 1998, the odds of any one company suc-cessfully receiving venture capital are less. In 1998 the odds of any one company successfully receiving venture capital were 7 in 1,000, or 0.7 in 100. The 2000 survey tells us that the odds are 5 in 1,000, or 0.05 of 1 percent, a significant decrease.

A significant group—about 20 percent of the total venture capitalists who participated in the survey—were extremely active, funding more than 12 deals per year. This "active" group funded, on average, 19 com-panies per year out of the 2,800 companies reviewed each year, for a funding percentage of roughly 0.7 percent—the same as the average for all venture capital firms two years ago. This shows the most active ven-ture capital firms have been able to cope with the increased flow of deals coming in and have stepped up their investment activity to keep pace.

The highest rate of funding was a firm that said it funded six compa-nies and received about two plans per week, or 100 per year. The firm funded 6 percent of the deals looked at, or roughly 1 in 17. The top 25 percent of respondents, in terms of percent of deals funded, averaged 11 fundings per year and reviewed about 600 plans per year. They funded roughly one in 50 of the companies they reviewed.

Among the venture capital firms that received a great number of plans per week (an average of 50, or 2,500 per year), the percentage funded was almost exactly the same as the group as a whole. The chances of being funded do not necessarily improve by contacting a less active venture capital firm, or a smaller firm. The large funds have the personnel and systems in place to process the immense amount of information they receive.

From the Entrepreneurs' Point of View

"Entrepreneurs going for capital must understand 'details' as the chances today of getting financed are extremely difficult."

"There are way more projects than money available and not enough investors available to look at various projects."

"It is definitely harder to get money now."

"VCs have taken worthless projects and with greed in mind, have funded these projects at the expense of small businesses."

"Venture firms in the dot.com start-ups are looking for real revenue streams and profitability."

"Dot.com businesses are taking money away from 'traditional' start-ups."

"VCs are not investors, they are investment managers rolling the dice for the 'real gamblers.'"

"The projects and 'management' that I have seen funded are beyond belief."

More Companies—More Time to Close?

Because the volume of new companies contacting venture capitalists has increased so much, one might assume this could affect how quickly deals are getting done. Among those who said that the number of companies had "greatly increased," two-thirds said the average time to closing was under 90 days, not significantly different from the average for all those surveyed. Those who said the number of companies contacting them had stayed the same or declined reported average times to closing almost identical to those who said the volume of plans had greatly increased.

So it doesn't look like the greater volume of companies to review has resulted in more time being required to close a given investment, which is some comfort for the entrepreneur.

CHAPTER

7

Earthbound Angels

Increasingly, Individuals Want In on the Venture Capital Game

The attractive returns of venture capital firms are beginning to draw more and more wealthy individuals into the venture capital arena, the financing of early-stage companies. Angel investors have been somewhat hampered in the past by the difficulty of finding high-quality deals. The Internet is changing this in a big way: A growing number of online networks allow accredited investors (people with a threshold level of income and net worth) to link up with companies seeking capital. The same generation of self-directed investors that has been gravitating to online trading services such as E*Trade and Ameritrade now is looking more and more at investing in private, early-stage companies.

The influx of angel investors is an extremely favorable development for entrepreneurs. Generally entrepreneurs have a difficult time finding or hooking up with wealthy individuals—investors who do not advertise the fact they are in the business of putting money into deals. The nature and risk profile of early-stage investments is very different, however, from investing in even the most exotic public companies. Small-cap public stocks may have a limited amount of trading activity, and thus it is difficult for an investor to exit. With venture capital investing, sometimes no exit whatsoever is possible for years.

Because online venture capital investing is such a new industry, it remains to be seen whether it will become a significant contributor to the overall venture capital investment in the United States. We don't have an answer to the question: What happens when a significant number of these early-stage companies simply don't make it in the marketplace and the individual investors lose the total amount of capital they put in?

Many day traders in the stock market have had to learn to adjust to the increasing volatility of the technology sector of the market; in fact, many sectors of the equity markets seem to be becoming more volatile. Even with volatile conditions, however, equity investors can take solace in the fact that stocks of good companies generally rebound after taking a bad tumble. With venture capital deals, however, some just stay down and never come back.

Although the venture capitalist mentality is accustomed to dealing with a negative outcome, how will individuals react?

Whether they find deals online or through traditional networking methods, individual investors making angel investments in early-stage companies will increase as long as the equity markets keep creating more and more millionaires or billionaires.

What Entrepreneurs Don't Know About Angels

Angel investors are responsible for the majority of the companies that get funding. Many entrepreneurs think the only way to obtain capital is to contact one or more of the few thousand venture capital firms in the United States. They are ignoring a market of angel investors that numbers in the tens of thousands and is likely to grow much faster than the number of venture capital firms will.

Angels have a much broader investment focus than the technology-driven venture capital firms. It is not an overstatement to say that, within the universe of angel investors, there is a potential investor to fit nearly every type of company and situation.

Angels now include a generation of younger investors who have made significant money in earlier investments or in Internet companies. They are not necessarily retired CEOs who are looking to get involved in a company again. Today's angel investor can be younger than the entrepreneur.

Angels seek to be active in companies, too, just like their professional investor counterparts in the venture capital firms. Entrepreneurs often envision selling passive securities to accredited (wealthy individual) investors and then just running their company the way they want, the way they always had. In fact, however, one of the major motivations for these wealthy individuals is the desire to get involved in guiding the company toward success, not just in participating in the returns.

The following profile of an angel investor was developed by The Center for Venture Research at the University of New Hampshire, which does research on angel investments:

- The "average" private investor is 47 years old with an annual income of $90,000, a net worth of $750,000, is college educated, has been self-employed, and invests $37,000 per venture.

- Most angels invest in companies within 50 miles of their home or office and rarely put in more than a few hundred thousand dollars.

- Ninety percent of these investments are made in small, mostly start-up firms.

- Nine out of 10 investors provide personal loans or loan guarantees to the firms they invest in. On average, this increases the available capital by 57 percent.

- Angel investors have higher incomes and are better educated than the average citizen, yet they are not often millionaires. They are a diverse group, displaying a wide range of personal characteristics and investment behavior.

- Investors expect an average 26 percent annual return at the time they invest, and they believe that about one-third of their investments are likely to result in a substantial capital loss.

- Investors accept an average of three deals for every 10 considered. The most common reasons given for rejecting a deal are insufficient growth potential, overpriced equity, lack of sufficient talent of the management, or lack of information about the entrepreneur or key personnel.

The Securities and Exchange Commission—the SEC—has its own definition of what an angel investor must be, although the SEC calls it an accredited investor. An accredited investor as defined in Rule 501(a) of Regulation D includes "any natural person whose individual net worth, or joint net worth with that person's spouse, at the time of his or her purchase exceeds $1,000,000" or "any natural person who had an individual income in excess of $200,000 in each of the two most recent years or joint income with that person's spouse in excess of $300,000 in each of those years and who reasonably expects for each the same income level in the current year."

ADVICE FROM AN ANGEL INVESTOR/ENTREPRENEUR

Neil Senturia, CEO of Mohomine, Inc., San Diego, CA

How did you go about raising capital when you started your first company? "I started my first company in October of '95. If I could have raised venture capital on day 1, I would have, but I was an ex–real estate developer who had an idea to deliver high-speed Internet and e-mail in public places, sort of like Superman jumps into a phone booth, checks his e-mail, and flies off to save Metropolis. When I went looking for money, what I got from venture capitalists mostly was something between polite neglect and outright hostility.

"So I went out to raise angel money—the first million dollars. It took me seven months. I probably contacted 100+ people. I eventually got 23 people to put up $950,000. Of the 23 people that invested, I knew personally only three of them. I got referred into a network where people I know referred me to people I didn't know, coast to coast. I had a friend, a starting point, not unlike six degrees of separation. I had one person I started with who knew a guy who would say, I'm not an investor but call these guys. It took seven months, 120 packages were sent out. The average investment was probably $25,000 to $50,000."

How much of the decision was based on one of their friends going in on the deal as well? "That was important. Groups of three or four of the investors knew each other."

So they relied on the judgment of their peers? "Absolutely. Let's fast-forward, after selling that company I took six weeks off. Then met a group of bright young technical people and started a second company. The investment model was the same model: $1 million to get started. But this time it took three days and nine phone calls, and I turned away half a million dollars. Of these nine people, eight were investors from my previous company. Was I that much smarter now? No. The investors viewed it as: We made a lot of money last time."

Did the fact you were going to be involved on a day-to-day basis make a difference? "I'm a relatively known quantity, not in Silicon Valley, but in San Diego. So yes."

Why do angel investors band together in networks? "Formal angel investors groups are more numerous today than they were five years ago, by a wide margin, exponential, even. There is a desire by monied people to have some semistructured forum or method to see deal flow. This is an interesting dilemma because deal flow is the problem for the venture capitalists as well. Now, what they'll say is, that's not quite really true, we get really 2,000 to 3,000 plans a year. But a flow of really good deals is still a problem.

"Here's the dilemma for the angels. Remember when I was raising capital, I made nine phone calls. I didn't go to a formal band of angels. There are now groups of angels in San Diego, L.A., San Francisco— there are angels galore. I go to a lot of these angel investment conferences. To some extent the deals you see presented may not necessarily be the best deals. That doesn't mean they are not good deals. It's somewhat self-selecting.

"The problem with the angel round is that it needs to be followed very shortly by a bigger round, a more substantive round, a more professional round. After the angel round, rather quickly you find you're running out of money. This round is designed to get the company started, test the idea, build out a portion of the management team. They quickly go from the angel round to having to compete in the venture round or first round. Lots of companies don't get past that. They get the first million, but not the next four."

What holds them back? "Lots of start-ups are not companies, they are *features*. Many of them come to angel investor meetings and just present a feature, not a company. It may be good technology, may be wonderful. It is usually just something someone is going to buy— a piece of software, a product."

What is your overall view of the funding of early-stage companies? "Like democracy, it's not a perfect system, but it's the best we've got. There is something to be said for survival: This may be a little too Darwinian, but if it was too easy, then everybody would do it.

"How do you get in the movie business? The best way is to have someone in the business to introduce you around. Maybe your cousin is an actor, or your uncle is a script editor. Every year 100,000 people come to California wanting to get into the movie business, with absolutely no contacts. A certain percentage get in anyway. The system is delightfully imperfect. But you can come from Des Moines with no relationships and $50 and get in the business.

"There are systems such as angels networks, but it is still difficult to get to the right investors. This system is flawed, but lots of companies do get started anyway. The winnowing process is often done through success by duress—the company is running out of money so I better figure out what to do next. I wouldn't try to change the system."

How has angel investing changed in the last year? "We had a true inflection point in April, 2000. Prior to that there had been a mad dash for angels to get into companies. Valuations were high. They all wondered, where can I put my money out and earn a 30, 40, 50, 60 70 percent return?

"Every business magazine had a story about Joe Johnson having invested in something and made a 7,000 percent return—and his real business is fixing washing machines. In April the world changed. A huge number of companies funded in the fourth quarter of '99 and first quarter of '00 are running out of money and are having a difficult time getting money and there's no quick fix available to them. It used to be a lot of these companies thought the exit strategy was, I hope I can find someone dumber than I am, to pay more than I did for this stock.

"There is a problem with the current start-up mentality. They think they are in a sprint, but building a company is actually a longer race than that. These sprinters have skewed the expectations of entrepreneurs whose races are much longer. You don't just run a 100-yard dash and say: Where's my money? Young entrepreneurs are getting false advertising of the way things really work.

"For every eBay there's an Intel, companies that have lasted a long time, with huge skills, that will last. I don't know if eBay will be around in 30 years. I may not bet against it, but . . .

"We are starting to see a return to family values, let's call it the willingness to work for a number of years to build a real company. Not products, not applications, not features, but companies."

Are You Sure You Want an Angel Investor?

With angel investors, the personality fit is particularly critical. How well can you get along with the investor? People investing their very own money—often money they worked extremely hard to earn in the first place—creates a more personal situation than money invested by a firm that does this many times per year. Venture capital firms have an organized approach to dealing with portfolio companies in terms of reporting requirements, amount of time spent with the company, schedule of meetings. Angel investors are likely to have fewer investments, and the "rules of engagement" are less specified: The angel may become more involved than you wanted. A partner in a venture capital firm is unlikely to call you and ask, "How's my company doing?" An angel investor may well express it that way.

The other extreme is cases where the angel investor may not be there to help you when you really need advice and counsel; the investor could be off doing something else.

We know of a wealthy individual who made investments in companies as a way of allowing his children to gain top management experience. When he put the money in, one of them was installed in a key position on the management team. For the entrepreneur, this was the worst of all possible worlds: an investor with high expectations, an inexperienced manager being brought aboard in an important role, and a family member there every day to report back to Dad. There has to be easier money out there than this.

An angel investor looks at other factors than venture capitalists do when making the decision to invest. They evaluate the ego satisfaction they will get from being involved. This can take several forms: the satisfaction of helping the young company succeed, passing on knowledge or experience, and being able to tell friends and business associates about what they are doing. The entrepreneur talking with potential angel investors has to be cognizant of how the company and the relationship can provide this ego satisfaction, or the investment is not likely to take place.

One angel investor told us that in reality, a wealthy busy person would be better off investing his or her risk capital with one of the venture capital firms rather than try to take the time away from the core business activity to find and analyze the investments themselves. But then the investment would belong to the venture capitalist's portfolio; the angel would not have the same pride of ownership in the equity of the start-up companies being funded.

Venture capital firms view their reputation as being extremely important. They don't want entrepreneurs going around the country—or the

Internet—talking about how terrible they were to work with. Angel investors don't necessarily adhere to the same code of conduct. A widely variable group of "characters" populates the angel community.

HOW ACTIVE ARE ANGEL INVESTORS?

Entrepreneurs wonder whether it is possible to generalize about the relative level of involvement in a company of angels versus venture capitalists. Some entrepreneurs are viewing the involvement in a positive light, hoping the investors will contribute their expertise, knowledge, and contacts. Others, however, are really asking, "How much will the investor interfere with how I want to run the company?"

Some people involved in the financing of early-stage companies will say that angels, on the whole, get far more involved than traditional venture capital firms. They are contributing their own money, after all, and are therefore more likely to want a voice in the day-to-day operations or to participate in the strategic planning of the business, rather than just a seat on the board of directors.

But there certainly are other angels, however, that are looking at the deal purely as an investment—just like buying shares of a company listed on Nadsaq—and are too busy with their own companies to spend much "quality time" with an entrepreneur.

Because venture capital firms devote their full-time efforts to the business of funding and growing companies, it can be said with certainty that they seek out a certain amount of active involvement in the companies they invest in. They do not want to run the companies, however.

With either type of investor, angel or venture capital firm, the entrepreneur needs to find out what this level of involvement will be prior to the transaction being completed, so there are no surprises later on. Conflict with an angel who tries to be too actively involved or disappointment when an investor does not provide the promised contacts or help can then be avoided.

Part of the planning process for an entrepreneur prior to starting to raise capital is to identify areas where he or she might need help, candidly discuss these areas with the prospective investor, and then ask if they are willing to provide assistance. Investors may have a wide range of expertise and contacts that are not readily apparent.

But you'll never know unless you ask.

DEAL TALES: NAKED CAPITALISM

A beautiful young woman we know who had invented a personal care consumer product that had a potentially huge market developed a unique approach to finding angel investors. To finance the seed funding for her venture, this enterprising lady worked as a stripper in one of those high-class "gentlemen's clubs" whose clientele is predominantly upscale businessmen. From the ranks of her admiring customers, she easily recruited several potential angel investors to help her launch her product.

What perplexed her was the valuation of her deal. She called us the day before her meeting with one of the investor candidates, wondering how much a piece of her pure start-up venture was worth. $100,000? $250,000? She had no idea. We told her this depends on whether the investor believed her sales projections and production cost figures, and that it was highly subjective—and then wished her luck.

The next week she called back with the exuberance of recent success still fresh in her voice. She said the investor had come to the club where she worked, watched her dance all night, and told her afterward, "I definitely want a piece."

We daresay.

ADVICE FROM AN ANGEL

John S. Baker, Angel Investor, San Diego, CA

What angel organization are you involved with? "I am a member of San Diego Tech Coast Association—a 'club' (for lack of a better word) of serious angel-level investors. We have a pretty rigid system for bringing an entrepreneur along to the point that he can present properly before the group complete with Term Sheet and all.

"There are similar groups in Orange County and Los Angeles and in the San Francisco area. The groups share their list of qualified companies; this increases the deal flow and exposes the company to a greater number of potential angels."

Why do you prefer to be angel investor as part of the group instead of going it alone? "By being associated with this group, I get a better flow of deals . . . and there is a lot of interaction with other members which helps flesh out areas in which I am less strong."

Do the angels work together? "Everyone in the group is expected to help in the due diligence tasks for companies which are in the system. I have served on two—a fascinating learning process."

How active have you been as an investor? "I am in four deals; two are now profitable, the third is generating revenues, and most recent one (two months ago) is meeting milestones and is about to complete its second round. None have paid off for me yet, but I am happy with the prospects."

Do the angels provide other kinds of mentoring assistance to entrepreneurs? "In San Diego we have a group called CONNECT, which is associated with UCSD. CONNECT helps companies grow in a variety of ways, but one very useful capability for me is their "Springboard" program. Springboard helps an entrepreneur hone his business plan by presenting before a small group of people representing his industry and experienced angel investors. Survivors of the Springboard program will now be channeled into the Tech Coast program, so it all adds to the number of deals we see."

Finding the Perfect Match

The narrow technology focus of many venture capital firms leaves many entrepreneurs out in the cold. If you have a more offbeat company, such as an independent record label you need expansion capital for, where do you go? Finding angel investors can be a far more difficult project, because they have much less visibility than venture capital firms; they don't show up on any entrepreneurial radar. This is where matching services come into play. Matching services perform a screening function, linking companies with wide-ranging investors based on criteria such as industry, stage of the company's development, and amount of capital being sought.

There are scores of these matching services around the country, but a few have been around long enough to have a track record. The following are a few well-known services.

- *America's Business Funding Directory* (www.businessfinance.com) is an online matching service that is initiated by the entrepreneur each time he/she wishes to search for an investor. The entrepreneur then gets a list of "matched" financing sources and investors to contact.
- *ACE-Net, Angel Capital Electronic Network* (www2.sba.gov/ADVO/ acenet.html) is sponsored by the Small Business Administration

(SBA) of the federal government. ACE-Net is actually comprised of a number of local networks that match based on their own local investor database, not a national database.

- *GEVentureMine.com* (www.geventuremine.com) was established in summer of 2000 and is relatively new but is backed by GE Equity, a major debt financing source. Entrepreneurs agree to pay a finder's fee, a percentage of the capital raised, to GEVentureMine.com if an investor is found through this matching process.

- *Private Equity Network, Nvst* (www.nvst.com) allows entrepreneurs to post a description of their company for access by Nvst's network of Accredited Investors.

- *The Elevator* (www.theelevator.com) posts companies' 150-word "elevator pitch" to a password-protected area for review by angel investors.

- *The Capital Network* (www.thecapitalnetwork.com), is one of the oldest networks. Intermediaries and service providers, as well as venture capital and private investors, can participate to be matched.

HOW THE MATCHING SERVICES WORK

Entrepreneurs complete an application and provide an executive summary or, in some cases, a brief description of their company. The application includes questions on what stage the company is at, what industry, how much capital is required, and where the company is located. These questions are the screening parameters for the investors. The application can be completed online for most services. There is usually an application/registration/membership fee paid initially of between $100 and $750, and there can be a finder's fee or percentage of the investment due as well. The percentage can vary from 1 percent to 10 percent, but it is paid only when the capital is invested in the company.

Entrepreneurs also can sometimes post their complete business plan online as well. Several services work more as investment bankers; they screen the companies, accepting only those that they feel will be most successful in obtaining capital.

Investors, if individuals, must certify they are accredited as defined by the Securities and Exchange Commission, which means they must meet certain net asset and income requirements. They also complete an application and in most cases pay a membership fee, which can range from a few hundred dollars to $3,000. In some cases they must also open a brokerage account with the matching service or a subsidiary broker dealer.

At this point the process diverges depending on the service used.

Some services provide an automated matching service. The investor is notified of any potential matches based on the application questions. The investor can then view online in a password-protected area of the service's web site the executive summary of the company, the complete business plan, and/or contact the company directly for further information.

The other method requires investors to go to the web site and input their investment parameters each time they wish to see if any companies match.

Offline matching services do the matching through a computer and then e-mail or fax the investor the information of the companies that match. If the investor is interested, the service tells the investor the entrepreneur's contact information and also tells the entrepreneur the investor's name and contact information. It is then up to the two principals to initiate any further discussions.

ADVICE FROM AN ENTREPRENEUR

Jonathan Green, President, smallcapstocknews.com, San Diego, CA

From your experience with angel investors, why do they join angel groups? "Angels join networks to expand their net of potential deals and opportunities. It is far more effective to use a bigger net to achieve success than one lone fishing pole. It's about looking at many to find few."

How do these networks benefit entrepreneurs? "The advantage for the entrepreneur is that we can go to one place and present and get feedback all at one time. Often this is the best, if not the only, opportunity for the entrepreneur to get the time to meet with these individuals at one time in which they are open, willing, and interested in receiving the presentation and plan.

"I would say many angels involved in strong deal flows do in turn seek out a number of angel groups to join. Others who do few deals often rely on friends and family to bring them various deals."

Have you noticed any trends in the development of angel groups? "There is more of a consolidation going on now in regard to angel networks. There is a reorganization going on in this industry in the Southern Cal area. Angel groups are taking a much more systematic approach to their activities. By combining angel groups, often they increase the ability to operate more efficiently. In addition, this allows groups from up and down the coast the opportunity to review others' business plans and share ideas as well."

The Internet Expedites the Financing Process

The exciting new approaches to corporate finance are bringing large numbers of investors into the marketplace—angels who are hot after the stunning investment returns they see the venture capital firms achieving. The financial innovators serving this market are speeding up the funding process for entrepreneurs, and as competition among the online finance services grows, it will most likely result in significantly lower costs of acquiring capital for early-stage companies.

ADVICE FROM AN EXPERT

David Nussbaum, CEO and Founder of EarlyBirdCapital.com

How has the Internet changed the traditional and sometimes stodgy world of investment banking? "Venture capital is profitable—risky, but profitable—nobody would argue that. It is a simple concept; people invest in start-up companies for the opportunity to realize extraordinary profits. While I would balk at using the word 'stodgy' to describe investment banking, it is safe to assume that the entire IB world, in the past, has been a closed club. For years individuals languished watching institutions profit from exclusive IB deals.

"Common sense tells you that the more people that participate in VC deals, the more potential profits get diluted from the big guys. Obviously, Wall Street contingents do not enjoy losing any profit, and since industry professionals realized the potential in their early-stage investments, they acted accordingly. But along came the Internet, and the walls on Wall Street began to get knocked down. The Internet has begun to level the playing field, allowing individual investors access to high-quality VC deals over the Internet, without the need of high-power financial contacts.

"The Internet is universal, and its reach has surpassed everyone's imagination—this has had a direct impact on the private equity world. Private equity, in years past, received very little press, but the technological boom/bull market of the 1990s has created a tremendous appetite for early-stage investments—before a company makes a media-splashed IPO. Subsequently, the advent of the Internet, many would argue, has created a wiser and more aggressive investor—the timing was right to revolutionize the industry.

"The Internet has not just changed the IB industry, it has overthrown years of conformity and created an opportunity for the masses to participate. Venture investing will never be the same."

Do you see any significant future changes? "This is a tough question. America, as a society, a race, and an economy is constantly evolving. Today's solutions are tomorrow's problems. But I think recent events at the SEC (Regulation FD) have shown that the financial industry will continue to empower the individual. The advantage institutions have in certain situations is astounding, and the regulatory agents are realizing that this does not help their goal of efficient markets.

"It would be tough to predict a revolution with the same force as the Internet has had on venture capital and the entire investing community."

Angel Networks

Angel investors sometimes form loosely associated groups that meet once a week or once a month to review business plans and in-person presentations by invited entrepreneurs. For the most part each individual angel makes the decision to invest independently, and the network makes no investments on a consolidated basis. While venture capital firms don't belong to these networks, often partners of venture capital firms do belong and make their own personal investments, outside of their venture capital firm.

You can locate these types of organizations through your local chamber of commerce, Small Business Development Office, or Service Corps of Retired Executives (SCORE). While a few of the angel networks have web sites, most don't.

Lately, in an attempt to take advantage of the interest in investing in Internet and e-commerce–based companies, several angel networks have been established on a for-profit basis, where the founders charge both the entrepreneurs and the investors a fee.

ADVICE FROM AN ANGEL

Carol Sands, Managing Member, Angels' Forum, Palo Alto, CA

What is the Angels' Forum? "We are a preferred money source. At least as it stands today our investments are limited to only those companies in the Bay Area. The Angels' Forum is a group of 25 very active angel investors who are investing their own personal money in start-ups, having made their own money in a start-up environment as well. So, the idea is that they can look the entrepreneur right in the eye and say 'Yes, I do understand. Yes, I have been there before.'

"And one of the core elements is that the time that we choose to spend with the start-up hopefully is more important to the company than the money we're investing, although none of us will deny the importance of money."

How would a company get selected to present to the group? "It's not easy. And actually, finding an angel, I think, is one of the hardest things to do. The reason is that if you find the right angel, not only are they a money source, they are also your 'champion.' And it's the champion part, in the long run, that will make all the difference in the world.

"I define champion as someone when they wake up in the morning they say: How can I help this company? When they are meeting someone for the first time, they are thinking: How can this person help me help this company? When they are going through their Rolodex, they are saying: Who in my Rolodex can help this company? It is that kind of incredible channeling of energy to the company that a champion can bring.

"When they run into a VC friend of theirs they say: By the way, I've invested in this company and here's what they are doing. Or they run into a college buddy and say: Hey, I've invested in this company and they are looking for this type of person, do you know anybody? It's all those kinds of things. In the early stages of a company the number-one thing for every entrepreneur, I think, is coming to the realization that there are not enough hours in the day to personally do everything that needs to be done, and the ability to ask for help from somebody who can actually provide it is absolutely essential."

How critical is the personality fit between the angel and the entrepreneur? "With champions it's essential. With the rest of them it's not important. If a person is only going to be a money source, that's all that counts—how green is their money. If they're going to interact with the entrepreneur and provide advice and counsel, then the willingness of the entrepreneurs to accept that advice and counsel is directly proportional to the chemistry between the two."

Are some angels more active than others? "I want to clarify that I don't mean being involved in the company as in 'taking over management.' I don't think an angel should ever do that. A good angel is the mentor, the coach, the advocate, but they don't ever put on the team jersey and actually step onto the basketball court."

What makes angels want to get involved in start-ups and risk their money? "You have to define what kind of angel you are talking about because there are a whole bunch of different types of angels, and one of the big issues for beginning entrepreneurs is understanding the subtle differences between the various angels.

"There are people who have time but not money. There are individuals that have helpful and useful advice. There are others who have people connections. Those who can validate your concept but not do much else because they don't have business expertise. Others can't validate your concept but definitely have the business expertise.

"The single most important thing an entrepreneur does, and quite frankly the gating factor that will determine success, is their ability to have the right team around them. Any entrepreneur who starts this process off believing 'I can do this all by myself and I don't need help' is absolutely stupid and will never receive the funding they are seeking because everyone else understands they are doomed.

"The question is, how do you go about attracting all this? From an investment point of view from Angels' Forum one of the things we know from our own personal success is those who have strong relationships in other parts of their life are the ones who are most likely to be successful as entrepreneurs because they know how to leverage the relationship."

How do you go about selecting companies to present? "To get in front of the Angels' Forum is extraordinarily difficult. You have to have not one but two angels behind you, having convinced them to support you and sponsor you to the group."

When do companies make formal presentations? "Weekly. We are basically a professional angel group. We function as if we were a venture capital fund except for the small detail—we're not. A venture fund in my book is defined as someone who is investing other peoples' money; we're investing personal money. But we use the same format, the same disciplines, the same procedures, and then we blend in our own methodologies of working with the entrepreneur, which predominately come from personal experiences with what kind of help we needed and wanted and could receive when we were entrepreneurs. Then we apply it to the portfolio of companies we invest in."

How many companies would present or participate? "We have a weekly partners' meeting that runs about six hours. These are a blend of talking about existing portfolio companies and looking at new investment opportunities, so it depends. The week varies depending on what's happening with the portfolio companies."

These sessions sound very intensive. "Absolutely."

Not a 20-minute, hi, how are you, here's what we're doing presentation. "Well, sometimes it's like that. If we are testing with the group whether there is an interest in this industry, or in this company, we might bring somebody in for a short presentation, to just kind of take the temperature. Other times we may have serious questions about where you're going and how you're going to get there and we're trying to understand. That might be an hour or an hour and a half presentation just like in a venture fund when you're brought in front of the partner group.

"In addition to our weekly meeting, we also work in small subgroup committees. We make take something offline and say we need to look at this technology a little bit deeper and send a group of the technology-oriented individuals to look at it. Or we just don't understand the market here so let's have our sales and marketing angels go offline and meet with the entrepreneur and report back.

"Some committee work and some group work."

If an entrepreneur is fairly well connected and has some referral sources to meet angels one on one, what's the advantage of going with an organization like yours? "If you can ever get an angel to pay attention to you, take it. The advantage of working with Angels' Forum is that we have a 'Three Musketeers' philosophy of life—all for one, one for all. Once you are backed by the Angels' Forum, if you need my personal area of expertise, you have it. Access to my Rolodex, you have it. It doesn't make any difference if I'm personally in that particular investment, what's important is that the Angels' Forum is in the investment, and all 25 of us have made the promise to each other.

"That kind of power gets to be a very defining source for a lot of our portfolio companies very quickly. Once you get the funding, you're into the life of the start-up. There are problems and questions and opportunities and crossroads that come along, and it would be nice talk to someone who has been down that path before.

"Or at least listen to you and say, 'Yes your logic is right.' Or the one that actually I find is much more important is to be able to tell the en-

trepreneur that there are no good answers to this particular problem—
each solution has complications and there is not one that is obviously
better than the other. So, how do we work together to manage the
process."

Within your group you have expertise in all the business disciplines? "Yes. The group was put together specifically to address all
the different parts of a start-up's life. In addition to having been CEOs,
we have people with a background in sales and marketing, operations, engineering, human resources, and finance. We were very purposeful when we put the group together to have multiple industries and
multiple job expertise in the group. We wanted this expertise resident,
right there."

**What would be different about obtaining funding and expertise from your group versus working with one of large venture
capital funds in the Bay Area?** "The difference is that in the very early
stages in a company's life, there are a set of pretty predictable situations
that come along that we routinely deal with and have resources available. Quite frankly, the frequency of the issue gets you to the point that
you are quite good at dealing with it and you understand all the nuances of the situation.

"We provide a level of expertise and involvement that most of our
VC brethren can't do just because of the sheer intensity that an early-
stage investment requires versus a later stage. If they are at a point
where they are putting $10 million in a seed round, the company is
probably pretty mature."

The main parts would be together at least. "Right. Whereas we
are used to dealing with companies with incomplete management teams
and where the strategy is not locked down. Crossroads are coming
around hourly rather than every six months."

**Why would an entrepreneur seek out Angels' Forum versus
other forms of early-stage funding, either another angel group or
other private funding from an individual?** "The one thing I can predict for sure is that every single one of our investments at some point will
get into trouble. What I can't predict is when or what the trouble point
will be, and so what I think the Angels' Forum offers the entrepreneur is a
much broader base of expertise and a stronger probability they can help
you through that trouble period because of their relationships in the business community."

**Are we seeing more organizations like yours around the
country?** "No. I think there are a lot of hobbyist angels who are casually investing in companies and are implying that they will be
around to help the company through the growth process. When you
look at these different angel groups, a large majority are focused on

providing a social time for the angel investors, and there is nothing in the way the group is structured that encourages or provides a place to talk about past investments or to group-solve problems that current investments are having or encourage the angels to physically go see the companies.

"None of them I'm aware of are organized like our group. Almost all of the groups I know and interact with are centered around the fun of the hunt of finding a company to invest in. None are focused on what you do after the investment. That's a reality that the entrepreneur needs to be aware of: that most of these are just collection points for money. Which is not a bad thing. You just need to be realistic about your expectations."

At the very least it makes it easier for entrepreneurs to make contact with investors. "Absolutely. Having that kind of access to investors on a group basis, so the probability is relatively high that you can do one-stop shopping, is important.

"I'm constantly reminding our entrepreneurs that learning how to ask for help from the right resources is one of the most important things every entrepreneur needs to learn how to do."

Is there anything else you advise entrepreneurs? "Never burn a bridge. A funding source who says no to you today may say yes to you later on and/or could be a funding source for your second or third or fourth entrepreneurial adventure."

ADVICE FROM AN ENTREPRENEUR

How did you get started on your search for angel investors? "Due to the scope of the concept we developed, we needed to pursue seed capital from day 1. Our initial investors were sought from people with whom we had existing business relationships and/or related business experience, such as our printing company, etc. Upon securing our initial investors, the 'daisy chain' process was implemented to secure more investors. We went from five to 40 investors and have secured $3.6 million in a series of three angel investment rounds."

What was your most productive method of finding an angel investor? "I have found current investors to be the best source of referrals to potential investors and that a personal presentation to each angel investor has yielded the best response."

How did you deal with the issue of revealing enough information about your company to get them interested but not revealing

proprietary information until the angel investor would sign a nondisclosure? "Given the nature of the company and the type of the potential investor, a judgment call was made in every situation on an individual case-by-case basis as to whether or not an NDA [nondisclosure agreement] would be required. For example, with a potential investor who works with an Internet company that builds sites, we would require an NDA before any disclosure; with a retired banker who had no possible ulterior motives, we would not require one."

What was most frustrating in your search for angel investors? "The amount of time it takes away from running the business. It serves as a significant distraction from achieving the core goals of the business. One of the strategies we used to try to alleviate this was using funding intermediaries. However, those relationships were often very unfruitful and caused further displacement of time, and we ended up raising the money ourselves anyway. I recommend that you pursue angel money and venture capital money directly through referrals and strategic partners."

How long did it take you to find the angel that invested? "It took two months to get our initial investor, and I have found 40 more over a 12-month period."

What area of your business plan or business model did the angel investor question the most? "The predominant area of angel questions always come in relation to our sales plan/revenue model because ultimately, their ability to monetize their investment is tied to your ability to perform against the stated revenue objectives. Understanding your market and how you will actually penetrate that market and generate revenue is critical to securing any investor."

If you could give one piece of advice to other entrepreneurs looking for angel investors, what would it be? "The most important element in securing and working with angel investors is dealing with them in a completely candid manner. You must be forthright with the negatives and positives of the business model and the company's performance, building a relationship of credibility and trust."

Angels and Referrals

Angel investors rely on referrals even more than venture capital funds, because angels try to keep a low profile and do not "advertise" for deals the way venture capital funds do. The latter are listed in venture capital directories, have an Internet site, or participate in venture capital conferences.

If you were a multimillionaire who enjoyed dabbling in venture capital investments, you would certainly not announce that to the business world as a whole. Can you imagine how many people would contact you? Angels rely on discreet referrals from a small number of professionals they trust. That is why it has traditionally been so difficult to find angel investors.

Angels do a lot of networking within the business community in order to find suitable companies for investment. Wealthy individuals have seen the amazing returns some venture capitalists have been earning and want to get in on that investment action themselves. But just as it has been difficult for entrepreneurs to locate angels, so it has been a challenge for these new angel investors to gain access to a broad range of entrepreneurial investment opportunities. In the future, the Internet may become the primary source of deals for angel investors.

WHAT VENTURE CAPITALISTS SAY ABOUT GETTING START-UP CAPITAL FROM ANGELS

An increasingly popular scenario is to raise a modest amount of capital, perhaps $500,000, from wealthy individuals. This capital helps the company get its technology or product development further along, thereby making the company more valuable, and possibly less of a risk, to the venture capital funds that might provide the next round of investment. A lower risk can translate into higher valuation; in other words, the company will not have to give as much equity to the investor who comes in the second round.

If angel investors are increasingly getting involved in financing start-up companies, what advice do the venture capitalists have for entrepreneurs about obtaining capital from this source?

"All capital is not created equal. You really need to care about who your money is raised from, rather than how much or at what valuation. In creating a start-up there are so very many things to attend to that entrepreneurs should seek as much help as possible—investors are an ideal source of this help, as their incentives are

aligned. *Passive capital is probably the most expensive kind you can raise. You need to find active investors who are well connected, experienced, knowledgeable about your market, and familiar with the process of starting companies—the operational, strategic, and human factors that are part of starting a new company."*

"Entrepreneurs should be cautious about raising too much money from angel investors that don't have experience building businesses or working with venture capital firms."

"Be careful when raising 'angel' financing from unsophisticated investors. Increasingly, we find companies that have raised a significant amount of 'angel' or 'nonprofessional' money at staggering valuations. If a company comes to us and says, 'Well, we raised $4 million in our last round at a $100 million valuation,' the deal is dead on arrival. One way to avoid this problem is to raise angel money through a convertible instrument whose ultimate valuation is determined by the valuation of the professional round."

"Don't take the easy money. Get someone who will ask the hard questions going in."

ADVICE FROM A VENTURE CAPITALIST

Jeff Allen, Managing Director, Rocket Ventures,
www.rocketventures.com

Does it make sense for an entrepreneur to seek out angel money first, before the professional round of capital? "An entrepreneur has to do what he or she needs to do to get the company running. If individual investors are willing to get the company to the stage where venture capital firms would be more interested, then they should do that. Where VCs [venture capitalists] have a problem with angels is with the structure of deals and valuation. Lots of companies have brought on angel money but have not been wise in the use of funds and haven't completed a significant set of milestones in building the company out. They take enough money to get halfway through product development; they don't have a complete product or a complete team, so they haven't really accomplished anything with the money they were given. Typically this is a problem of not raising enough money: They've only taken enough to build out office space and infrastructure. That doesn't produce a whole lot of value for the company. An entrepreneur comes to the door and has a team of four to five people and they are in the middle of product development and are running out of cash. Angels have priced the deal too high and the company has not accomplished anything as yet.

"Until they've accomplished something, there's no reason to invest at the price the angel investors have set for it. The angel investors don't want to see the price of the shares go down so they block decisions and convince entrepreneurs not to take the money from the VC [venture capital] community, and it drags the process out very long. I've seen companies that fall into this trap, and they don't go anywhere for a long time. In fast-moving markets, they end up losing the market."

———————————————

8

Venture Capital Decision Making

The Most Important Factors in the Investment Decision

It's not the product, the size of the market, or even greed. It's the people.

Venture capitalists were asked to rank five important factors that influence their decision to invest, with 5 being the highest rank you could award a factor, 1 being the lowest. The important factors were:

- Quality of the management team
- Size of the company's market
- Proprietary, uniqueness, or brand strength of the company's product
- Return on investment (ROI)
- Company's potential for growth

According to the venture capitalists' responses, quality of the management team is by far the most important factor in the decision. VCs invest in people, not products. Virtually tied for second place are the factors of growth potential, return on investment, and size of the market. In last place is product uniqueness.

Table 8.1 shows us the different ways of looking at how venture capitalists ranked these factors. The first column shows the average rank of quality of management is nearly three times the importance of uniqueness of product. And you can see the middle three factors are clustered close together.

Column 2, percentage ranked factor 5 or 4 (high rankings), shows that the ranking of quality of management was the result of the majority of VCs ranking that characteristic highly, not that some VCs gave it a high ranking and the rest just gave it an average ranking so that the overall rank was the highest.

Finally, column 3 shows the inverse of column 2: Very few VCs ranked quality of management as a 1 or 2, a low ranking.

Table 8.2 shows the change between 2000 and 1998, when investors were asked to do this same ranking. While quality of management remains in first place, the average score dropped a bit from 1998, and there was more of a variance from the most highly ranked to the lowest ranked. Additionally, Product had a lower point score in 2000 than in 1998.

In the 1998 survey, many venture capitalists scored all the factors at 5, while in 2000 more gave an absolute ranking as the survey requested.

Table 8.1   Factors in Decision Making

	Average Rank	% Ranked 5 or 4 (High Rankings)	% Ranked 1 or 2 (Low Rankings)
Management Quality	3.4	37	2
Growth Potential	2.2	17	17
Return on Investment (ROI)	2.0	19	25
Size of Market	2.0	18	21
Product	1.2	9	35

Table 8.2 Change in Ranking of Investment Factors

Year of Survey	2000		1998	
Factors	Score	Rank	Score	Rank
Management Quality	3.4	1	4.1	1
Growth Potential	2.2	2	3.3	3
Return on Investment (ROI)	2.0	3	3.5	2
Size of Market	2.0	3	3.3	3
Product	1.2	5	3.0	5

Quotes from Venture Capitalists
"I hate to put all 5s, but this is true. We look for all of the above—those are the parts that make up the companies we invest in."

"The company must possess all of these factors!"

In 1998 the percentage of respondents that awarded 5 to a factor were as follows:

Management	52%
ROI	42%
Market Size	27%
Growth	25%
Product Uniqueness	19%

In 2000, the third-place ROI had a score of 1.4 points less than Management. In 1998, the difference between Management and then second-place ROI was only .6 points. Does this mean venture capitalists are less greedy in 2000? Probably not. It may mean a strong ROI is more of a given, or expected, than it was in 1998.

These results indicate that all of these factors are of importance to venture capitalists, with quality of the management team by far the most important and product the least important. This relationship has remained steady since 1998. The factors of Growth Potential, Return on Investment, and Size of the Market were all ranked fairly closely together for both years, indicating that entrepreneurs must address all of these factors in the business plans they write and the in-person presentations they make to venture capitalists. The tendency of some entrepre-

neurs to dwell solely on what they perceive to be their product's uniqueness does not serve them well when they are seeking funding.

Venture Capitalists Are from Mars, Entrepreneurs Are from Venus

As clearly seen in Table 8.3, entrepreneurs think money is uppermost in
the decision to invest; they believe Return on Investment is the most
important factor in the investor's decision to invest. In second place is
Quality of Management, then Growth Potential, Market Size, and Product.

For entrepreneurs, there is only a 1.5 point spread between the
highest-ranked factor and lowest-rated. While the difference between ROI and Management is only .2, it's interesting to look at
how that ranking took place. Sixty-six percent of entrepreneurs gave
ROI either a rating of 4 or 5, only 52 percent gave Management a rating
of 4 or 5, with 3 being the most common rating. It seems that entrepreneurs recognize that management is important but don't quite realize
how important.

Entrepreneurs and venture capitalists disagree on four out of the five
rankings. Only Product received a similar ranking—last place. Venture
capitalists don't differentiate much between the middle three ranks of
Growth, ROI, and Market, while entrepreneurs have a wider point
spread and rank the VCs' third choice, ROI, as their first choice.

Product received a 4 or 5 ranking from 23 percent of the entrepreneurs but from only 9 percent of the venture capitalists. While both

Table 8.3 Comparisons of Entrepreneurs and Venture Capitalists

Factor	Entrepreneurs		Venture Capitalists	
	Rank	Score	Rank	Score
Management	3.6	2	1	3.4
Growth	3.3	3	2	2.2
ROI	3.8	1	3	2.0
Market	2.6	4	3	2.0
Product	2.3	5	5	1.2

groups agree that Product is the least important factor, more entrepreneurs rank it highly.

Entrepreneurs are confused and frustrated when trying to figure out what venture capitalists really want.

"Most of the VCs I have met in the last year are egotists who have suspended all rules of courtesy."

"They [VCs] live to the beat of their own drummers."

"An entrepreneur with no investment capital of his/her own, even though he/she may have an excellent product, the ideal marketplace, and excellent estimates for growth and expansion, has a snowball's chance in hell in bringing his idea to fruition."

ADVICE FROM A VENTURE CAPITALIST

Bill McAleer, Partner, Voyager Capital, www.voyagercap.com

What are the most critical factors when making the investment decision? "We look first of all at what is unique about the opportunity. And we try to evaluate how large a market the company is operating in. Management team is of course critical. In most cases, the company does not have a complete team, but at least the start of one. That is why the face-to-face meeting is so important to the venture capitalist. It is difficult to evaluate the management team from just the discussion of their background in the business plan or in a telephone conversation."

Why Do Venture Capitalists Say No?

And do they ever change a no to a yes?

Once again, management is foremost. Not only is it the most critical factor in the decision to invest, it's the most common reason why investors decline to invest.

The overwhelming reason why they refuse to invest, given by 40 percent of venture capitalists, was *lack of an experienced, complete, management team.* Several VCs cited the entrepreneur's need to build a team with depth and experience before contacting a VC. The venture capital firm is willing to contribute the expertise of its partners as well as capital, but it will not back companies with glaring weaknesses in management. These firms are looking for talented people to back, people with previous records of success.

In contrast, venture capitalists who invest in very early-stage companies recognize that a complete management team is not feasible. To those VCs it's not such a glaring fault.

The next most frequently mentioned reason for declining to invest (17 percent) was that *the company did not fit their investment criteria*, the industry(ies) on which they focus, or the geographic area. Many entrepreneurs use a shotgun approach in contacting VCs, believing the more the better. However, failure to research what industry venture capitalists focus on usually results in contacting the wrong audience and is a waste of time and money. A related reason for venture capitalists refusing to invest is that the company is too early stage: The entrepreneur did not know that the venture capital firm does not invest in start-ups, for example, but contacted the firm anyway.

The four main investment criteria for venture capitalists are:

1. Industry the company is in
2. Stage of the company
3. Size or amount of the investment
4. Geographic restrictions.

Tied for third place was that the *size of the market the company was in, or the need in the market that the product serves, was too small* (13 percent). The chance of building a significant, valuable enterprise is smaller. The fact that *the company has no competitive advantage or has a noncompelling technology* also was frequently mentioned (13 percent).

Strategic weaknesses (10 percent) was an important reason for declining. The company said what it planned to do but not how it was going to do it. The steps to execute the business strategy were poorly thought out or incomplete—there was no clear execution strategy (10 percent).

Other reasons for failure to invest include:

- The company is too small and will not grow large enough (10 percent).
- The industry has no barriers to entry for competitors (6 percent).
- The risk is too high relative to the projected return (6 percent).

- The company has low margins or the industry is facing margin pressure (4 percent).

Less frequently mentioned reasons were:

- The entrepreneur put too high a valuation on his company's stock.
- The company is not profitable.
- The company faces huge, entrenched competitors.
- The entrepreneur was not referred to the venture capital firm.
- The entrepreneur did a poor job presenting the company in a meeting.
- The entrepreneur viewed the venture capitalists only as a source of money, not as a value-added partner.

ENTREPRENEURS HAVE A DIFFERENT UNDERSTANDING OF WHY VCs SAY NO

Table 8.4 compares what entrepreneurs said to what investors said.

Although both groups mentioned lack of management, it was clearly of more importance to the venture capitalists. Whereas investors' real reasons for declining related to flaws in the company itself—the market, the competitive advantage, the execution strategy—entrepreneurs tended to think the reasons had nothing to do with their company but with external factors. Entrepreneurs blamed the decline on the venture capitalists not being willing or able to understand, or seeking unreason-

Table 8.4 Why Do VCs Say No?

Factor	Venture Capitalists Say	Factor	Entrepreneurs Say
Lack of management	40%	Lack of management	20%
Didn't fit criteria	17%	VCs won't take the	12%
Market too small	13%	time, were too busy	
No competitive advantage	13%	or cannot understand	
Weak strategy	10%	our product/ technology/business model	
		I don't know	9%
		ROI too low	8%
		Poor business plan	8%

ably high returns, or because the entrepreneurs could not articulate their vision in the business plan. Entrepreneurs were also more diffuse in their responses than were venture capitalists.

Entrepreneurs cited several factors the venture capitalists did not mention at all, such as:

> "They themselves [VCs] don't know exactly what they are looking for in a new venture."

> "They [VCs] don't understand what the company does initially. Venture capitalists would rather have an introduction from someone rather than look at a company that was not introduced. It's a close clique."

> "They [VCs] are unwilling to spend any time to personally investigate the management and the project."

> "Most lack experience in a particular area and do not understand the 'new' technology of today. They [VCs] are fat and rich. And they have no vision beyond the end of their noses. Not all, but most."

> "Investors say no because of misrepresentation discovered during due diligence—whether unintentional or through entrepreneur dishonesty."

> "Companies do not provide credible evidence that they will provide a return on investment to investors."

> "A lack of time to review information given to them. And prospects fail to follow up."

> "They [VCs] have no understanding of the proposed product/service."

> "They [VCs] have the wrong vision: they actually want to sell money, not to create a business."

> "The venture capitalists are too busy and can't organize themselves so they let [lower] priority projects slip and they lose them. Then they chalk this up to some other reason."

Will a "No" Ever Become a "Yes"?

Do venture capitalists ever change their minds? Occasionally yes, but very occasionally. If the venture capitalist is intrigued by the technology or potential market, or sees a gap in the entrepreneur's business model's logic and that gap is later closed, he or she might consider investing at a later date. Entrepreneurs should not interpret this as an open invitation to keep presenting to the venture capitalist in the hopes that eventually he or she will cave in and invest. If VCs don't say under what specific circumstances they will change their mind, then the dialogue is closed.

DEAL TALES: IF I KNEW SPIELBERG, I WOULDN'T NEED YOU

Dennis K. was an energetic, driven, "Type A" entrepreneur who was very impatient with the whole process of raising capital. He had developed a broadband technology that facilitates the delivery of entertainment to the home. He thought he had all the bases covered in his management team—technical, finance, marketing—but when he began contacting venture capitalists, he found he had a glaring weakness—no one in his company had contacts with the companies that develop and license entertainment content. He had developed a wonderful pipeline with nothing to pump through it. He also found that it was difficult to get any constructive feedback from the venture capital firms. All he heard was "Sorry, but we decline." How could he improve his pitch if he wasn't ever told what he was doing wrong? Being an aggressive individual, Dennis didn't hesitate for an instant to pick up the phone and call a senior partner of a major venture capital firm—or try to get through at any rate. He seldom talked to anyone but the receptionist or a secretary, or was sent directly to that conversational black hole called voice-mail. His frustration began to boil over.

Finally, one day he got through to a junior partner at a major Southern California venture capital firm. She patiently listened to Dennis' pitch, then told him that her firm couldn't consider an investment in his venture unless he had already aligned himself with someone significant in the entertainment business, "someone like Steven Spielberg," she said. Dennis was becoming seriously confused. He thought the venture capital firms had contacts necessary for marketing and distribution, and all he needed to do was supply the technology, the "idea."

"You mean," he sputtered, "if I go out and get Steven Spielberg or David Geffen or somebody like that to join up with me, then and only then would you consider investing in me?"

"Yes," she replied. "Then we would consider investing in your company, if you had that sort of powerful strategic alliance in place."

"I know I'm just the entrepreneur here," Dennis said, now starting to lose his temper. "But it seems to me, if I had Spielberg on board, why would I need you?"

Investor Feedback Is Not Always Forthcoming

Let's say you are a highly charged entrepreneur, armed with a clear, concise, fairly dazzling business plan, ready to contact venture capitalists. You do your research, finding the investors whose published criteria match your company to a tee. To your delight, your company turns out to be in a "hot" area for investment. In no time at all you have compiled a list of nearly 100 venture capital firms that could be suitable investor candidates. You have polished your executive summary so much you need sunglasses to look at it.

You have decided the best course of action is to contact a small number of venture capitals at a time, no more than 10 to 20. The idea is to get their feedback after reading your executive summary, to find out if your "pitch" is getting through to them, whether you have adequately expressed the merits of your company as an investment. You find out some of the firms accept an e-mailed executive summary, others prefer postal mail. Remember, the object of the contact letter is to get the venture capitalist to request your full business plan, which will lead to further discussions, it is hoped. You send out the first 20 and wait, and hope. You expect that out of this first 20 letters, you probably will get five to seven positive responses and convert these into one to two really strong potential investor prospects.

So what happens?

	E-mail Decline	Postal Decline	Request for Full Plan	No Response
First Week	3	2	0	15
Second Week	2	1	0	12
Third Week	1	1	0	10
Fourth Week	0	1	0	9
Cumulative	6	5	0	9

What went wrong here? No one requested your business plan after receiving that wonderful executive summary you anguished over for weeks? And nine out of 20 venture capitalists didn't even bother to acknowledge receiving your letter, didn't even give you the courtesy of a decline. That was rather rude, wasn't it? And why does it take them so long to get back to you?

If you treated your potential customers that way, you wouldn't have any business. But that's the point: Many VCs don't believe they need your business, only that you need them.

So what about the decline letters? Surely they told you their reaction to your deal? Now you will have the information you need to hone your presentation a little better and strike a responsive chord in the next batch of 20 VCs you contact.

Welcome to the big leagues, Mr. Entrepreneur. Most of the decline letters will tell you absolutely nothing. They will be form letter responses created by a secretary to deal with that tidal wave of business plans and summaries that washes up in the VC's office each week.

The letters will have vague statements about your company not being what they were looking for and of course wishing you "the best of luck in financing your venture." One of the most pompous of these letters we ever saw was from a venture capitalist in Washington, D.C., that told our client: "Your company does not comport with our investment objectives." We had to scramble to the dictionary to find out what "comport" meant.

The only way to get any meaningful feedback is to call the venture capitalists who declined, persist until you get to talk to a partner, and ask directly why they did not want to pursue talking with you. And then do the same with the ones who did not respond at all. You can learn a lot from finding out these specific reasons for a decline, because often the problem is simply a failure to communicate.

And then you have to pick yourself up, forget about the earlier rejections, and begin contacting more investors.

An innovative approach to saying no came in the mail recently to us. Let's call it the preemptive strike. It was from the managing director of a venture capital fund whom we had never met. It said:

"Thanks for your letter. Unfortunately, this is not an area of focus at this time. We'll keep you in mind. Continued luck on your venture."

The letter was nice enough, but (1) We never wrote to him and (2) We aren't starting any ventures. Apparently what he was doing was contacting us ahead of time, and telling us no, just in case we started a venture sometime in the future. Just getting the rejection out of the way now.

CHAPTER

9

No, It's Not Location, Location, Location, But It Is Management

I t's a given that management is critical to obtaining venture capital investment, but what constitutes a quality management team?

What Is Quality Management?

The question was asked open ended with no suggested qualities or choices given. The venture capitalist was free to name only one quality—and several did just that—or write a paragraph. The majority of VCs named at least three or more qualities. Many different responses came back to this question. The results were as follows. (The number to the right represents a scale of how frequently each was cited relative to each other.)

117

Relative Frequency of Mention

Successful experience or proven track record	9.5
Integrity, honesty	3.0
Dedication, commitment, passion, energy	3.0
Vision and ability to articulate vision	2.3
Knowledge, skill level, intelligence	2.0
Leadership ability	1.0
Ability to build a team	.75
Marketing focus	.50
Made investment in company	.50
Winning attitude	.50
Industry contacts	.50
Good references	.25

As you can see in Figure 9.1, quality of management means *experienced*, according to an overwhelming number of venture capitalists. Only 17 percent of them did *not* include successful experience or proven track record in their response. Curiously, the VCs felt compelled to designate integrity or honesty as a characteristic rather than as a given. This may be the result of past history with entrepreneurs who made less than full disclosure to them during the initial meeting stage and the fallacies discovered during the due diligence phase.

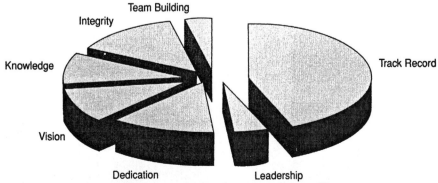

Figure 9.1   Key Components of a Quality Management Team

DEAL TALES:
FOLLOW THE YELLOW BRICK ROAD . . .

Late in December one year, we were writing the strategic plan for an extremely successful company. We interviewed each key member of the management team, asking them about the company's plans for the future. They were all personable and helpful, except that whenever we asked a question about how the company develops its strategies, we were told, "Oh, you'll have to go see (the CEO) about that. He's the visionary, the architect of our strategy. We merely follow him." "Wait until you talk with (the CEO)," they said. "Our best ideas always come from him." After we heard this five or six times, we began humming: If and ever a WHIZ there was . . .

We couldn't wait to meet this strategic genius, whose brilliance we had read about in the business press. Almost shaking with anticipation, we sat down with the CEO one afternoon, and waited for the Great Man's words of wisdom. What we heard was a rambling, two-hour, free-association monologue on topics ranging from his favorite Broadway musicals, sushi bars, herbal remedies, John Wayne movies, and, of course, how truly remarkable he was. It turned out the fountain of knowledge we had been seeking was at best a trickle. He was just a guy behind a public relations curtain. A rich guy, but just a guy nonetheless. This company had simply enjoyed a temporary monopoly in its industry and had made a fairly obscene amount of money in a very short period of time. There were no strategies, really, and no strong CEO. The lesson we learned: You don't need great powers to be a Wizard, just great publicity.

What VCs Are Looking for in a Management Team

A Proven Track Record
"A CEO that has been there, done that."

"Integrity, energy, brains, experience, a proven track record."

"A CEO with a success or two and at least one failure."

"People start achieving in kindergarten. We need to know their history of personal achievement."

"The CEO has had high functional responsibility, if not CEO level, at a company that sells to the same customer base."

"Prior success with taking other companies through the IPO or acquisition stage."

"Small-company experience."

"Industry contacts."

"Management experience with another fast-growth company."

"Having a clear concept of execution; evidence they can execute their business plan."

Personality Traits

"A good sense of humor."

"High self-confidence with minimal arrogance."

"A dynamic individual who will not accept failure."

"Efficient, effective, mature, dynamic, flexible, diverse."

"Follow-through, flexibility, and responsiveness to the board of directors."

"Ability to adapt."

"Personality."

"Self-awareness—particularly aware of what they do and do not know."

"Unquestionable ethics, relevant experience, a sense of humility."

"Decisiveness, ability to delegate, willingness to consider new ideas and opinions of others."

"Risk takers."

"A sense of reality. Common sense."

Marketing Ability

"The management team knows why customers in that industry will part with their money."

"Ability to be flexible and relate to changing market conditions."

"Ability to monitor and adapt to changing market conditions and evolving customer needs."

"The ability of the managers to capture a significant share of a fast-growing and rapidly changing market."

"A VP of marketing that knows why customers in that industry will part with their money."

Desire

"Drive to win and a history of winning. Passion about the venture. A big ego but it doesn't get in the way of hiring smarter people or relinquishing control. A deal maker/negotiator/doer. Unusual energy and commitment. Smart both in intelligence and street smarts (tactics). An instinct for making money."

"Their desire to make money is bigger than their desire to control the company."

"Being devoted to your concept and willing to make your venture work no matter what it takes."

Team Player
"A well-rounded team that complements each other."

"Ability to recruit and motivate a talented team."

"Team longevity."

"A team that covers all the bases and is complementary in style."

"At least three to four competent managers must already be in place."

"A founder who has willingly stepped aside, yet maintains the intensity and the motivation to help make it happen."

Finance
"Have their own funds already invested in the project."

"Cash management skills."

"An understanding of the need for a liquidity event for the investors."

Accept No Substitutes—Dealing with a Lack of CEO Experience

What can entrepreneurs do if they don't have experience as a CEO, or if their management team is not complete? Although a number of different responses came back, indicating this is a difficult question for venture capitalists to address, the responses broke down into these major categories:

The founder should step aside and bring in an experienced CEO	40%
The founder should ask the venture capitalist for management assistance or let the venture capitalist recruit a CEO	35%
Assemble a board of directors or an advisory board composed of CEO-type individuals	15%
Have such a winning business model or great idea that it outweighs any management team deficiencies	7%
Obtain CEO experience before seeking venture capital	3%

It seems venture capitalists accept no substitute: 75 percent specified that the founder should hire a CEO, or step aside and have the VC hire a CEO. While assembling an advisory board is a step in the right direction, it won't compensate for the lack of a strong CEO. And only a mere 7 percent would say they would accept a great business concept in lieu of a quality management team.

WHAT VENTURE CAPITALISTS SAY TO DO

"They should try to align themselves with a retired CEO who could serve as chairman of the company on a part-time basis and also serve as their mentor."

"Without an experienced CEO, they should lower the price they expect for their stock, because the venture capitalist views the risk as higher."

"They should make as much progress as possible before seeking funding."

"We invest in early-stage companies, so we do not expect the team to be complete."

"They should show a willingness to be coached by the venture capitalist."

"They should demonstrate they can learn and grow with the company, or they should get out of the way."

"We would not fund a company without an experienced CEO."

"They should step aside willingly and recruit a CEO."

"If the market is large and the technology is sound, we believe that you can attract high-quality management to the company, so an incomplete team does not prevent us from investing."

"We would not fund if the management team were incomplete."

"No problem. One of the values we add postinvestment is introductions and work on rounding out the management team."

"New entrepreneurs rarely have experience as a CEO. Having worked as an executive (not the CEO) for a well-managed company is a bonus. Management teams seeking early-stage venture capital are never complete. It's not a problem, but the managers must be able to attract top-quality talent quickly to round out the team."

"We prefer to have no CEO and an entrepreneur willing to hire one than to have an inexperienced or underqualified CEO."

"Typically, early- to midstage companies don't have fully developed management teams. As such, if the entrepreneur's business model is attractive and he can demonstrate a willingness to bring in other potentially more capable managers, VCs are willing and often embrace the opportunity to assist in the process."

"The first step is for them to admit they need help."
"The CEO should step aside willingly."

Common Weak Spots in Management Teams

Since venture capitalists decline to invest most often based on the lack of a quality management team, and they define quality management as CEO experience and a track record, it stands to reason that a lack of CEO experience would be the most common weak spot in a management team.

But VCs see several other characteristics as common weak spots.

Lack of CEO Experience	66%
No previous track record of building a company	49%
No sales/marketing experience	44%
Lack of financial management experience	41%
Too focused on product or technology	38%
Inflexible	30%
Lack of general business experience	30%
Greedy	23%
No previous history of the team working together	23%
Team is too young, not seasoned	21%
Not willing to disclose information to investors	7%

Quotes from the VCs on the Subject of Management Team Weaknesses

"They are too focused on product or technology to the exclusion of other equally critical variables."

"Lack of general business experience including financial, marketing, team building, people skills, operations, multitasking, meeting a payroll, and accountability to investors and/or a board of directors."

"The existing management team is not willing to step aside for someone with more experience."

"The team has no experience in the business area they are proposing to tackle."

"Unrealistic expectations."

"They have a good product/technology but have no concept of its market."

"All of the weaknesses cited are pretty common. No company is perfect. The question is whether they can overcome their challenges and/or if we can provide the solutions they need."

"You see all of these weaknesses."

"Usually, the CEO does not lack CEO experience but may lack relevant CEO experience. Or many times the team comes to us without a CEO in place."

"No sales/marketing experience is not a big deal to us. Usually this part needs to be hired in earlier VC investing."

"Regarding their unwillingness to disclose information, we do not sign nondisclosure agreements, so if they don't give us enough information, we just move on."

"We don't require that management be capable, just that they be coachable."

"CEOs must have a sense of urgency. Most think they have lots of time."

"Another weakness: arrogance."

One venture capitalist checked off "greedy" twice.

FROM THE ENTREPRENEUR'S VIEWPOINT

Do entrepreneurs see the same weak spots in company management teams? No, they don't, which should come as no surprise.

It seems entrepreneurs are a little more generous than venture capitalists, as you can see in Table 9.1. They rate a general lack of business experience as the most common weak spot, followed by lack of a

Table 9.1   Characteristics Comparison

Management Characteristic	Rank by Entrepreneurs	% of Entrepreneurs	Rank by Venture Capitalists	% of Venture Capitalists
Lack of general business experience	1	46	7	30
No track record	2	44	2	49
No CEO experience	3	42	1	66
No financial experience	4	40	4	41
Too focused on product	5	34	5	38
No marketing experience	6	31	3	44
Inflexible	7	26	6	30
Unwilling to disclose information	8	21	11	7
No team history together	9	20	10	23
Greedy	10	15	8	23
Too young or unseasoned	11	9	9	21

track record, no CEO experience, and no financial management experience.

Lack of marketing experience is ranked as much less serious, falling to sixth place by entrepreneurs, while it's ranked in third place by venture capitalists. While the order of rank changes, both entrepreneurs and VCs place the same four characteristics in the last four places.

Again, this points out entrepreneurs focus on product/technology/service and not how to get the customer to buy the product/technology/service.

The only characteristics that are ranked the same are No Track Record, No Financial Experience and Too Focused on Product, rankings 2, 4, and 5 respectively. Two characteristics are ranked only one space apart; Inflexible is ranked seventh by entrepreneurs and sixth by VCs; No Team History is ranked ninth by entrepreneurs and tenth by VCs.

The crucial difference is that VCs place a much higher value on CEO experience than entrepreneurs.

Putting Your Team Together

Fortunately, there are sound strategies entrepreneurs can employ to construct a well-rounded management team.

ADVICE FROM A HUMAN RESOURCE EXPERT ON BUILDING A MANAGEMENT TEAM

John Younger, President, TriNet's Venture Talent, www.trinet.com, ePowered HR for Fast Companies

The Importance of Friends and Family: "Read an important book before you build your management team—your personal address book. Call up friends and family. But when you've exhausted your personal contacts, you'll need a heavy-hitting approach: a professional recruiting and staffing partner."

Finding the Right Partner: "The right recruiting partner will have the expertise and experience to deal with your specific needs. This includes a track record of success in a very small niche—entrepreneurs looking for compatible, talented people with which to surround themselves.

"Why is this important? Because a knowledgeable firm will be able to guide you through a series of crucial steps.

"1. *Pore over the business plan and prioritize key hires.* If you have software that needs to be designed and brought to market, don't worry about a director of communications just yet. Focus on hiring key technical talent.

"2. *Allow several months to find top-level executives such as a CEO.* A good firm will write out a job description for key hires that runs several pages, pinpointing the precise fit for the company-to-be and its objectives. It's important not to stumble when finding such individuals, so anticipate a long hiring ramp.

"3. *Expect top-level executives to bring aboard their own team members.* For example, a CFO may have accountants and analysts already in tow—an invaluable asset when you're on a hiring spree.

"4. *Use the right technology to make the process scalable.* Automated job postings, databases, and a variety of sourcing techniques will ensure that you can keep the pace when you need to fill up cubicles."

Telling a Story: "That all may sound great—but once you *find* the talent, how do you attract them? There's one way you and your recruiting partner can attract talent: have a story worth telling and a vision worth following. Your management team and even the first few dozen employees aren't likely to get technical about the compensation package. They're there because:

"They want their work to matter.

"They want to work with good people.

"They want to take a risk in order to make a difference.

"You know your vision is compelling, so practice telling the story that accompanies it. Stock options and salary can come later. With a good story at the tip of your lips, you just may find that talent is yours for the taking."

ADVICE FROM VENTURE CAPITALISTS

Larry Kubal, Managing Director, Labrador Ventures,
www.labrador.com

What do VCs recommend to entrepreneurs about building their management teams? What resources are available for entrepreneurs to use? "Clearly, a key entrepreneurial trait is leadership ability. Part of leadership is the ability to recruit. At Labrador Ventures, we look for entrepreneurs who seek out people who are brighter and more capable than they are to add to their management teams. The golden rule of recruiting is to attract the best people possible who also fit well with the chemistry of the team. Leadership also involves being the keeper of the evolving corporate culture that is affected whenever a new member joins. As a recruiter, an entrepreneur needs to be opportunistic and to network, network, network. Entrepreneurs should ask VCs how they help in finding talent to round out management teams and seek examples from their portfolio of companies."

What should they think about as they are putting together the team? "Putting together an effective management team is more an art than a science. The chemistry of the team is as important as the capabilities of the individuals involved. Here are a few general guidelines to follow:

"1. Avoid overlap in team responsibilities and even in areas of operational interest.

"2. Look for flexibility and the ability to work in unstructured situations effectively.

"3. Get the best people possible whose capabilities are ahead of the curve of what the company currently requires.

"4. Recruit people who are smarter and more capable than you are.

"5. Seek individuals with similar values and work ethic.

"6. Hire people you want to see every day."

Gerry Langeler, OVP Venture Partners, www.ovp.com

What resources are available for entrepreneurs to use? What should they think about as they are putting together the team? "Build your management team as if your life depended on it—because your corporate life does. Great teams can adjust and succeed even when the original plan is flawed (as it almost always is!). Fair teams will go to their graves trying to prove the old plan was right. When you bring on each new senior member of the team, ask yourself: 'Is this a world-class person, or am I filling a slot on an organization chart?' Sometimes you might have to do the latter in the short term—but know that you are!

"Finally, ask yourself: What are the characteristics of a successful CEO of a high-growth start-up? If that description doesn't match what you are, admit it up front and look to your venture backers for help in finding someone whose skills do match for that position, now or down the line. Some of our best deals, for us and their founders, came from that model."

Valerie J. Anderson, General Partner, Catalyst Partners, Inc., www.catalystpartnersinc.com

"Make sure you use a legal firm that is experienced in venture capital financings in your industry. You will spend two to three times the usual fees if the lawyer on the company's side doesn't understand standard terms for these types of financings."

WHICH COMES FIRST, MANAGEMENT OR MONEY?

Entrepreneurs face the dilemma of how to entice first-rate management without money, and they can't interest venture capital money without the management.

Outsourcing some of the functional areas of management is a possibility until the company can afford and requires full-time executives. In the area of accounting, the entire back office can be outsourced through companies such as PhoenixResources.com. The entrepreneur doesn't have to worry about payroll, accounts receivable, and getting the bills paid. The accounting functions can also be integrated into an e-commerce system that tracks credit card billings, customer processing, and such. Fulfillment houses can be hired to maintain inventories and pack and ship products.

Certain firms, such as TatumCFO.com, provide part-time, as well as full-time and per-project chief financial officers who have experience in many different industries and in start-ups.

Marketing, public relations, and Web design can also all be contracted for at the appropriate time.

But that still leaves the huge gap of CEO. Most entrepreneurs, while they would like to be the CEO, don't have the qualifications that VCs are looking for: track record and experience. One alternative is for the entrepreneur to recruit a CEO who can commit and contribute to the company but not start drawing a salary until the company is funded.

ADVICE FROM AN ANGEL INVESTOR/ENTREPRENEUR

Neil Senturia, CEO Mohomine, Inc., San Diego, CA

What is the CEO's job in an early-stage technology company? "The principles are, first, don't ever run out of money; second, hire the absolute best people you can surround yourself with, the best and the brightest. The difference between a good programmer and a great programmer is not $30K, it is $30M. Seek, demand, and nurture greatness. You do not have to love him or her, you have to be in awe of their skills. Only hire 'As.' You seek out PSR people—poor, smart, and want to be rich. Third one is, don't run out of money. That's all there is to your job. If you do that really well, you can build a great company."

ASSEMBLING A TEAM OF ADVISORS

Many entrepreneurs like to have a board of advisors to bounce ideas off of, commiserate with, and strengthen their company's management team. That board might consist of a fellow CEO, an attorney, a consultant, an accountant, and industry experts. If there is a gap in the company's management team, an advisor can temporarily fill this gap until the company grows to the point where it can justify a full-time executive.

The board can meet informally on a monthly or every other month basis, or each advisor can be contacted as the need arises on an individual basis.

This group can come in handy in making introductions to capital sources. Its members also can be useful in evaluating the terms and conditions submitted to you by capital sources, even if they don't participate in the actual negotiations. Questioning the potential investor's letter of intent for reasonableness and suggesting counterproposals to submit are two areas in which the advisors can be especially helpful.

When assembling the board, entrepreneurs shouldn't make the mistake of using the board positions for family and friends, unless those friends are well qualified in their industries. Just having a board won't make a difference; having a quality board will.

Finding Investors Where They Work and Play

T he funding of early-stage private companies has been an extremely inefficient market—just ask any entrepreneur who has ever looked for money. Entrepreneurs' efforts to obtain capital are hampered by lack of access to investors and because the process is excruciatingly slow. The frustration level can reach the boiling point as entrepreneurs read statistics that venture capital investment in the United States has never been higher, but all the magical doors to the capital kingdom seemed closed to them. Despite the rising tide of investment, it is *not* easier for the typical entrepreneur to find capital.

Tapping into Capital on the Net

The speed and networking capabilities of the Internet have been harnessed to address this problem, and the future for capital-hungry companies is looking brighter all the time.

Entrepreneurs were quick to embrace the Net because they saw the potential for instant access to millions of potential customers for their products and services. It took a while, but now venture capitalists and wealthy individuals or "angel" investors are beginning to use the Internet as a tool to conduct the business of finding investments.

Capital seekers often contact just a few investors at a time, so only a small fraction of the potential investors ever know the entrepreneur is out there looking for them. Many good companies remain underfunded, unable to reach their full potential, or receive less than a fair value for their equity.

The Internet streamlines the capital-raising process in several ways. Capital seekers are able to research venture capital firms directly through the firms' web sites. The Internet breaks down regional barriers, allowing companies to swiftly link up with sources of capital all across the country. The Internet allows the company to get in front of large numbers of investors quickly and efficiently.

The online capital sourcing services can be characterized as catch, match, and hatch.

Catch a Venture Capitalist on the Net

Most venture capital funds now have web sites, making it possible to submit information about your company, in some cases your whole business plan, by e-mail. These sites contain valuable resources to learn about the firm's investment preferences, the investment process itself, and about the partners of the firm. Several online directories of venture capital firms exist; three are PricewaterhouseCoopers (www.pwcmoney tree.com), The Capital Connection (www.capital-connection.com), and The National Venture Capital Association (www.nvca.com). These directories link to hundreds of venture capital firms. By visiting them, capital seekers can quickly determine whether the investment parameters of the venture capital firm are a good fit with their company and not waste time contacting investors who are not.

WaldenVC (www.waldenvc.com) has a particularly informative and comprehensive site. Patricof & Co. (www.patricof.com) even has an automated procedure for quickly formatting and submitting information about your company.

Match

Vcapital.com (www.vcapital.com) is a web site that is associated with nearly 350 venture capital firms. An entrepreneur can see which venture capital companies are members, what their investment parameters are, and what companies they have invested in. Unfortunately, no contact or address for member venture capital firms is provided. Entrepreneurs pay a fee to join, and their executive summary will be matched with the member venture capitalists. Vcapital.com sends the executive summary to the VCs, who may then contact the entrepreneur if they are interested.

Other matching services are covered in Chapter 7. Many of these matching services have venture capital companies as members even though the main thrust is accredited investors.

Add Capital, Wait for Company to Hatch

Business incubators or business accelerators take the process one step further and assist with developing the company: strategic planning, building the management team, providing capital, and even guiding the fledgling all the way through an initial public offering. A pioneering firm was IdeaLab (www.idealab.com), which recently raised $1 billion for its venture capital arm. eCompanies.com (www.ecompanies.com), Incubate.com (www.incubate.com), and duoDesign (www.duodesign.com) are other examples in an ever-growing arena. Some of these firms are built on the model of holding companies; they seek to invest in Internet companies that can complement each other in a synergistic fashion. Internet Capital Group (www.icge.com) and CMGI (www.cmgi.com) are two well-capitalized entities that fit this profile.

Business incubators are divided into nonprofit incubators, sometimes associated with a university, and for-profit, private business incubators.

NONPROFIT BUSINESS INCUBATORS

While not usually a source of capital themselves (although there are exceptions), business incubators can provide access to capital. Business incubators are usually nonprofit organizations that help young fledging companies by providing shared office resources and, more important, by providing management assistance, consulting, mentoring, and business and technical support services.

Most incubators have admission standards and accept only what they feel are companies with the most potential in the area the incubators focus on. While most incubators are high-tech oriented, incubators exist for every type of business. There is even an incubator for businesses focused on the arts.

The company completes an application and, if accepted, physically moves to the incubator building and shares office equipment, telephone, reception area, and office staff for a monthly payment, which can range from less than $100 to more than $500. In addition, many incubators require an equity position in the companies they accept.

The goal of the incubator is to graduate businesses from the subsidized incubator environment to the business community as viable thriving companies, usually in two to three years. According to the Impact of Incubator Investments Study of 1997, 87 percent of incubator graduates are still in business.

PRIVATE, FOR-PROFIT
BUSINESS INCUBATORS

For-profit, private, business incubators are privately funded and managed. They provide office space, mentoring, access to capital, and other assistance to those companies who are accepted. Many of these business incubators invest in their hatchlings or have an associated fund that invests. Their objective is to accelerate the time it takes to get a company's products or services to market, many times in less than six months, and often in no more than 90 days, and, of course, make the incubator a tidy profit. Private incubators have been founded by venture capital companies, entrepreneurs, and corporations.

Some private incubators require entrepreneurs to physically relocate their companies to the incubator's offices, while others don't.

Private incubator fees can include a monthly service fee for telephone, computer usage, office space, and administrative services as well as fees for professional assistance. The incubator company often takes an ownership position in each company it hosts.

An advantage of the incubator is that often member companies can take advantage of professionals, such as attorneys, accounting firms, marketing firms, and others, who are willing to provide their services at a discount rate or, more likely, for an equity share.

Another advantage is that if the incubator has a positive track record of hatching successful companies, a bit of a halo effect may be generated to new member companies. In other words, when the new member company is ready for an IPO or for a significant infusion of venture capital, it benefits from the success of the companies before it.

Many of the private, for-profit incubators accept outside investors. A few are publicly traded.

Private Incubators in Alphabetical Order

Aktivate (www.aktivate.com), calls itself a venture accelerator. Companies must be early-stage funding, new economy, and New England based.

Cambridge Incubator (www.cambridgeincubator.com). Businesses must be an e-business concept with a transactional element, start-up seed stage, which means a prefinancing valuation less than $5 million, a product/service that can be in beta release within a few months, and must relocate to Cambridge Incubator, located on the edge of the MIT campus in Cambridge, Massachusetts.

Divine Interventures (www.divineinterventures.com), founded in the summer of 1999 by Andrew Filipskowski. Divine focuses on information technology companies located in Chicago.

DuoDesign (www.duodesign.com), provides up to $450,000 in cash and or services over a six-month period to Internet start-ups and then helps the company find angel investors or venture capital. DuoDesign also provides consulting services in marketing, Web design, and e-commerce to established companies. Incubator companies are housed at the facility in Evanston, Illinois.

Ecompanies (www.ecompanies.com), founded by Sky Dayton and Jake Winebaum in May of 1999, is located in Santa Monica, California. Ecompanies concentrates on Web-based start-ups. Companies don't have to relocate to Santa Monica. You can submit your idea or company through their web site.

Ehatchery (www.ehatchery.com), founded by Jeff Levy in Atlanta, Georgia. It has invested in five companies so far, all Web related and all located in Atlanta, Georgia.

Hotbank (www.softbank.com), founded and backed by Softbank Venture Capital. Companies must relocate to the Boston-based facility. Referrals of Web firms, business-to-business Internet companies, and wireless technologies are accepted from universities, venture capital companies, and angel investors. There is no Hotbank web site. Contact through the Boston office of SOFT-BANK Capital Partners, Charles R. Lax, General Partner, 1188 Centre Street, Newton Center, MA 02459, phone: 617-928-9300, fax: 617-928-9305.

Idealab (www.idealab.com) is probably one of the original Internet incubators. It was founded by Bill Gross in 1996. Currently there are 50 companies under various stages of incubation. Idealab is headquartered in Pasadena, California, and has additional offices in Boston, New York, and Silicon Valley. The bad news is that according to Idealab's web site, it is not currently accepting new companies. The good news is that their affiliated venture capital company, Idealab Capital Partners (www.icp.com), will review new companies for potential investment.

I-Hatch (www.I-hatch.com), founded in February of 1999 by Chip Austin, Brad Farkas, and Derek Reisfield, focuses on early-stage Internet companies located in the northeastern United States in e-commerce, new media content, Web-enabling technology, network infrastructure, and Internet services. You can submit an executive summary of your business plan through the web site.

Ihatch (www.ihatch.com), not to be confused with the incubator I-Hatch, will physically incubate companies located in central Florida.

It invests in information technology companies on a global basis. Seed financing ranges from $250,000 to $1 million. Early stage up to $5 million.

Incubate.com (www.incubate.com) is located in Arizona but open to companies located elsewhere, preferably in the Southwest. Established in February 2000 by R. Bruce Whiting, this hatchery's management team is experienced in start-ups, having invested in several well-known Internet companies previously as well as manufacturing and computer-assisted design. Its services can range from just obtaining the angel capital required through traditional incubator services. Companies do not have to relocate to Incubate.com's physical facility in Tempe. Contact it through its website.

iStartVentures.com (www.istartventures.com), founded in January of 1999 and located in Seattle, Washington, prefers to be called a business accelerator rather than business incubator. Prefers early-stage Internet-related companies. It is not mandatory that companies relocate to the iStartVentures offices in Seattle, but it is strongly encouraged. iStartVentures does not charge its portfolio companies any additional fees for officing.

Katalyst (www.katalyst.com) likes to be called a net accelerator and focuses on the business-to-business segment of the Internet. It is located in Radnor, Pennsylvania.

LabHeads (www.labheads.com), of Phoenix, Arizona, was founded in May 1999 by Christopher Matthieu. LabHeads.com currently has about 20 businesses under its wing. Its focus is to take ideas, create a company, and then sell the entity.

Phase 1 (www.phase1.com) was established in 1997. Companies must be housed at the incubator's facility at 12 Laurel Avenue, Laurel, MD 20707, phone: 301-206-2224, fax: 301-598-0769, info@phase1.org.

Think Tank.com (www.thinktank.com) was founded by Scott Blum in 1999. Not much is included about its company preferences, how it works, or what services it provides.

Venture Frogs (www.venturefrogs.com) is really an investment fund founded by Tony Hsieh and Alfred Lin. They do offer incubator office services and advice at their offices in San Francisco.

VentureWorx (www.ventureworx.com) says that it finds Web-focused business ideas, molds those ideas into e-business start-ups, gives the start-ups operational support and expertise, and then takes them public or merges with a company at a valuation of $100 million. It doesn't say anything about if or how it invests capital into companies. VentureWorx is located in Charlotte, North Carolina.

PSEUDOINCUBATORS

Some consulting firms present themselves as "pseudoincubators." They provide services to help entrepreneurs that are similar to a real incubator. They find the capital, legal help, accounting services, and the like and perhaps even put together a business plan.

The fees can include an up-front or retainer of several thousand dollars plus a share of ownership in the company and a percentage of any capital raised paid as a cash fee.

There is nothing wrong with a consulting firm providing these services or charging those fees. The problem is that a few position themselves as legitimate incubators, and they're really consulting firms in incubator clothing.

Other firms provide a matching service between the services that start-up companies need and the service providers. The service providers have agreed to either forgo their normal fees or drastically reduce them and trade the services for ownership in the start-up they assist. The matching service then also takes an equity position in the start-up as payment for their matching service. Advice4Stock.com and Venture Accelerator (www.avce.com) are two such matching services.

Small Business Investment Companies

Small business invesment companies (SBICs) are venture capital companies that receive the majority of their funding from the federal government's Small Business Administration (SBA). They are licensed and must adhere to certain rules and guidelines. An SBIC is founded by people experienced in providing capital to growth-oriented companies, usually with a background in venture capital. For every $1 they invest of their own funds, or from funds they've raised, they are eligible to obtain $2 to $3 of funding in the form of an SBA matching fund loan to the SBIC. For example, if the SBIC contributed $2.5 million as their equity share, the SBA would lend the SBIC $7.5 million so the total funds available for the SBIC to invest would be $10 million.

SBICs can restrict themselves to certain industries and stages of company that they prefer, just as venture capital companies can. They also very commonly will invest only in companies in their geographic location.

The funds they provide can be in the form of a loan or equity infusion. They must invest some portion of the total funding as equity and are limited by SBA regulations to a minority position in any company that they invest in. Since SBICs have to repay the SBA on a regular basis, they probably are more interested in creditworthy companies that have a very high probability of performing well.

Venture Capital Clubs and Entrepreneur Organizations

Venture capital clubs and entrepreneur organizations focused on finance offer entrepreneurs a structured way to access venture capital and sometimes private investors. Meetings are held monthly and are comprised of a networking session, educational session, and then presentations by entrepreneurs who are looking for investors. Fees can range from monthly dues of $25 to one-time presentation fees of $500. Venture capital companies, private investors, professional service providers, and intermediaries belong as well as entrepreneurs.

You can locate these types of organizations through your local chamber of commerce, Small Business Development Office, or SCORE (Service Corps of Retired Executives).

How to Find Capital If You Are Not a High-Tech Company

Ideas from the Venture Capital Firms
"The methods employed are no different than in the high-tech industries. Networking is the key to finding capital no matter what industry the company is in."

"There are plenty of investors looking for deals in non-'sexy' industries too."

"Be creative."

"Right now it's tough. The number of venture capital firms that focus on early-stage, nontech companies is a small universe. Angel investors are typically the best sources of capital for these type companies."

"They can call us! Most of our investments are in manufacturing, service, transportation, and warehousing."

"There are a lot of firms with focuses beyond high tech. You just need to find them. Be persistent. Look for niche venture firms in the appropriate space."

"You can check most VC firms on the Internet. VC guiding web sites."

"There are VC firms for every type of investment. "

"Seek out specialty funds: retail, consumer products."

Some VCs Suggested Angel Investors
"Use friends and family until you establish market validation."

"Also, in Silicon Valley, you have many, many, many rich individuals who will invest."

"Take a modest amount of angel money."

"Angel networks."

"Look in the prospectuses of comparable public companies for names of investors in a section called principal stockholders."

Do Research and Find Investors on the Internet
"Use the Internet to search for venture firms who invest in other businesses."

"Matching services."

"ACE-NET."

Use Service Providers
"Go through an intermediary or service provider (accountant, lawyer, etc.) Investment banks."

Seek Funding from Large Corporations
"Corporate VCs—business development divisions of large corporations."

"Talk to industry players."

"Strategic investors in your industry."

Other Suggestions

"Traditional banks."

"SBA loans and even banks, maybe smaller ones willing to look at higher-risk loans."

"Find out if banks ever make loans to start-ups or early-stage companies, and if so, who."

"Get the SBA to help: www.SBA.gov."

Researching Investors

Besides the venture capital web sites, several books, most likely at your public library, or available for purchase at a reasonable price, list venture capital firms, addresses, contact person, telephone numbers, investment parameters, and companies they previously invested in. *Pratt's Guide to Venture Capital Sources* by Stanley E. Pratt, *The Gold Book of Venture Capital* published by Kennedy Information, and the *Directory of Venture Capital* by Catherine E. Lister and Thomas D. Harnish are three available in printed form as well as on disk or CD.

Many news services and newsletters can keep you updated on the world of venture capital, completed transactions, new funds, and new management. Try *Deal Flow* (www.redherring.com), *The Daily Deal* (www.thedaily deal.com), and *Internet VC Watch* (www.internetvcwatch.com).

Scan back issues of the business section of the local daily paper and weekly business papers such as the *Business Journal*. Look for announcements of companies that are looking to make acquisitions or have made investments. In just a two- to three-week time span, in one city companies looked to expand by acquiring/investing in companies in the areas of advertising, child care, financial services, and consumer products. Also look for articles that announce an expansion or opening of a new company or service. A new sports equipment company announced their product and gave the names of the major investors of their new company. A restaurant company that was announcing the franchising of their restaurant concept did the same thing.

Look in the trade publications of your industry for CEOs and high-ranking executives who are retiring. Sometimes these retirements are not voluntary, and the executives would like to remain involved in the industry. Or an executive may get bored with retirement.

Approach people in a nonaggressive, positive manner. Don't ask them directly to invest. Explain how your company's growing or how you're starting this great new company, and ask if they know of anyone who may be interested in helping. When the person asks: Help how? mention you need marketing expertise, a finance executive—whatever area you do need help in. Of course, be sure to mention you're also looking for capital.

Join trade associations and your local chamber of commerce, even if you're just a start-up company. Membership fees won't cost more than a few hundred dollars. Joining gives you creditability and an immediate network of memberships, which can number in the thousands, with built-in networking opportunities to reach those members.

Making the Most of the Media in Your Search for Venture Capital

Increasing the company's visibility and establishing the company's management as experts in their field has several advantages when searching for venture capital. It adds a level of creditability and widens the company's potential network of contacts.

Publicity is not advertising. You have no guarantee that a press release will be picked up, and you have no control on how the information in the press release is used. It could be the basis of an extensive interview and feature story, or it could simply be one- or two-sentence announcement. How the press release is utilized is completely up to the editor and reporter of the publication.

ADVICE FROM AN EXPERT: VENTURE PUBLICITY EQUALS VENTURE PROSPERITY

Todd Brabender, president of Spread the News Public Relations, Inc., www.spreadthenewspr.com

"If advertisements were free in this media-driven society in which we live, smart entrepreneurs would spend their time compiling creatively effective ads to generate widespread publicity for their ventures.

"Ideally, that would lead to subsequent investor and/or consumer interest and a great start for your venture.

"Advertising, as we all know, is far from being free. But that doesn't mean you can't use similar principles to create free or low-cost publicity for your ventures. An entrepreneur seeking venture capital increases his/her chances of generating interest from a strong investor if the venture has received media exposure. (That PR principle works similarly for the VC seeking a strong investment opportunity as well.)

"The integral first step to self-promoting PR, especially in a new venture, is a seemingly simple yet integral process I call 'media notification.' There are no hidden, groundbreaking meanings to this obvious term. It means taking advantage of the ever-expanding media market to benefit your venture most effectively. Although it is very unlikely, you could pay for an advertisement that beckons the ideal venture capitalist to invest in your idea. But why pay outrageous ad rates when, given the right media pitch, thousands of editors, reporters, and producers will compile mini-ads—in the form of broadcast stories and print articles—for the simple cost of a media release or low-cost media campaign?

"Unlike superficial advertisements, media notification placements profile the product or venture; the principals behind the venture; and—oftentimes the strongest publicity element—the human interest story behind the birth of the venture.

"Media exposure and publicity can be looked upon as a prevalidation of marketability and often lend strong credibility to the venture. The fact that a venture received media exposure, whether it was pitched by a PR professional or a novice, means the media professional saw merit in the venture as well. And most times media professionals, especially those in the specific trade media, are very qualified judges of their industry.

"There are over 70,000 media outlets and more than one million editors, reporters, and producers in North America alone. However, only a fraction of those media professionals and their respective media outlets are applicable to your idea, venture, or investment. The key to an effective publicity campaign is finding those media professionals in the right media markets. Do you know where they can be found?

"Be advised: Bigger does *not* mean better when it comes to media pitches and placements. Sure you could target *Time, Newsweek,* and *People* magazines for publicity—all general-readership publications with circulations of over 3 million. But even if you landed a story there, do venture capitalists who invest in your type of venture really read those types of magazines? Your ideal media target may very well be a trade-specific magazine with a circulation of around 2,500. In all likelihood, you would probably get more investor interest from the smaller, more focused publication. But do you really know what your media market is or how to find it? You would know quite easily if you compiled some basic media market research. Simply go to any library and look up the SIC (Standard Industrial Classification) codes relating to your product or venture. Cross-reference that information with media outlets that correspond to those codes. Then compose your information in a one-page 300- to 500-word media release. In writing the release, answer the basic questions or who, what, when, where, why, and how. Be confident, but keep superlatives (best, finest, most . . .) to a minimum. Nothing turns off a reporter/editor more than a media release that reads more like an ad campaign. Provide the media with 'newspegs' that will give them a reason to cover your campaign. Unique, unprecedented aspects, newsworthy nuggets that let the editor/producer know that it is a unique story his audience needs to hear.

"Better yet, go to the source—ask a PR specialist to assist you. Many PR pros can help you compile very meticulous media market research and even launch a campaign for a very reasonable fee. PR specialists or smaller PR firms oftentimes have low-cost service packages specifically for that reason. A word of caution: Beware of the so-called press release distribution services that promise to simply pitch your release to thousands of media outlets for one price. Many, although not all of them, are what I call 'pitch n' ditch' services that simply purge your release to an e-mail list of media outlets. This practice affords your release no exclusivity and provides no follow-up media contacts, media relations, or tracking of print/broadcast placements—all integral to the success of your entire marketing campaign.

"If initiating a PR campaign is a project you feel you can take on yourself, by all means, do it! The best businesses/ventures cultivate wonderfully reciprocal relationships with as many media professionals as possible. I recommend that every entrepreneur and venture capitalist do the same. Then sit back and wait for the venture capital and/or consumer interest to come pouring in."

WHAT TO INCLUDE IN YOUR PRESS RELEASE

A press release is not an ad. Think of what would interest readers of the publication (TV, trade publication, etc.) about your company. What you have to announce is not the important factor; it's what the readers of the publication want to know that is. A press release covers the five Ws: who, what, where, when, and why. Who is doing it, what are they doing, where are they doing it, when is it being done, and why? Cover all five Ws, the critical information, in the first paragraph of your press release. Then expand on that information, giving the most important information first, in subsequent paragraphs. If space is short, the press release will be cut from the end forward, which is why you don't put important information toward the end.

ADVICE FROM AN EXPERT ON INTERNET PR

Adam Sherk, moderator, Internet Public Relations Discussion List, (www.adventive.com/lists/ipr/summary.html)

"With new Internet businesses launching every day, many e-commerce categories are getting crowded fast. A typical category today may have two or three major players that have secured substantial funding and are making a serious run. In addition, there are any number of less established companies desperately trying to break in and be competitive with limited resources.

"If your company is still in the process of securing funding, there is no way that you will be able to compete in the advertising arena. Whether through banners or e-mail ads, TV spots or billboards, your major competition is going to gain large-scale exposure that you cannot afford to match.

"But through public relations, particularly online, any Internet company is capable of making a strong impact. Internet PR does not level the playing field—money still makes a difference—but there are many opportunities that can be secured at nearly any budget level.

"Whatever your target audience may be (Internet industry professionals, potential investors, consumers, etc.), a successful Internet PR campaign will increase visibility and build credibility for both your company and its key executives. Published media mentions can help significantly in bringing about an action: securing venture capital, developing partnerships, generating sales, etc. The concept is simple: If people have heard of you, they are more likely to do business with you.

"Tactics that will enable to you secure online publicity include:

"*Marketing activity pitches.* Generating mentions in the Internet industry trade press is a good way to position your company as an active player in a particular category. Publications such as www.digitrends.net, Digitrends Daily, www.internetnews.com/IAR/, InternetNews.com, Internet Advertising Report, www.siliconalleydaily.com, Silicon Alley Daily, cover marketing campaign launches, new partnerships, and major advertising buys on a daily basis.

"This is one area where money does still make a difference. The message that company X is kicking off a $20 million marketing initiative or is partnering with portal Y for a special cobranded section of the site is going to be better received then something on a much smaller scale. But it is absolutely possible to achieve mentions regardless of the scale of the activity.

"A typical online trade publication may feature 5 to 10 news items each day, so if you frame the pitch in an interesting and relevant manner, you have a chance of breaking in. Journalists will prefer to know budget information, but you do not have to disclose it.

"In addition to the direct exposure of the publicity secured, your company will also benefit by association. There is value in being featured in the same publication as better-established and more active companies; it indirectly places you in the mover and shaker club.

"*Round-up Articles.* Many Internet industry publications publish 'round-up' articles that provide a general overview of a particular e-commerce category and mention the key sites within it. Even if your company is ranked near the bottom of the list (articles will often include the top 5 or top 10 players), it is very important to at least be included in the mix.

"Research the journalists who are currently covering your industry, and send them some form of introduction package about your company. While this may or may not result in a story that is specifically about your company, the main objective is to get on their radar screen and, it is hoped, be included when round-up articles are written. You can also check the editorial calendars of major media outlets to see if an article on your category is currently planned.

"*Executive Visibility.* Many Internet companies use the strategy of making a 'star' out of their founder or chief executive. You may not be able to create a profile at the level of a Jeff Bezos or Jerry Yang, but there are plenty of online opportunities to gain exposure for Internet executives.

"For example, www.channelseven.com, ChannelSeven.com, publishes a weekly feature called '7 from Seven,' in which they ask the CEO of an Internet company seven questions related to his or her business activities. Another outlet, www.strategyweek.com, StrategyWeek.com, broadcasts streaming radio interviews with Internet executives.

"Again, the more established the company, the more interest there will be in interviewing the executive, but you can make it happen. If you can demonstrate why your CEO is a visionary or how he or she is moving your category forward, the story should be compelling enough to draw interest. And frankly, with the extremely competitive nature of e-commerce today, if you can't demonstrate these things, your business is probably in trouble.

"Another way to gain exposure for company executives is through article placement. Sites such as www.clickz.com, ClickZ.com, www.internetday.com, Internetday.com, publish articles written by Internet executives every day, and others like www.dmnews.com, DMNews.com, with their own editorial content.

"The articles must be genuinely informative and noncommercial in tone in order to be published. In many cases you should not even plug your company in the body of the article; let the author byline and biography do that. Publishing articles on a regular basis increases the visibility and credibility of both the executives and the company, and is particularly effective if you are positioning an executive as an expert in a particular area.

"While the publications that do interviews are typically only interested in top executives, article placement can be used to increase visibility for a number of executives at your company. If your executives are too busy or lack strong writing skills, have someone on staff ghostwrite the articles."

Expanding Your Own Network

Aggressive networking helps you put the power of numbers behind your capital search. Many entrepreneurs have discovered that it isn't the first investor you contact, but maybe a friend of a friend of a friend of the first investor, who will actually become your financial partner. How do you build a network? By turning each no into two or more prospects, by simply asking the investor, "If you aren't interested in a company like mine, do you know two other people who might be?"

With this technique, you are taking advantage of the obvious fact that venture capitalists tend to associate with other venture capitalists. They dine together (you can recognize them: They're the ones who get seated first in the restaurant). They belong to the same clubs (usually located behind high fences and thick hedges), and their children go to the same schools (always private).

You also are using the psychology of rejection in your favor: Most people don't like to tell other people no, so by asking for two more names you are converting a no into something that allows them to feel they have been helpful.

Investors on the lookout for companies to invest in contact accounting firms and law firms. Often their own clients will have expressed an interest in investing in growth-oriented companies. Your attorney and accountant can network for you in their circle of contacts. It's to their benefit for you to find an investor; it means growth for your company and probably more work and therefore fees for their professional services.

Several venture capitalists mentioned that referrals from law firms and accounting firms were important in their search for companies.

ADVICE FROM AN ENTREPRENEUR

Rudie Young, Founder and CEO, www.e-aquatic.com, and formerly an angel investor in the entertainment industry

You didn't begin your capital search until after you launched your web site. Why did you wait? "I thought it would improve our chances of finding capital if we could demonstrate to prospective investors that we had a working web site and that we are doing business."

What do you find to be frustrating about the capital-raising process? "The fact that most angels and venture firms encourage entrepreneurs to send in their executive summary or their business plan but nearly 80 percent of them never respond back. They should at least let the entrepreneur know that they're not interested in his/her business, instead of not replying at all."

Do you have any suggestions or insight to share with other entrepreneurs who are out looking for capital? "Finding capital is similar to investigating a crime scene: Follow up on all leads. Do as much networking as you can through your business affiliations, your law and accounting firm (if you have one); if not, get one or both. Don't let any negative views discourage you; consider the source. You and only you can make things happen for your company."

What is your approach to building your management team? "This is often difficult for entrepreneurs, but you must be able to identify your own limitations and then surround yourself with the best management talent available to you.

"Most entrepreneurs want to be the CEO, but many do not have the necessary experience running a rapidly growing enterprise. A smart businessperson knows when to step aside and let someone else be responsible for the CEO position.

"As the founder of a company, you should put your own money and sweat in it. Investors should not be expected to take a risk that the founder is not willing to take."

Get Out Your Track Shoes

Finding capital is now more of an open process, not just available to the members of the "club." With the advent of Internet-based finance portals, all business owners can proactively access sources of capital.

Formerly, looking for capital seemed like running a marathon in lead sneakers; the Internet is giving entrepreneurs a brand-new pair of wings. Although finding capital is still not a sure thing, it no longer requires quite the Herculean effort it has in the past.

11

Getting to the Big Show: Venture Capital Conferences

Chambers of commerce, software associations, entrepreneur networks, capital networks, and venture capital clubs sponsor events, usually called venture capital conferences, that expose entrepreneurs to potential investors. Venture capital companies attend these events to proactively seek out companies to invest in, rather than waiting for the companies to come to them. Seven percent of the venture capital firms surveyed said conferences were the most common way they had found the companies they had actually invested in.

ADVICE FROM AN EXPERT

Douglas Dunipace, Esq., senior member and chairman of the Commercial Practice Department of the law firm of Jennings, Strouss & Salmon, P.L.C., Phoenix, Arizona, and chair of the 2000 Arizona Venture Capital Conference

"Regional conferences, such as the Arizona Venture Capital Conference held in Phoenix in December each year, can provide entrepreneurs a variety of benefits, some of which may not be easily recognized at first blush. These conferences bring together venture capitalists, angel investors, and other financing sources in a single location for an event-packed couple of days.

"The most obvious beneficiaries of these conferences are the companies who are selected to tell their story in 10 to 15 minutes each to a captive audience. Standing before a group of venture capitalists and other financiers is only the tip of the iceberg. Prior to the presentation, the presenting companies have been mentored by teams of experienced businesspeople, accountants, lawyers, and other professionals. In that process, the presentations are dissected, tested, and refined over a period of several weeks. The result is a presentation that puts the company's best foot forward and can serve as a solid basis for future or expanded presentations. In feedback sessions, presenting companies often rate the mentoring process as the most valuable aspect of the venture capital conference opportunity.

"The company that is selected to make a presentation at a venture capital conference significantly enhances its likelihood of receiving funding. In its first eight years, the Arizona Venture Capital Conference has facilitated over $162 million of venture financing for presenting companies. Other regional conferences have resulted in similar benefits to the companies presenting there.

"The benefits of participating in a venture capital conference are not limited to the presenting companies. By attending the conference and observing the company presentations, entrepreneurs and others looking for capital have an opportunity to see what a polished presentation should include. Additionally, the Arizona Venture Capital Conference and others have other sessions specifically targeted at presenting alternative financing avenues. In these seminars, entrepreneurs are provided timely information about both public and private avenues for business financing. They also hear directly from representatives of financial institutions about their criteria for investing in new or expanding companies.

"Finally, most venture capital conferences are structured so that all the attendees, whether presenting companies or not, have an opportunity to meet and interact with representatives of venture capital and other financing firms. Many relationships which result in investments down the road were first established through attendance at a venture capital conference.

"Not every company is an appropriate candidate for venture capital financing. However, attendance at a venture capital conference will help the entrepreneur determine whether his or her company could attract venture capital and, if not, what other sources of financing may be available."

Process of Applying

To get accepted at a venture capital conference, entrepreneurs submit an executive summary of their business plan in the format requested by the organizing entity. Applicants must stay within the conference's guidelines of what they will accept. If the specifications are no more than five pages single spaced with print no less than 10 pica, don't submit five and a quarter pages. And obviously meet the deadline. Don't count on flexibility in their submission rules.

There is almost always a fee to participate. Sometimes the fee is split into a minimal fee, less than $100, due upon submission and then an additional fee, due if the company is selected as a presenter. But some events charge the entire fee with the submission regardless of whether the company makes it to the final round.

A panel often screens submissions and selects the finalist companies. Approximately 10 to 20 finalists are given between 10 and 15 minutes each to give their pitch to the audience of venture capital partners, angel investors, and service providers. Each finalist is assigned a team of coaches or mentors. These mentors help the entrepreneurs refine and polish their presentations during weekly or biweekly meetings. The entrepreneurs then have at least one dress rehearsal in front of a small group of VCs. Occasionally an entrepreneur requires a second dress rehearsal.

About 200 to 600 people attend the presentations. Not all these attendees are investors; in most cases the majority are attorneys, accountants, intermediaries, consultants, and other entrepreneurs.

These conferences have resulted in successful fund raising of tens of millions of dollars.

Depending on the conference, it may be valuable for an entrepreneur to attend, regardless of whether their company is selected. There are usually social and networking events, lunches, and seminars, that allow entrepreneurs to meet the other attendees and investors.

If for no other reason, entrepreneurs should consider attending to see the other entrepreneur presentations. These presentations have been formatted to appeal to venture capital companies, and, as mentioned, the performances have been mentored and coached.

ADVICE FROM AN ENTREPRENEUR ON PRESENTING AT A CONFERENCE

Owen P. Doonan III, Chairman, THE-Group, The Handicapable Executive Group, Duxbury, MA

Was it a worthwhile experience? "Yes."

What was the most difficult aspect of presenting? "The first 30 seconds. Opening with a well-planned dynamic and audience-grabbing statement. Some people are concerned about audience questions, but I am glad when there is a flurry of questions, because it verifies that my presentation is on track. Good solid answers are the key to winning in the venture capital arena."

What did you find most surprising? "The time it took to complete a funding after basic agreements were in place. A well-reasoned question of a VC would be 'What is your time line from receipt of business plan through actual release of funds?' "

Would you do it again? "Of course. Sharing the wealth by investing in business is the American way!"

How did the coaching or mentoring of your presentation help you? "Actually, I am an experienced coach/mentor with over 25 years in the investment banking business. For a change of pace, I did it for my-self this time!"

Any tips on getting your application accepted as a finalist? "Treat your cover letter, business plan, and accompanying material as if it were a marketing piece for investors. Words that come to mind in-clude: professional, solid, impressive, confidence building, exciting, worthwhile, sure thing."

ADVICE FROM A VENTURE CAPITALIST

Matt Nelson, Director, Fund Development, Village Ventures, Inc.

"At Village Ventures, our target markets are ones that have largely been ignored by traditional sources of venture capital. In these markets, we find that supporting and attending venture conferences are ways to ig-nite awareness and interest in places where they did not exist before. Not only can these forums build a sense of community, but you can learn a great deal about new products, services, and strategies. This all comes from one event—an efficient method of gaining insight and locat-ing new opportunity.

"Although the formats at most fairs allow only a brief look at each company, these introductions are invaluable, and provide a quick avenue to new and exciting deal flow.

"Benefits are there for entrepreneurs as well. Presenting to a broad audience saves a great deal of time and expense in the search for funding. The ideal fair gives its participants a venue where capital and opportunity can begin to come together."

Patrick Sheehan, Partner, 3i Group, www.3i.com

Do you attend VC conferences? How valuable are they? "Occasionally I attend them. They are not that valuable normally. I would be surprised to find an investment from a presentation at a conference. If you are a late-stage investor, it may be a different answer. Conferences can be quite useful for networking. I wouldn't overestimate their usefulness overall."

Screening

Entrepreneurs are sometimes dismayed by the competition to become one of the presenting companies. In most conferences, only a fraction of those companies that sign up for the conference are actually chosen to present, and the screening process can seem bureaucratic: rigid submission criteria in a standard format that may be difficult for an entrepreneur to adapt a business plan to.

Usually the conference organizers provide a suggested outline for the business plan or summary to be submitted. There may even be coaching sessions or other organized events prior to the conference to get entrepreneurs ready.

The screening panel is generally made up of venture capitalists, accountants, attorneys, and other professionals. At some conferences, the panel provides constructive criticism regarding the entrepreneur's business plan summary, but the selection process of some conferences takes on a definite political aspect: People familiar to the organizers may have the inside track on becoming presenters. For an entrepreneur, another frustration is that a new barrier is put up between their company and meeting the investors: the screening committee that decides which companies merit being included on the roster of presenters. Relying on an often-anonymous panel of strangers to evaluate your company's business plan or executive summary is not a comfortable feeling.

Imagine the confusion this Internet entrepreneur felt when he got back these screening panel comments after working hard to shrink his business plan into the eight-page summary required for submittal:

The Company

Good space, details not clear

Good concept, not unique

I like the founders having put money in the deal

The Product/Service

Sounds like 100 other concepts

Unclear on proprietary nature

Is this unique?

No focus, no basis

Not clear on details

The Market

Nothing new here

Tremendous competition, already established players, need better detail on how you compete

Management

Sound OK

Questionable experience in market

No domain experience

Management good

Financial Projections

Where are the P&L details?

Provide greater detail on use of funds

The screening panel gave him an additional three-quarters of a page (!) to answer these questions. Most of us, looking at this, would make the reasonable assertion that this was not quite fair. In order to explain all of these areas, the panel would have to read his entire 35-page business plan.

But with venture capital conferences, rules are rules.

ADVICE FROM AN ENTREPRENEUR

Bill Dawson, Entrepreneur

Was presenting at a venture capital conference a worthwhile experience? "Not from a funding standpoint as prospective investors were more interested in promoting their capabilities and identifying what other opportunities currently exist in process that their competition was pursuing (qualified leads). Looking back, it would have been better to identify the various investor resources, their investment objectives and industry preferences, and direct the contact directly afterwards."

What was the most difficult aspect of presenting? "Conveying the description of the business without diverting into extensive technical detail."

What did you find most surprising? "I wasn't surprised."

Would you do it again? "Not in the format of a company presentation."

How did the coaching or mentoring of your presentation help you? "By developing a presentation, you review or finalize your own business plan and objectives and identify issues to resolve."

Any tips on getting your application accepted as a finalist? "Any entrepreneur who is interested in reaching investors in this format needs to understand the audience expectations and capabilities prior to presenting the opportunity. The opportunity should be matched as close as reasonably possible to investor objectives, including validation of the opportunity. Also, many times the presenter goes into extensive technical detail about the product or service without defining how a market will be accessed and the opportunity realized. From an investor standpoint, I look at the technical details as implementation strategy after the opportunity is defined."

ANOTHER ENTREPRENEUR'S OPINION

Roberto Guerrieri, CEO, UGIVE.com

Was it a worthwhile experience? "Absolutely! It forces you to refine your pitch so it fits tight not only to investors but to your target market."

What was the most difficult aspect of presenting? "Don't underestimate practice. Practice makes perfect."

What did you find most surprising? "Nada."

Would you do it again? "Yes, it is great exposure and a launching PR pad for your company."

How did the coaching or mentoring of your presentation help you? "Excellent! As an entrepreneur you are so close to your product/service that sometimes your message gets confusing. The mentor team is a fresh perspective for a simple, clear story."

Any tips on getting your application accepted as a finalist? "Make sure your application talks to what is getting funding today, not yesterday."

Venture Capital Conferences

January

2001 Venture Capital Conference
Boca Raton, Florida
Phone: 305-446-5060
e-mail: forum@flvencap.org
www.flvencap.org

February

Investor's Choice West
Salt Lake City, Utah
Phone: 801-595-1141

March

New Jersey Venture Fair
Jersey City, New Jersey
Phone: 609-452-1010

North Florida Venture Capital Forum
Jacksonville, Florida
Phone: 904-730-4726

SciTech Conference
La Jolla, California
Phone: 888-960-1800
Fax: 619-558-9371
www.scitechsymposia.com

Virtual Venture Capital Conference
Held entirely online
e-mail: conference@capital-connection.com
www.virtualventurecapitalconference.com

April

Connecticut Venture Fair
Stamford, Connecticut
Phone: 203-256-5955

May

Innovest Venture Capital Conference
11000 Cedar Road, 4th Floor
Cleveland, Ohio 44106
Phone: 216-229-9445
Fax: 216-229-3236
e-mail: tkraus@edinc.org

Investor's Choice International
Maui, Hawaii
Phone: 801-595-1141

Marin Technology Venture Forum
Sausalito, California
Phone: 415-331-7262
www.marinventure.com

Silicon Valley Venture Entrepreneurs
Santa Clara, California
Phone: 619-853-8555

June

AEA Financial Conference
Atlanta, Georgia
Phone: 516-594-3000 ext. 15

Canadian IT Financing Forum
Toronto, Canada
Phone: 604-538-6015
Fax: 604-538-6790
e-mail: pstand@inforamp.net
www.CanadaIT.com

European Private Equity Investor Conference
Phone: 1-800-599-4950
Fax: 212-967-8021
e-mail: imattson@srinstitute.com

Long Island Capital Forum
Melville, New York
Phone: 516-432-9133

Venture Capital Investing
San Francisco, California
Phone: 516-594-3000
Fax: 516-594-5979
e-mail: CathyF@ibforum.com
www.ibforum.com

VentureOne Exchange
San Franciso, California
VentureOne Corporation
Phone: 415-538-2659
Fax: 415-357-2101
e-mail: rtoilolo@ventureone.com

September

Business Incubator & Technology Showcase
Morristown, New Jersey
Phone: 973-267-4200
Fax: 973-984-9634
e-mail: clara@vanj.com

Mid American Venture Capital Conference
180 North LaSalle, Suite 2001
Chicago, IL 60601
Phone: 312-855-0699
Fax: 312-855-9356
e-mail: ilvcconf@aol.com

October

Cal IT-Europe
Cadogan International Conferences Ltd.
117 Charterhouse Street
London, UK EC1 M6AA
Phone: + 44 171 336 8710
Fax: + 44 171 336 8703
e-mail: cadogan@iii.co.uk

Software Investment Conference
San Diego, California
San Diego Software Industry Council
6965 El Camino Real #105-510
Carlsbad, CA 92009
Phone: 760-930-9163
Fax: 760-930-9164
e-mail: sdsic@sdsic.org

Southwest Venture Capital
Dallas, Texas
The Capital Network
3925 W. Braker Lane, Suite 406
Austin, TX 78759
Phone: 512-305-0830
Fax: 512-305-0836
e-mail: paul@ati.utexas.edu

Venture Oregon
Oregon Entrepreneurs Forum
2611 S.W. Third Avenue
Portland, OR 97201
Phone: 503-222-2270
Fax: 503-241-0827
e-mail: info@oef.org

November

VentureNet
Westin South Coast Plaza
Costa Mesa, California
e-mail: Bill@scsc.org
www.venturenet.org

December

Arizona Venture Capital Conference
Phoenix, Arizona
Phoenix Chamber of Commerce
201 N. Central Avenue, 27th Floor
Phoenix, AZ 85073
www.azventurecapitalconf.com

CHAPTER

12

Do Referrals Open Doors?

Do You Really Need a Referral?

We have all heard that it's critical for an entrepreneur to be referred to a venture capital company in order to be taken seriously. Right? Well, maybe not.

We asked venture capitalists this question: What's the most common way you have found the companies you have actually invested in?

Thirty-four percent of the VCs said referral by another VC. Not surprising, since venture capitalists like to invest with other venture capitalists to spread the risk. Additionally, the majority, over 70 percent in second quarter of 2000 according to PricewaterhouseCoopers' venture capital survey, goes to second-round and beyond financings. The VC involved in the initial funding, rather than the company's entrepreneur, often introduces later-round financings to other VCs.

Table 12.1 shows direct contact by the entrepreneur themselves was

Table 12.1   How VCs Find Companies to Invest in

	Venture Capitalists Say		Entrepreneurs' Perception	
Referral Source	%	Rank	%	Rank
Another VC	34	1	18	3
Direct by Entrepreneur	30	2	20	2
Intermediary	17	3	64	1
Attorney	7	4	13	4
Accountant	7	4	9	6
Events	7	4	10	5

cited by 30 percent of the VCs and ahead of referrals by intermediaries (17 percent) and referrals by accountants and attorneys (13 percent). Interestingly, only 7 percent of the VCs said events like venture capital conferences were the most common way they had found the companies. A few VCs said that they had found the companies primarily through their own personal network.

The results do not add up to 100 percent, since even though the question was phrased as "the most common way" several respondents designated more than one way. Venture capitalists have an independent streak.

Perhaps smaller, more regionally oriented venture capital firms are more accessible by direct entrepreneur contact than the top-tier firms. Such is not the case. No such correlation is apparant from the responses of specific venture capital firms. Top-tier firms aren't any more—or less—approachable directly by entrepreneurs.

The Entrepreneurs' Viewpoint

The great majority of entrepreneurs think the most common way venture capitalists are introduced to the companies that they eventually invest in is through paid intermediaries or finders. The intermediary community has done a good job of convincing entrepreneurs it's their way or no way, since that form of contact is cited by entrepreneurs more than three times any other method, while VCs rank intermediaries in third place and significantly below direct contact by the entrepreneurs.

There could be a number of explanations why entrepreneurs believe intermediaries are so important. Many start-ups do not have the capital available to retain a law firm and/or accounting firm, so that avenue of referral isn't open to them. Quite a few intermediaries work on a success-fee basis and only get paid if they find investors. So the entrepreneur doesn't have to take cash away from other functions in order to use an intermediary. And then there is the possibility that entrepreneurs prefer to use intermediaries because they don't want to be personally rejected by the VC. The intermediary faces the rejection and has to hear "No, thanks."

There are a number of effective ways to contact venture capitalists. Entrepreneurs sometimes are told that the only way to get through to a venture capitalist is by using a referral. This does not seem to be the case. Direct contact is fine, according to a significant number of VCs. Entrepreneurs sometimes wonder whether it is worth the time and expense of attending venture capital conferences and other networking events. Yes! By doing so they can make contacts that eventually result in deals.

Referrals: The Great Debate

Our survey results show that venture capital firms disagree with each other about whether a referral is necessary in order to contact them. But those firms that recommend referrals are adamant on the point, as these comments from the VCs indicate.

> "*If they cannot get a referral, they probably do not have a plan that would interest anyone. Referrals can come from their attorney, accountant, banker, etc. If they are not sophisticated enough to have a qualified service provider that has ties to the VC community, they are unlikely to get funded.*"
>
> "*Referrals are the only way.*"
>
> "*Networking: Associate with quality lawyers and accountants.*"
>
> "*Have their attorneys and/or accountants recommend them to venture capitalists whom they know.*"
>
> "*Only referred deals are reviewed.*"
>
> "*Referrals are critical.*"
>
> "*Of all the deals that come to us, only the referrals have been financed.*"

"There is nothing more important than a referral. I would never send a business plan cold without a referral. Network until you can get a referral."

"The most credible source of deals are other private equity shops and other VCs."

"To get your plan in front of the right person it is important you have some kind of referral. Any way you can, try and find a friend or a former associate who knows the investment professional who can green light a deal."

Several of the VCs who have been interviewed in the media have stated that they would never invest, or haven't ever invested, in a company that was not referred to them. However, their responses on the survey included direct contact by entrepreneurs as one of the most common ways their firm had found companies. This contradiction is a little puzzling.

WHOM COULD YOU ENLIST TO INTRODUCE YOUR COMPANY TO AN INVESTOR?

It has been said that there are only six degrees of separation between any two randomly picked people on earth. In other words, it would take only six contacts before there was a direct personal link between any two total strangers anywhere. So why do entrepreneurs feel that finding a personal referral to a venture capital company is an impossible task?

In the Entrepreneur's Own Words

"Most entrepreneurs are not educated about the process. It is important that entrepreneurs know the ins and outs. The current venture capital industry is a closed society. If you do not know anyone, you are always on the out looking in."

"We don't all live in Silicon Valley. It's too difficult to meet VCs elsewhere in the country."

"Very good ideas don't get funded without introductions from well-connected people, either people with whom the venture capital group has invested in the past or angels who they have followed as second-round funding before."

"There seems to be a large element of politics and person relationships involved in choosing investments and sometimes a lack of understanding of the underlying business."

"Venture capitalists are throwing money at concepts that have not been tested or

proven and leaving good concepts on the table because they know someone who knows someone."

Professionals Who Could Introduce You to Investors

Attorneys

Accountants

Consultants

Executives of a VC's portfolio company

Finders, brokers, intermediaries

Other venture capitalists

Investment advisors

Insurance agents

Business associates

What makes a referral valuable is the relationship the referral source has with a given investor, the implied "warranty" that they would send only quality deals to the investors and that your company qualifies.

What's in it for the person making the referral? This depends on the type of referral source. Some professional service providers assist their clients with making contact with investors as part of the overall services they provide. Their motivation is that without capital, you are a small company; with capital, you have the potential to become a major client. You may be charged for the time they spend making the introductions on your behalf. Others may ask you to pay a referral fee, a percentage of the transaction when the deal closes or stock in your company or both.

One cautionary note: Venture capital funds are hesitant to pay intermediaries a significant percentage of the capital they put into a deal. If you do offer to pay a finder's fee, make it something reasonable, such as 2 to 3 percent of the capital, not 10 percent. The venture capital fund will not allow 10 percent of the capital to be paid to a finder, and this can cause conflict when the deal is moving toward a close. One well-known Internet intermediary has observed that it is strange that venture capitalists object to paying finder's fees to people who cause transactions to take place, when the partners of the VC fund are compensated on a percentage basis for successful transactions. Logically, in an environment where venture capitalists say there is "too much money chasing too few good deals," they should be willing to pay handsomely for a good deal being brought to them. But it's not necessarily so.

Referrals have become more of an issue because venture capital funds are receiving more deals than they can keep up with, and they need some mechanism to establish a pecking order to sort through the reams of paper that come into their offices. A method they employ is to give a higher priority to those transactions that come from someone they already know.

Apart from that, there really is no particular advantage to using a referral source. In mergers and acquisitions, having investment bankers serve as buffers between the buyer and seller can be extremely valuable to solving contentious issues and keeping the deal on track. And they are richly rewarded for their work. Keep in mind after that transaction closes, the buyer and seller may never have to meet again.

We are asked many times to refer deals to VCs. Our response is that it may get the executive summary read more quickly, but doesn't have any effect on whether the company gets capital.

Venture capital deals are quite different from mergers and acquisitions transactions, because the ultimate goal is to create a partnership between the venture capital firm and the company. The venture capitalist is vitally interested in getting to know the entrepreneur and his or her team, not talking through a third party.

Networking

Networking is a valuable way for entrepreneurs to expand their own contact base. Trade associations and professional associations are especially useful.

ADVICE FROM AN EXPERT ON USING ASSOCIATIONS TO NETWORK TO YOUR BEST ADVANTAGE

Ed Denison, Director, Arizona Software and Internet Association, www.azsoft.net

"Most industries have not-for-profit trade associations that exist to provide value to their industry. They are invaluable tools for you to use to network to your best advantage.

"Most associations follow the value chain for the industry they serve. The association members are the individuals and/or industry companies, vendors, and support services companies that specialize in that industry. Each provides value to you in your quest to find capital. Fellow industry members, your peers, are perhaps your best networking opportunity to find capital. Many of them have been through the process already and can provide you leads on where they were well received or received the cold shoulder. They may suggest which venture capital companies do deals in your own industry and deals in a similar stage of development to your company. Vendors to your industry know who is hot and who is not! They can tell you who has been recently funded.

"Surprisingly, many vendors also invest in customer companies or forge partnerships that include investments. Support services companies, such as law firms or accounting firms, are also a source of information. They know local specialists in your field that can provide expertise to you. They also have a network of funding sources you can utilize.

"Most associations with a significant membership that are looking for investors have programs that assist in this process. Many put on investor conferences that match investors with member companies. During this process they often provide mentor teams of professionals that donate their time to prepare the company for its presentation. Other associations have Special Interest Groups [SIGs] or roundtables that meet to allow people looking for capital to come together to learn the process. My own association has monthly meetings with entrepreneurs that go over the entire process from business plan preparation to preparing for the IPO. There is normally not a charge to attend these SIGs. Many associations have Web pages that identify those that can help you find capital locally.

"Networking does not just happen easily for many of us. We have to work at it. Making the effort to go to the meetings at 7:30 A.M. or for cocktails or dinner when we are tired is difficult. Most entrepreneurs work very hard and are focused on their company. However, you must network to help your company grow. I promise you that every hour you spend will provide huge value to you and your company. Bring lots of business cards. Go up to strangers, stick out your hand to introduce yourself. Find out what their issues are and see if you can help them. They will more than return the favor in the future.

"The Internet is a terrific way to identify the association best for you. If you are in the technology or information technology space, go to www.itaa.org, and click on their regional affiliate section to find the association in your locality. Local service providers are also good sources to discover the best association. Check out the local press to see what groups are active and particularly scan the activity section.

"Trade associations are great ways to meet the people that can help your quest. In return, they are looking for memberships and participation in their activities. This is the making of a terrific arrangement."

BEWARE OF THE GATEKEEPER

The emphasis on referrals as a means to gain access to investors has spawned an entirely new impediment for entrepreneurs: gatekeepers. These people position themselves, generally in a localized area, as the only ones who can make the key referral for an entrepreneur to an investor, particularly the larger VC firms. The gatekeepers' reputation grows and grows—as if their power to open doors is magical. Entrepreneurs will point one out at networking meetings and whisper: "Only he can get you in to see the VC."

Technology-savvy but non–financially oriented entrepreneurs often fall prey to gatekeepers. Gatekeepers can find the most fertile ground in areas of the country that are not well trafficked by venture capitalists, making investors seem all the more remote and access all the more difficult to obtain.

In our heavily populated and prosperous city, entrepreneurs have a legitimate complaint that it is difficult to get major venture capital firms to pay attention to the technology companies here. We have seen gatekeepers emerge and disappear several times over the last 10 years. A new one appeared on the scene recently who uses this highly overrated influence to earn lucrative finder's fees or to insinuate himself into deals and earn equity in the companies.

The truth is that gatekeepers have no more access to venture capitalists than scores of attorneys and accountants and other service providers in your community. You don't need gatekeepers; they need you.

BEWARE OF THE PROFESSIONAL CRITIC

Everyone agrees that team building is one of the keys to entrepreneurial success, filling in the missing pieces, adding talent and experience to the management group. Thoughtful entrepreneurs often believe they need to bring in "gray hair," people a generation or more older than they are who have that air of "been there, done that."

Sometimes the gray hair is added to the advisory board of the company; other times the person has a more formal role. The experience these individuals add to the team can be terrific, indispensable, phenomenal. However, if you look closely, there are many shades of gray. Entrepreneurs need to understand there is a distinction between acquiring valuable experience over the years and just living a long time because your family had outstanding genetics.

Some of these retired CEO-type people just love to attach themselves to inexperienced entrepreneurs and slowly take over. And one of the methods they use is to disparage all the work that was done prior to their fortuitous arrival on the scene. The company's marketing strategy is all wrong. The R & D cost estimates are flawed. The organizational setup is all wrong. The business plan needs to be redone. The professional critic will of course offer to fix things, for a substantial equity interest in the deal. The question entrepreneurs need to consider is: Does this person really understand the problems and challenges of entrepreneurship?

We witnessed several weeks of cruel torture by one of these guys whom an entrepreneur we had known for a long time had enlisted. The entrepreneur was getting ready to contact venture capitalists, and asked the professional critic to look over the company's business plan. The entrepreneur called the critic to get a reaction. The critic said, "There were some areas of your plan I had difficulty with."

"What areas? Please tell me," pleaded the insecure entrepreneur. The critic hemmed and hawed—and said, "Well, I'll just let the VCs tell you what's wrong," until the entrepreneur all but offered majority control in his company in exchange for the critic's wisdom.

Another time a client of ours asked us to meet a retired CEO who had offered to come on board and mentor the entrepreneur. The client wanted our opinion on whether the guy could add any value to the team. There was a definite feeling of hostility in the room when we began: The guy clearly didn't want his position in the company eroded by our opinion, people 25 years his junior. He began talking up how great he was, looking at us as if to say, "I eat little folks like you for breakfast." We asked him how long he had been mentoring entrepreneurs. "Two years or so," he replied. "What's your experience?" he asked, as if ready to laugh at whatever we said. "We have a combined thirty years of advising entrepreneurs," we said.

In this case, experience was the best teacher.

If You Just Absolutely Cannot Find a Referral, Then What?

Venture capitalists recommend the following to entrepreneurs who don't have a referral, to improve their chances of getting their company considered.

An excellent business plan	23%
A striking executive summary	21%
Know what the VC wants, and make sure your company is a perfect fit	13%
Attend venture capital conferences and meet investors there	9%
A referral is the only way	9%
Have a great management team	6%
Send the plan overnight mail to get attention	6%

VCs Agree: The Business Plan Is Key

"A well-prepared business plan."

"A professional-looking package."

"An exceptional business plan."

How To Impress the Venture Capital Firm with Your Plan

"We are impressed by business plans with airtight assumptions."

"Get to the point. We receive so many business plans that it is difficult to spend a lot of time with each trying to figure out if there is a good company underlying the verbiage. You should be able to summarize your business in about five pages and describe it in a reasonable amount of detail in about 25 pages. If you can't, you probably do not have enough focus. Consider hiring a professional, either a consultant or an agent, to help you draft the plan."

"A concise business plan with detailed marketing strategy."

Get in the News

"Create a newsworthy business event/result that gets picked up in the press or generates word-of-mouth interest in your company."

Conferences

"Attend conferences or other networking events/meetings where they would have the chance to meet and interact with VCs in an informal setting. Make sure your 'elevator' speech is ready to go."

"Participating in a venture capital fair or conference."

"Network, attend events where venture capitalists will be."

"Present at VC-oriented shows."

Use an Intermediary

"Hire someone who knows how to raise money."

13

Intermediaries and Other Wild Things

Finders, Intermediaries, Finance Consultants, Money Brokers, and Investment Bankers

Starting a company, or managing an ongoing company, is already more than a full-time job. Finding venture capital takes time and energy, often time and energy that could be devoted to your company. Many entrepreneurs are great at networking and developing contacts for their business but hit a stumbling block when they try to raise capital.

People who find money for companies for a fee are called finders, intermediaries, money brokers, corporate finance consultants, or investment bankers. The fees they earn are called finder's fees, introductory fees, contingency fees, commissions, brokerage, or success fees.

Finders and money brokers find the investor and make the introduction.

Intermediaries also assist in the negotiations process and will help structure the term sheet and review the letter of intent.

Corporate finance consultants do the above and help prepare the business plan or offering memorandum.

Investment bankers become involved in mergers and acquisitions, assist in taking a company public, as well as finding investors.

Many people use the above terms almost interchangeably. Here we will simply use the term "intermediary" to mean any of the above.

Fees

Finder's fees vary quite a bit. They can include an up-front fee of several thousand dollars and an ongoing monthly retainer, plus a cash fee based on the amount of the capital raised, plus an equity position in the company or warrants. Or the fee can be simply a percentage of the capital raised.

The services provided can also range from providing a list of potential investors that the entrepreneur contacts, to the preparation of a business plan, contacting investors, assisting with negotiations, and structuring the deal.

The classical Lehman's formula fee of 5 percent of the first million of capital raised, 4 percent of the second million, 3 percent of the third million, 2 percent of the fourth million, and 1 percent of all money after that may not apply. Double Lehman is common, as is a straight 10 percent of the money. Finder's fees can be expensive. Paying someone $100,000 to get you a net of $900,000 seems like a good deal, until you have to write that $100,000 check.

Intermediaries often require an up-front fee or retainer, which can range from a few hundred to a few thousand dollars. Sometimes this fee will be deducted from the success fee or finder's fee. Some consultants who prepare business plans are also intermediaries and will prepare the business plan for free or for a great discount. Sometimes consultants will accept equity in the company as their fee for completing the business plan.

FEE AGREEMENTS

The fee agreement or contract can be exclusive, which means if the capital is found, it doesn't matter if the intermediary was responsible or made the introduction, he or she gets paid the fee.

Nonexclusive fee agreements mean that the intermediary has to find the capital source, introduce them, and gets paid only if the capital source makes the investment or loan. The term of the agreement can be up to 12 months. There also will be a clause that says if anyone that the intermediary introduced makes an investment after the term of the agreement expires, but within a certain time period afterward, which can range from 12 to 24 months, that the obligation to pay the intermediary fee remains.

WORKING WITH AN INTERMEDIARY

The intermediary should tell you the identity of every person he or she is contacting about your company. You have the right to know who is being provided that information, even if the information is blind (your company's name is not revealed). There may be people who you do not want contacted or people you have already contacted. Ask to see a list of potential contacts. The intermediary may respond that his or her contacts are proprietary and can't be divulged. The fear here is that you will either circumvent the intermediary and contact the investor yourself or that you will share that list with others and the intermediary's sources will no longer be proprietary. You can agree to give the intermediary a letter that states you won't do either of these things.

ADVICE FROM AN EXPERT ON QUALIFYING AN INVESTMENT BANKING FIRM

Jim Arkebauer, Venture Associates, Denver, CO, www.ventureA.com

"The process of selecting or qualifying an Internet investment banking firm should not differ too much from what has always been the selection/qualification process. Inquire about the track record, how long the firm has been in operation, ask for some references, determine comfort ability with the principals and the types of financings that have done in the past.

"Most investment banking firms have industry/business niches that they are most comfortable in dealing with. These are usually areas that they have experience in or in which they have financing contacts. This, plus a prospect's management team's qualifications are keys to determining if an investment banking firm can assist a prospective client.

"The primary service that an investment banking firm brings to any deal is the fact that they are experienced in the process. They have been through it many times before and are knowledgeable about what works and what doesn't as well as the pitfalls to avoid and what short cuts can be taken."

Should you hire someone to find the capital for you? Yes, if you don't have the time, don't enjoy making sales presentations, or are intimated by interacting with people with money or access to money. But before you do, exhaust all the readily available sources of capital, such as venture capital companies, banks, and small business investment companies (SBICs) yourself. And remember, anyone who is working on a commission or success fee is only going to work on those deals that are hot—that generate a lot of interest from the intermediary's contacts. As soon as it cools down, the intermediary has to move on. Intermediaries have to work on the transactions with the greatest likelihood of success, or they don't earn an income.

ADVICE FROM AN EXPERT

David Nussbaum, CEO and founder of EarlyBirdCapital.com

As a successful investment banker, what would you recommend to entrepreneurs to help them select an investor? "This is a common question, and luckily it has a simple answer. The rise of popularity in venture investing ($19 billion invested in Q2 2000) has created an overabundance of eager VCs looking for profitable investments. While this is good for the entrepreneur, a young start-up must be wary of an investor's intention. A small company should avoid unfocused, money-hungry investors who care little about their business goal and concentrate merely on equity and return on investment. While these factors are always important, since a VC obviously wants an investment return, an entrepreneur should want more than his/her unfocused cash. The phrase 'mentor capital' has risen to prominence in the venture world and quickly distinguishes a good investor from an unfocused investor. Mentor capital means an investor cares about growing the business and works closely with management to strategically nurture the start-up, thus creating a viable operation. This key difference is important to any entrepreneur who has worked painstakingly to develop a feasible business plan.

"Another important factor is contacts—which naturally adheres to the concept of mentor capital. A start-up needs more than cash—it needs valuable 'face-time' with potentially big clients and later-round investors. These opportunities may be hard pressed if the VC has few connections in the business that he/she is investing in. A VCs Rolodex is almost as important as his checkbook.

"Finding an investor that provides mentor capital is key to developing a positive VC relationship."

You must determine two things about potential intermediaries: their level of competence and whether they really have any investor relationships.

If you are uncomfortable making a sales pitch to investors, there is nothing wrong with enlisting the aid of someone who does that every day for a living. But remember, the first contact with the investors is the first impression you will be making. When you interview a prospective intermediary, you need to determine whether this is the type of person you want representing you out in the venture capital marketplace.

Many books or articles on finding capital tell the entrepreneur to ask the intermediary these questions:

- How many deals have you closed?
- How much capital have you raised?
- Can you give the names of three companies you have raised capital for that I can talk to?

These questions are all right, but they don't get to the heart of the matter. The real issues for you are:

- Does the intermediary have strong relationships with investors? Do they trust the intermediary's opinion? Does the intermediary have contacts in the world of venture capital, or is he or she simply going to a searchable database, culling out those VCs whose investment parameters are similar to your company, and sending a letter out?

- How hard is the intermediary willing to work on your behalf? What is the marketing approach? How does the intermediary plan on contacting each potential investor and then following up?

- Does the intermediary appear professional, someone you would like to have representing you? Does the person's appearance fit with the image you want for your company?

- Is the intermediary knowledgeable about your industry, so he or she can talk intelligently with an investor? Investors can ask technically specific questions; will the intermediary be able to answer them?

What intermediaries have done in the past is not necessarily an accurate predictor of how they will fare for you. A person just starting out as an intermediary may be hungrier and work harder.

Also keep in mind that venture capitalists don't like to pay exorbitant fees—of any kind—but they especially don't want a substantial amount of investment going to pay off an intermediary.

Intermediaries on the Internet

Quite a few investment banking or intermediary sites are now online. The services range from simply providing an automated matching service to full-fledged investment banking including private placements.

ADVICE FROM AN INVESTMENT BANKER

Jim Arkebauer, Venture Associates, Denver, CO, www.ventureA.com

Has the Internet changed investment banking? "I would suggest that the Internet has changed the investment banking world by making investment bankers as well as almost all other financing sources more accessible. E-mail and web sites have opened up an easier line of communication from entrepreneur to financing. Obviously, the first step has been just the plain fact that these sources are more available (via lists). It used to be a considerable project to track down names and contact information.

"I believe that the Internet will continue to impact entrepreneurial financing in a positive way. As it does in many other areas, the Internet opens and frees up the financing process. Witness the increasing numbers of direct public offerings [DPOs] and the sites and/or firms which seek to facilitate DPOs. This also applies to private placements and what is currently called angel financing. Prior to the Internet, there was no way that entrepreneurs could let the whole world know about their project and that they were seeking financing."

Where to Look on the Internet

AngelStreet.com (www.angelstreet.com) is an Internet-based investment bank that matches accredited individual investors and institutions with private capital investment opportunities. Angelstreet.com solicits a venture capital company to be the lead investor and then offers its accredited investor members the opportunity to invest with the venture capital company.

CapitalKey Advisors, LLC. (www.capitalkey.com) blends cutting-edge Internet technology with traditional investment banking services to provide small and emerging businesses with professional advice and effective access to capital. Fees are a percentage of the capital raised, no retainers, no up-front fees.

Early Bird Capital (www.earlybirdcapital.com) is an online investment banking firm assisting companies looking to raise early-stage financing between $3 to $5 million. Companies are screened, and only those that are accepted are presented to member investors.

The Garage for Start-ups (www.garage.com) requires the entrepreneur to complete a preliminary application, which is then reviewed by the principals of garage.com. The companies are further screened with a personal interview set up either in person or by telephone. Only companies with high growth potential are accepted after a thorough due diligence process by garage.com. Once accepted, a mini-plan is displayed in a password-protected area open to member-accredited investors. A percentage of the capital found is charged by garage.com to the entrepreneur.

Off Road Capital (www.offroadcapital.com) is not for start-ups but for established companies looking for $3 to $15 million expansion capital. Companies accepted by Off Road Capital are then offered to the network of accredited investors. Those investor members pay a membership fee, open an account with an affiliated financial institution, complete an application, and go through a credit check.

Venture Highway (www.venturehighway.com) provides a matching service between entrepreneur members and investor members. Entrepreneurs pay a quarterly fee to have their executive summary posted and 1 percent of the investment made by any investor introduced through their matching process. Investors can view the executive summaries based on their investment parameters. If they would like the business plan, they must contact venturehighway.com to provide it. Then they are provided the business plan and the entrepreneur is notified.

Yazam (www.yazam.com) offers investment banking services to Internet-related companies. It recently merged with First Tuesday, an organization in Europe that introduces entrepreneurs to investors at informal networking meetings. Entrepreneurs submit their business plan to Yazam and are notified of a preliminary interest by Yazam. If interested, Yazam then performs extensive due diligence and if satisfied will accept the entrepreneur's company as a client. Yazam works on an exclusive basis, fees are cash payment when funding is final and an equity position in the company, in addition to a seat on the company's board of directors.

14

So Many Venture Capitalists, So Little Time

How Do VCs Want to Be Contacted and What Do They Want to See?

Researching the investment preferences of venture capital firms is critical, so you don't waste their time or yours by sending information about your, say, communications technology to a venture capital firm that specializes in biotechnology companies.

Investment criteria are usually based on the factors of industry preference, amount of capital, stage of the company, and geographic location. Also look at what companies the venture capital firm has invested in, how much, and at what stage. The Pricewaterhouse-Cooper's (www.pwcmoneytree.com) quarterly venture capital survey is searchable by investee company sorted by industry, as well as by venture fund. Entrepreneurs can get a good idea of how much investment activity has taken place recently in their industry and in what regions of the country.

ADVICE FROM A VENTURE CAPITALIST

Dennis Spice, Managing Partner, Open Prairie Ventures, www.opven.com

How does a firm determine investment parameters and industry focus? How often does this change? "We're evaluating our strategy every week, to make sure there is no deviation from our goals we set out. One of our goals is to only invest in companies that have sharp focus. Many time inventors out of universities have six ideas or more. We want them to focus on one idea that is commercial viable. The entrepreneur must understand the others must stay on the shelf for the time being."

In midyear 2000, VCs started to turn sour on B2Cs (business-to-consumer Internet companies) and focus on B2Bs (business-to-business sites). How do you decide what industries or sectors to focus on? "We try to look in our crystal ball out fifteen years if possible to see where technology is headed. While the rest of the industry was turning off on B2C, we never really had focused on B2C anyway. We look at ourselves as a contrarian venture fund. When others don't see value added in a particular sector, we view it as a great time for us to get involved, and we can get in at a lower valuation."

Advice For the Denizens of the New Economy: What the VCs Say
"The business model and profitability still matter!"

"Net entrepreneurs don't spend nearly enough time thinking through their business models and how they will eventually reach profitability."

"Net entrepreneurs should spend less time hyping their companies and focus on the fundamentals of their business."

"Net entrepreneurs need to clearly show/discuss how they will (a) drive traffic/eyeballs to their site and (b) how they will convert site visitors into paying customers."

"Net entrepreneurs generally should shoot for markets in excess of $500 million ($1 billion+ is preferred)."

Ways to Get the Investor's Attention

Use E-mail
"A crisp overview or presentation that can be e-mailed."

"E-mail the executive summary."

Use Overnight Mail
"Send the plan via overnight courier so it gets greater attention."

"Referral really is the best way. Overnight mail to a specific partner would be second best."

Make a Phone Call
"Be able to say what your company does in 15 seconds or less."

Be Persistent
"Also, follow up your plan submission with a single call several weeks later. This gives VCs a chance to review the plan before they hear from you, does not harass them—please only call once—but gives you a chance to hear their thoughts, which may help you shape your company even if they decline to invest."

"Be persistent."

"If possible, follow up your fax or e-mail with a phone call. Personally, I prefer to be given a couple of days to review the plan after receiving it. Don't be pushy, though. Simply ask if the VC has received the plan, had time to review it, and whether he/she has questions. Don't believe the anecdotal stories about companies being funded because the entrepreneur called a VC every day for a year and/or showed up unannounced and refused to leave until granted an audience."

A License to Be a Pest!
"Call the VCs every day. Be persistent."

The Internet Is Becoming an Important Way to Contact Investors

We asked venture capital firms, "How would you prefer the initial contact by the entrepreneur (or their representative) be made to you?" As shown in Figure 14.1, e-mail is now by far the most popular way to make the contact, with 42 percent of respondents choosing that method. Postal mail followed next with 29 percent; the telephone was the choice of 17 percent of respondents; 8 percent suggested a fax contact; and 4 percent said they wished to be contacted through a referral.

Again, several venture capitalists were adamant that they only considered companies referred to them by a respected source.

The significant number of venture capitalists who prefer phone contact is interesting. Entrepreneurs might ask, "If I cold call a VC firm, will I really be able to get a decision maker on the phone?"

Intuitively it could be expected that making the initial contact through e-mail rather than postal mail might speed up the process. According to the respondents, this was the case: 29 percent of those who prefer e-mail for an initial contact reported that they closed deals within 60 days on average, compared to 19 percent of respondents as a whole. Contact by telephone also appears to expedite the evaluation process as well, with 71 percent of those respondents who preferred to be contacted by phone saying they closed deals within 90 days of contact, on average, compared to 64 percent for the venture capitalists as a group.

Among those who reported that they had been able to close a deal within 30 days of contact, 50 percent preferred to be contacted by e-mail, 29 percent by phone, 18 percent by postal mail, and 3 percent by referral. The percentage who preferred e-mail and phone was higher, and postal mail lower, than for the group as a whole. This "fast-closing" venture capital firms preferred to read a short executive summary or have

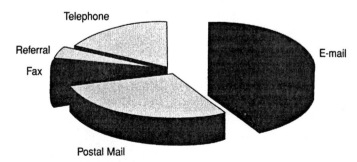

Figure 14.1   Initial Contact Preference

the company described on the phone initially, more than the group as a whole, and they had a lower preference for receiving a full business plan as an initial contact. More information on how long it takes to close a deal can be found in Chapter 20.

In the past two years or so, many venture capital firms have launched well-designed and complete web sites describing the funding process, the partners in the fund, previous investments, and current investment preferences. It is easier than ever for entrepreneurs to "do their homework" before contacting investors. And it is easier for them to be certain they contact venture capitalists that make a good fit with their company. Remember, the second most common reason VCs decline to invest is because the entrepreneur's company does not match their investment parameters.

Send Concise Information to Investors

When asked what information they would like to receive with the initial contact, the venture capital firms said:

2–3-page executive summary	56%
10–15-page "mini" business plan	22%
Full business plan	14%
Information by telephone only	7%
Cover letter describing the company	1%

Over twice as many venture capitalists prefer receiving an executive summary to any other information.

The respondents who wished to be contacted by e-mail much preferred receiving an executive summary as the first information (73 percent) compared to all respondents (56 percent). Those who said they wished to be contacted by postal mail were more likely to ask for the whole business plan (29 percent) than the entire group (14 percent). Even among those who wished to be contacted by mail, however, an executive summary was far and away the most preferred information to receive initially (54 percent). These results show the importance of making a strong impression with the executive summary, especially since the volume of submissions to venture capitalists is increasing so much.

The greatly increased volume of entrepreneurs presenting their companies may have forced the venture capitalists to make preliminary decisions in less time and on less information. Venture capitalists simply don't have the time to review an entire business plan. From the entrepreneur's standpoint, however, it is quite difficult to boil down all the key information about the company into a two- to three-page executive summary.

Note: The executive summary is considered fine for an initial contact, but investors still expect a full business plan to be available should they express further interest.

The preference for e-mail contact may explain why investors choose to see an executive summary initially rather than a full business plan. Most business plans would have to be e-mailed as attachments, which require time to download and print out. Executive summaries can be included as part of the initial contact e-mail with no attachments necessary.

The popularity of initial e-mail contact combined with the preference for an executive summary may indicate that the VC prefers a more efficient review process. No photocopying is required with e-mail; it can simply be forwarded. No paper is involved so there is no manual filing, and no clerical time or expense is involved in responding to the e-mail— no typing of a decline letter, stationary, or postage required.

Skeptical entrepreneurs might argue that the preference for e-mail might have to do with how easy it is to dispose of unwanted e-mail submissions using the delete key.

Several venture capital web sites utilize online submission of executive summary information. When using these online forms, treat them as if you were submitting hard copy. Cut and paste from your executive summary—which we hope has been polished to a high gloss; *don't* just wing it.

Venture Capitalists Recommend

"Brief, concise, one- or two-page executive summaries are the best way to grab attention and get us interested in reading more."

"A concise two-page executive summary that includes a five-year financial summary, in electronic form."

"A well-written, complete executive summary—three pages."

"Being able to concisely explain the business in two pages."

Contents of the Executive Summary

"Write a better executive summary than the typical ones we see—hit the key points."

"A crisp executive summary detailing a proven management team, a large, well-understood market, and differentiated and proprietary products or services."

"We read every business plan that comes in the door, so I would recommend a well-written executive summary that clearly outlines the company's value proposition to customers and plans to attack the market."

"Send an executive summary that outlines the people, market, and what makes their product or idea unique. Also, ensure the summary states the amount of capital required."

"Explain your success to date in your executive summary—sales, pipeline, alliances, etc."

"Be sure to include your contact information—you would be surprised how many people don't."

CHAPTER

15

Confidentiality: Prudence or Paranoia?

—

Maintaining confidentiality and protecting valuable intellectual property are two areas where entrepreneurs have significant—and justified—concerns, especially in this age of Internet start-ups, where entrepreneurs may come to the investor with just an idea. How do you protect your ideas?

It is a well-known fact that most professional venture capital firms will not sign nondisclosure agreements from entrepreneurs. An attorney familiar with venture capital transactions told us, "Entrepreneurs who ask a major VC firm to sign a confidentiality agreement make themselves look like rookies."

Venture capital firms are in the business of building companies in partnership with entrepreneurs, not taking ideas and building the companies themselves.

But there are gray areas. Entrepreneurs are sometimes concerned about venture capitalists using information from the company's business plan to benefit one of VC's existing portfolio companies in a related industry. What if you present your marketing strategies to a group of venture capitalists, they decline to invest in your company, but apply the logic of your strategies in the next planning meeting they have with a portfolio company?

Another nightmarish scenario for an entrepreneur would be to present a plan to investors who decline to put the money in because they view the management team as weak, but they see the opportunity in the industry or market space, go out and recruit a better management team, and enter the market. Not with the same strategy perhaps, but in the same market. So all the entrepreneur accomplished was to create a competitor.

Venture capitalists depend on a reputation of trust within the business community in order to get more deal flow. In this age of instant communication, imagine the bad publicity a venture capital firm could get if it went ahead and blatantly stole an idea for a venture from an entrepreneur who presented to the firm.

In general, the farther along an entrepreneur is in developing an idea into a company, the more milestones have been achieved, the more protection there is from having concepts stolen.

Entrepreneurs face a difficult balancing act between the need to maintain confidentiality and the goal of building a true partnership with investors. As an entrepreneur, you don't want to seem as if you don't trust the investor even before negotiations begin.

ADVICE FROM A VENTURE CAPITALIST

Jim Marshall, General Partner, Selby Venture Partners,
www.selbyventures.com

Why won't VCs sign confidentiality agreements? "We see too many similar deals to expose ourselves to the risk of signing a confidentiality agreement. This community [the venture capital community], while it has grown substantially over the past few years, is still relatively small. Our reputation is our most prized asset, and we'll do anything to protect it."

In the Internet world, when many companies start off as just an idea, how can entrepreneurs protect their proprietary concepts? "Being first or uniquely different in a category is usually better than any

IP [intellectual property] you could get. The best thing to do is work with investors who have good reputations and are known by qualified referral sources."

Jeff Allen, Managing Director, Rocket Ventures,
www.rocketventures.com

Why don't venture capital firms sign confidentiality agreements?
"The main thing is, there are so many business plans coming in and we read so many plans, that I don't think there are a whole lot of unique ideas out there. It's funny but they come in trends: you may see four, five, six companies attacking the same general idea, within a two- to three-month time period. They come in this wave. There is a liability issue. If we sign a confidentiality agreement, what's to prevent an entrepreneur from saying: 'You invested in a competitor to my company and you told them x, y, z about my company'? So many ideas are thrown around. We're in the idea business, and it becomes very difficult to manage. We never say anything specifically about one company to another company. This doesn't happen on the professional venture capital level. It's a matter of time and professionalism. The industry in general adheres to that.

"It's also a bravado or confidence thing. No venture capital firm would want to invest in a company that they think is not the best team to make the idea happen. My philosophy if I were entrepreneur would be, unless I have the best team around me to execute on this idea, I may not make it. So I need to get my act together, make sure I have the right technology and the right team, to convince the investor I am going to deliver on the plan I am presenting. That's what I look for in companies: If there are five or six companies in the same general space, I want to pick the one that is going to execute on their plan.

"Entrepreneurs need to come in and say, 'There are other competitors, but we're the team that is going to win.' Actually, the types of things we want to invest in are companies that have competition; it shows you there is a market for that particular product. It's a matter of evaluating whether that team will execute the best, and then structuring the deal."

Another VC's Views

"Angels versus venture capital firms. There are differences between the two. Angel investors are a different matter. Asking them to sign a nondisclosure agreement is a good idea. [It is] difficult to determine their trust-worthiness prior to meeting with them."

To the venture capitalist, the idea isn't the thing. It's the execution of the idea. The venture capitalists said that the ability to execute was one of the criteria of great management. They see many, many good ideas each year, but invest in only the few they believe the management team can execute, in a large market.

Intellectual Property—What Is It?

Intellectual property can be broadly defined as an intangible asset consisting of knowledge and ideas. Patents, copyrights, trade secrets, trademarks and, of course, ideas make up the major categories.

Patents can be defined as a government granting of the exclusive right to make, use, or sell an invention, usually for a limited period. One of the newest and most confusing areas of patents are those on business models.

Copyrights are the exclusive, legally secured right to publish, reproduce, and sell the matter and form of a literary, musical, dramatic, or artistic work.

Trade secrets are methods which can be formulas, processes, systems, or tools, that provide a company with a competitive advantage.

A trademark can be any visible sign or device used by a business to identify its goods and distinguish them from those made or carried by others.

Ideas themselves cannot receive intellectual property protection, unless a patent is granted for them. The way to protect an idea is to keep it secret, get a written nondisclosure agreement, or disclose only to someone who is trustworthy.

ADVICE FROM AN EXPERT ON INTELLECTUAL PROPERTY

Steven M. Weinberg, Weinberg Cummerford Legal Group, Global Intellectual Property and Internet Law, www.weinberglegal.com

How can entrepreneurs use intellectual property to increase the value of their companies to potential investors and to create a sustainable competitive advantage? "Many of the primary assets of new economy companies are intellectual property, including business methods patents, strong brands (trademarks), confidential know-how, and other trade secrets. Intellectual property can provide a company with the barriers to entry necessary to create sustainable competitive advantage. Intellectual property also can make a company more attractive to potential suitors or strategic alliance partners who may find the company's intellectual property attractive for their business. For example, portal sites are constantly looking for and buying new content, functionality, systems, and other material protected as intellectual property to make them more competitive. Thus, companies with strong intellectual property rights, where the rights create strong barriers to entry and make the owner a likely acquisition target, are more likely to attract investors than are companies without such rights."

Given that many venture capital firms will not sign nondisclosure agreements, what steps can entrepreneurs take to protect proprietary information while they are looking for capital? "As a general rule, venture capital firms do not sign NDAs not because they want to have the liberty to 'borrow' ideas but because they see so many similar business plans for so many similar ideas, they need protection against being sued. That being said, caution is still the rule. The issue is one of trust. It is better to first seek out venture capital firms through trusted professionals who regularly do business with the firms (such as your lawyer, accountant, business advisor, etc.). It also always pays to do a background check on the firm. What is being said about the firm on the street? Have they ever been sued for taking an idea? Are they known to be trustworthy? Do you know anyone who has worked with the firm? Have you checked references?"

Entrepreneurs are extremely concerned about having their business models or other confidential aspects of their company stolen by investors. How valid are these concerns? "It is rare that a business model is so unique that there is nothing like it. The odds are that a VC probably has seen something fairly similar to the business model before. And as noted earlier, VCs as a general rule are not in the business of stealing ideas."

Is it advisable for entrepreneurs to ask "angel" investors to sign nondisclosure agreements? How much protection do these agreements actually provide? "Nondisclosure agreements are only as good as the integrity of the person signing them and the financial ability to enforce them."

Many entrepreneurs use generic or "boilerplate" confidentiality agreements. Should the agreement be tailored to that specific company and the specific aspects of the business that are considered proprietary? "Since in enforcing confidentiality agreements many courts require that the material considered confidential must have been specifically identified to the party to whom the material is disclosed, it is often a good idea to tailor the confidentiality agreements."

Technology companies can often obtain patent protection. What types of intellectual property protection can an e-commerce company obtain? "Virtually all aspects of an e-commerce company may have components potentially protected by intellectual property law. If the company has novel methods of doing business (inventory control, distribution, customer service systems, etc.), patent protection is available. All content is protected by copyright, as is the look and feel of the site. Trademark law protects the name of the company and other branding elements. This is true not only in the United States but in many other countries."

Has the nature of what constitutes intellectual property changed in the dot.com era? "Yes. Global digitalization has given rise to many new forms of intellectual property rights. Examples include domain names, new genres of business methods patents, copyright management information rights, a whole host of new copyright rights, .com trademarks, etc."

If an Internet entrepreneur is just getting the company organized, what long-term considerations should go into the selection of a domain name and trademark? "An Internet company is no different than any other kind of company when it comes to branding. Built-to-last brands—i.e, those that are memorable and really stand out as distinctive—will last the longest. Brands that are too descriptive of the offering, or which sound like 'me-toos,' contrary to popular belief, do not create a marketing advantage. Instead, these weak brands get lost in the crowd. Just look at some of today's most popular e-brands: Dell, Intel, Yahoo!, eBay, and Cisco. None is descriptive, and all are memorable and distinctive."

ANGELS WILL SIGN CONFIDENTIALITY AGREEMENTS

Entrepreneurs often have individual investors—angels—sign confidentiality agreements before presenting any of the proprietary information about the company to them. It is also a good idea to put a general disclaimer, including confidentiality issues, in the beginning of a business plan.

Elements of Nondisclosure Agreements

Nondisclosure agreements vary in length and the amount of stern language used. Entrepreneurs should use an attorney to help draft a document that fits the needs of the company and is written for the types of investors who will be asked to sign it. The key point in many nondisclosure agreements are:

- The importance to the company of keeping the information confidential
- Specific definition of what information is confidential (prototypes, drawings, etc.)
- Length of time the investor is required to keep the information confidential

Information not covered by the agreement includes:

- Information already in the public domain
- Information the investor may have already had in his or her possession
- Information the investor may acquire from third parties

The investor is then asked to agree to:

- Keep the information confidential
- Not reproduce the information without permission
- Not disclose the information to third parties without permission
- Circulate the information within the organization only to people who need to see it for purposes of evaluating the investment
- Not use the information to create a technology or system of his or her own
- Protect the information from loss or theft

The nondisclosure agreement may also state that the investor is not granted any rights to use or license any of the confidential information, and the investor agrees to not use the information to the detriment of the company.

A Sample Disclaimer for the Business Plan

Note: The following is not intended to be legal advice. It is presented for illustration purposes only. Entrepreneurs should seek advice from legal counsel in preparing confidentiality agreements or other documents related to financial transactions with investors.

Note to the Readers of the Plan

The information contained in this Business Plan is proprietary and confidential. Any reproduction of this Business Plan, in whole or in part, without the prior written consent of _____ (the Company), is prohibited. The recipient of the Business Plan shall not directly or indirectly disclose any of the information contained in the Business Plan to any third party.

Transmittal of the Business Plan by _____ (the Company) does not grant any rights to recipient whatsoever to develop, manufacture, use, or market anything described herein.

The information contained in the Business Plan is believed by _____ (the Company) to be reliable. The reader must recognize, however, that projections about _____ (the Company's) future performance are inherently subject to a high degree of uncertainty, and no warranty of such projections is expressed or implied hereby. It is the responsibility of any prospective investor, joint venture partner, or lender to independently evaluate the feasibility and risk of entering into a business combination with _____ (the Company).

The reader of this Business Plan document agrees to keep the information in the document confidential, and to use it solely to determine whether the reader's organization has an interest in entering into discussions regarding a possible business combination with _____ (the Company). Should the reader's organization decline to participate, all materials presented to the reader regarding _____ (the Company) shall be promptly returned to _____ (the Company).

This Business Plan does *not* constitute an offer to sell any securities. Any such solicitation will be undertaken only under appropriate documents and pursuant to all applicable securities laws.

In these few short paragraphs, the entrepreneur has told prospective investors to:

- Keep their mouths shut regarding the confidential stuff they have read in the plan.
- Don't run off and use the ideas.
- The information may be wrong, anyway.
- We want our stuff back if you don't invest.
- Not to worry, SEC: we're not selling stock. We're just talking about our company.

ADVICE FROM A VENTURE CAPITALIST

Dennis E. Murphree, Managing Partner, Murphree Venture Partners, www.murphreeventures.com

"Many entrepreneurs don't understand why VCs won't sign nondisclosure agreements [NDAs] and fear that their ideas will be appropriated and used elsewhere. In the professional VC world, the chance of this actually happening is quite slim.

"Venture capital firms don't sign NDAs for fear that the entrepreneur could use the NDA as grounds for a lawsuit against them. VCs see hundreds, and even thousands, of business plans each year, and many ideas are somewhat similar to one another or have components that are similar. Many times a VC won't remember something similar from a previously submitted business plan and, in the case of the larger firms with multiple partners, may not even know that someone else in the firm has seen a similar idea in the past.

"Any reputable VC would never intentionally steal someone else's idea for three reasons: (1) No one wants the distraction and expense of a lawsuit; (2) there are too many opportunities to do 'clean' deals to have to worry with a 'messy' one; and (3) a VC's reputation would be soiled, possibly beyond repair, if the entrepreneurial community came to equate the firm with unethical behavior of that nature.

"A good reputation is what begets the opportunity to continually see the very best deals, and most VCs work very hard to enhance their reputation for honesty. They may be tough and they may be arrogant on occasion, but dishonesty is a stain which can never be whitewashed over time. Entrepreneurs need to realize that the vast majority of VCs are not looking to steal their ideas but rather to protect themselves when it comes to this issue of confidentiality. They would prefer to not even see a business plan rather than sign an instrument which could unwittingly put themselves or their firm in peril.

"One method that is sometimes used to protect the entrepreneur's intellectual property, and yet allow the VC to see if the IP has merit, is to have an independent third party, which both sides mutually agree to use, examine the intellectual property and answer the VC's due diligence questions as to its viability without disclosing anything inappropriate. This is not as good as direct examination on the VC's part but it is at least a partial solution should the two sides reach an impasse on an NDA.

"In the end, any entrepreneur should study a potential VC investor enough to know in advance if they can be trusted to deal with the entrepreneur on an open and honest basis. Talking to other entrepreneurs and to lawyers who have worked with a given VC in the past should be enough to give comfort as to whether 'stealing' an idea is really a risk at all."

16

The First Date: Meeting with Venture Capitalists

A Valentine Story

"Capital-Starved Enterprise Seeks Meaningful
Relationship with Wealthy Individual"

When seeking venture capital or when looking for romance, observing the proper etiquette improves the chances for success. When meeting a prospective financial partner for the first time, the company needs to dress itself up with an attractive business plan, showing off its tremendous upside. If the meeting takes place in a social setting, the first dance is crucial: The entrepreneur and the potential investor must make the all-important decision of who's going to lead.

Then there's the matter of compatible personalities. The path to true love is often impeded by the financial partner undervaluing the company's considerable assets. The company is wise to not give in too soon to the proposal; one mustn't appear "easy." Modern companies have been raised to be independent. They fear long-term equity commitments, get cold feet, and may even back out. The financial partner may be left at the altar, holding a wilted letter of intent.

On the other hand, some lucky couples who enter into a transaction with a spirit of give-and-take, form a lasting and prosperous partnership—till public offering do they part. The financial partner should remember to go gently. It may be the first time the company has ever been financed.

First Meeting Jitters

When an investor and an entrepreneur meet for the first time, there is inevitably a certain amount of tension in the air. For the entrepreneur, the reason for the stress is obvious: The meeting is very much like a job interview, and making a good first impression is critical.

Many entrepreneurs do not realize the importance of being prepared, of having an agenda put together, either in their mind or preferably on paper. Entrepreneurs should consider what major points to emphasize during the discussion and in what order they should be presented.

It is natural for the owner of a company to be focused on the company's challenges, but he or she should not forget that the mission is to get the investor interested in, and excited about, the company. Outlining the company's prospects for growth and profitability in the future and communicating enthusiasm are important in assuring that there will be a second meeting.

Coming off as too aggressive or blasé can backfire. An entrepreneur once started a meeting with a venture capitalist by saying "I'm in serious discussions with a number of other people, but since you made the trip, I thought I would give you a chance to tell me why you want to invest." This meeting did not last too long.

The flow of information in the meeting needs to go both ways. This is the entrepreneur's chance to: see how the venture capitalist works on a personal basis; ask the investor about his or her background; ask about other successful ventures he or she has been involved with; and determine his or her financial objectives and business philosophy. Investments sometimes do not work out well because of personal incompatibility, not because the company's performance was disappointing. Know who the investor is before closing the deal.

ADVICE FROM A VENTURE CAPITALIST

Patrick Sheehan, Partner, 3i Group, www.3i.com

How should entrepreneurs prepare for the first meeting with investors? "The first meeting's general purpose is to enable one or two members of the firm to walk away with a succinct summary of the proposition, in which the issues are clear. And there are always issues. Pretending there are not, is not helpful. The first meeting also is a chance for entrepreneurs—and they should not forget this—to do the reverse, so the entrepreneurs walk away with a distinct view of what the venture capital firm would be like to work with in practice."

In the first meeting do the partners get a feel for the management team or learn more about the company or products? "Management is an essential ingredient. If you had a bad feeling about the people, as unscientific as this sounds, I think you'd find most experienced investors walking away, even if they couldn't articulate why they felt that way. If you're backing a young company, you're putting money into something where the money will be there beyond the duration of any current plan; therefore, you have to have a high degree of faith in the individuals."

Can you spot a potentially winning team in the first meeting? "Belief in their ability to execute is probably one of the biggest green lights. Distinct from this is whether the company has an interesting idea, of which there are many. Where we see the ability to execute, we get enthusiastic, although it is not frequent to have meetings where you make that conclusion immediately and unconditionally. The more credible the people, the better. You can actually spot the reverse more easily."

Susan Mason, Partner, ONSET Ventures, www.onset.com

"Have a gut-level feeling based on potential customer feedback as to why your concept will be a winner. Market validation is the area we see that entrepreneurs are the weakest in; doing your homework with your potential customers will make your business model much stronger and more 'real.'"

ADVICE FROM AN ENTREPRENEUR ON
MEETING WITH VENTURE CAPITALISTS

"My summary of the overall experience is . . . be prepared! I mean this on many levels. Since you have about the first three minutes to wow the people you are talking to about your idea, you must be able to sell you and your idea quickly, concisely, and with passion.

"You need numbers—all of them, including costs, market value, burn rates, expected ROI, etc—short-term strategy, exit strategies (just in case), a management team in place, info on the competition, and more.

"My first meeting with VCs was brutal! I was unprepared to answer some of their questions on the spot. I had the information, but not on the tip of my tongue. I was passionate about the idea and its potential, but I was not effective in convincing the VCs. After the first five minutes, the meeting became a short lecture on what I needed to do before I try this again.

"My next attempt, with another firm, was more successful in that I was able to sell my idea effectively, I had the answers to questions, and they liked the idea. The problem was that the amount of money I needed was too small for this group. (I only needed about a million; their minimum was five.)

"Finally, a third company I spoke with told me that they liked the idea, but I needed to be farther along in the process before they could help. They said I needed seed money from angel investors first, and then, once initial funding had been found and the infrastructure was in place, they could take me to the next level.

"I have yet to find funding for the project. I haven't given up, but finding angel investors is easier said than done. It is a frustrating process but a great learning experience."

Be Prepared

The first meeting is a critical step.

Develop three scripts: a 30-second introduction of your company and that you're looking for capital, a one-minute pitch, and a 20-minute presentation.

Often the first meeting with an investor is on the telephone. The 30-second introduction is important to quickly introduce yourself, your company, and the fact that you're looking for capital in a coherent manner. You can also use this 30-second intro at informal business meetings, lunches, mixers, and networking events.

A clear concise one-minute summary says who you are and why the company needs capital, and explains the company's growth potential.

Finally write an outline or script for a 20-minute in-person presentation. Don't plan more than 20 minutes for the presentation itself. Introductions and small talk can take up to 10 minutes, and you don't want to plan on your meeting to last more than 30 minutes. If your product or service is so technical that it requires more than two to three minutes of explanation, then either send that technical information ahead or have it as a handout you present after your oral presentation.

ADVICE FROM AN ENTREPRENEUR ON MEETING WITH VENTURE CAPITALISTS

Steve Tsai, CEO, ActBig, Inc., www.actbig.com

What was it like at the first meeting with the venture capitalists? "Fortunately, we had been referred by our lawyer to the first VC we met with. Having a referral is key—it meant that (in addition to getting the meeting in the first place) we also got a warmer reception, more attention, and better follow-up than would have otherwise been the case."

How did you organize your presentation? "We had a relatively simple Power Point presentation that introduced: (a) who we were; (b) the basic case for our business; and (c) what we were looking for in terms of funding."

How long was your presentation? "About 15 to 20 minutes."

How long was the meeting? "About an hour."

How many people from your team did you bring? "At the time we had no team, so it was just us [the two founders]."

How did you prepare? "The best preparation was writing a full-blown business plan. Although we didn't present from the plan itself—and although I'm sure the VC never read it—going through the process of writing it meant that we had explored practically every angle we might get asked about.

"We also had quite a few people look at our Power Point slides and give us comments before we unveiled it to a VC."

What would you have done differently? "We would have spent more time investigating the companies that were already in the VC's portfolio. Key to getting a VC's attention is not only sparking their interest in your company but also in showing them why the fit is so right, i.e., what the synergies might be between your company and their existing portfolio."

Were you intimidated? "Nervous (because it was an important meeting) but not intimidated. Keys to *not* feeling intimidated are: (a) to be thoroughly prepared; (b) to remember that you know your own business better than anyone else does; and (c) to remember that VCs are mere mortals (e.g., like anyone, they will respond to a good story)."

What were some of the questions the VCs asked?
"Who's on your team?
"Who's your competition?
"What do you have that they don't?
"What's the market opportunity?
"How are you going to make money?
"What evidence do you have of market demand/acceptance?"

Were there any questions that surprised you? "None that I can recall. For the most part, the questions tend to be pretty straightforward and are aimed at uncovering the business fundamentals. For this reason, the best thing to do is to anticipate the questions (even structure your presentation around them) and knock them off before the VCs even ask."

Should you send your business plan ahead of the meeting or present it after the meeting? If the meeting will take place out of state, with travel expenses involved, send the business plan first. It can help qualify the investor's interest and you won't have wasted time and money. If the meeting is local, use your discretion, or let the investor decide which he or she would prefer. Some investors won't plow through any type of lengthy document until they've met the principals involved and have the incentive to then read the entire document. Others prefer to have read the business plan and have questions ready.

Don't depend on technology to glamorize the presentation and always have backup. Use Power Point or other presentation software, but make sure there are hard copies available just in case, for whatever reason, there is a glitch in either the presentation software or your laptop. You won't be left hanging with a blank screen and bored VCs. Leaving behind a hard copy of the presentation is a good idea in any event; it is a reminder of the important points of your business plan.

Keep in mind that while laptop presentations are fine for one-on-one presentations, the laptop screen can be difficult to see from any distance.

ADVICE FROM AN ENTREPRENEUR ON
MEETING WITH VENTURE CAPITALISTS

Taraneh Derak, CEO/President, Yubé, Inc., www.yube.com

What was it like at the first meeting with the venture capitalists? "I was extremely nervous before the first meeting. However, five minutes after the meeting began, I couldn't stop talking. The venture capitalists were extremely involved, and the session ended after an hour and a half instead of the 45 minutes they had originally scheduled us for.

"I truly enjoy this process. It gives me a chance to meet interesting people with extensive experience. Each meeting is filled with valuable feedback and information."

How did you organize your presentation? "We started with a well-defined strategy, then introduced the founders followed by problems and solutions; then market size and competitive landscape. We ended the presentation with a rollout plan and the funding we need to execute our plan."

How long was your presentation? "Twenty-five minutes."

How many people from your team did you bring? "All the founders (three of us)."

How did you prepare? "Research and practice, practice, practice . . ."

What would you have done differently? "I would have talked to more VCs before saying yes so that we would have had a better idea of what was available to us. And of course, negotiated better."

Were you intimidated? "Not at all."

What were some of the questions the VCs asked? "They asked about the founding team's background. This is very important. They also ask detailed questions about our vision and the competition landscape."

Were there any questions that surprised you? "Yes. One of the VCs we spoke with asked me about my nationality, family, kids, and future family plans! Of course, I responded to all the questions. I thought perhaps they had some concern about investing in a woman CEO with a husband and child."

Your Presentation

Break the presentation into four five-minute segments. The logic of the four segments is that in the first 10 minutes, you've covered the important points. If for some reason your meeting is cut short, the investor has been informed of these salient points.

THE FIRST FIVE MINUTES

Start with a brief overview emphasizing the strengths of the company, its management team, and the product, size of the market, and potential growth. Use the executive summary of the business plan as a guide.

THE SECOND FIVE MINUTES

Devote the second five minutes to building excitement about the product, why it satisfies customers, why the market is attractive, how the company will become a major player in the industry, and the potential growth and success of the company.

THE THIRD SEGMENT—FIVE MINUTES

The first two segments introduce the company, sets the background, and creates excitement. The third segment explains how the company is going to achieve this growth and success through the marketing programs, competitive advantages, proprietary aspects of the product, barriers to entry, and management team expertise.

THE FINAL FIVE MINUTES

The final five-minute segment discusses the specific revenue and expense projections and justifies the amount of capital requested and the uses of capital. It's not necessary to discuss specific terms, investment structures, return on investment, or paybacks now. You do want to have an exit strategy for the investor in mind, just in case you're asked.

Get the investor interested in the management team, the company, and the product. Practice makes perfect; rehearse until the presentation is polished but doesn't sound memorized. Have an accountant, attorney, or a good friend ask hard questions and critique the presentation. This may be the tenth time you have given the presentation, but it's the first time the investor has heard it. Be enthusiastic but not hyped.

If you have the time, videotape a dress rehearsal of the presentation.

At the end of the presentation, of course, ask for questions. But just in case there is a lag in the discussion, have an open-ended question, one that can't be answered by a simple yes-or-no response, that can be asked of the investors.

ADVICE FROM AN ENTREPRENEUR ON MEETING WITH VENTURE CAPITALISTS

Austin Erlick, Entrepreneur

How did you organize your presentation?
"1. Elevator pitch on company.
"2. Company history (financial, customers, employees)
"3. Business strategy and value proposition
"4. Differentiators
"5. Organizational structure
"6. Case studies"
How long was your presentation? "Thirty-five to 40 minutes."
How long was the meeting? "Two hours."
How many people from your team did you bring? "Two—CEO, CFO."
How did you prepare? "Tight concise presentation, be prepared for any question."
What were some of the questions the VCs asked? "Drilled into the following areas:
"Business model
"Key differentiators
"Financials and primary metrics
"Management team
"Case studies."
Were there any questions that surprised you? "No."

Be ready to answer the following questions in a positive manner.

- *Management.* What are the strengths and weaknesses of your management team? How are you going to fill any gaps in your management team? Be prepared to give a thumbnail sketch of each individual's qualifications and experience.

- *Product.* How is your product better? How is it legally protected? How much more research and development is required? If your product costs 50 percent more to manufacture or takes twice as long to complete development than you have projected, how will that affect your profits?

- *Competition.* What are the barriers to entry for your competitors? Why will your product succeed over your competitors? How will you establish a brand identity or unique product characteristic in the mind of your customer? XYZ company, which has a similar product failed; why won't you?

- *Market.* In 30 seconds or less, what are the demographics of your market? Why are you sure your potential market size is what you've said it is? Why are you going after this particular market rather than X market?

- *Marketing.* ABC company tried the marketing strategies you're suggesting and it didn't work; why do you think they'll work for you? Your marketing budget is substantially below what is going to be necessary to introduce your product; how did you come up with those numbers?

The bottom line here is that, ultimately, investors put their money in companies because they believe in the competence of the people involved in managing the company, not simply because they are impressed with the company's products or its market.

In the investment process, you are selling *you.*

ADVICE FROM AN ENTREPRENEUR ON MEETING WITH VENTURE CAPITALISTS

Gary A. Pudles, President, AnswerNet, Inc.
www.AnswerNetNetwork.com

What was it like at the first meeting with the venture capitalists? "It was very friendly. They seemed interested in hearing about our deal, and I do believe each one carefully considered our proposal."

How did you organize your presentation? "In all situations, I planned about a half hour (in three 10-minute segments) but kept it open for questions during the presentation."

How long was your presentation? "Most presentations lasted between 10 and 15 minutes. The VCs usually wanted to cover specific topics so the timing was always off."

How long was the meeting? "Between one and two hours depending on the interest of the VC."

How many people from your team did you bring? "Generally it was two or three. Myself (the CEO), the investment banker and sometimes the sales or finance person from our company."

How did you prepare? "By preparing a one-page agenda."

What would you have done differently? "Gone to different VCs."

Were you intimidated? "No, but in the beginning I was too anxious because I really needed the money commitment to begin the business."

What were some of the questions the VCs asked? "Why would I invest in you with all the dot.com companies out there? What is your exit strategy? What is your domain experience?"

Were there any questions that surprised you? "Not really."

17

Valuing Your Company: A Small Dose of Reality

Valuation of a Venture Capital Investment, or: How Much of My Company Do I Have to Give Up to Get the Money?

BEAUTY IS IN THE EYE OF THE STOCKHOLDER

An entrepreneur can employ rather complex financial analysis tools to establish the value of his/her company and its stock. Although the tools seem to apply a degree of scientific accuracy to the subject, they do not produce automatic results. In the case of an established company, it is possible to use three or four different methods and arrive at three or four radically different results. It is then up to the person doing the valuation to find an "average" among the results. For an early-stage company, the valuation question is even more problematic, because the valuation is

213

typically done based on projected future cash flows and what you can sell the business for in three or five or seven years, numbers that are inherently subjective in the first place.

A simple valuation is to say that if the investor invests $3 million for a 20 percent ownership position, the company is worth $15 million. If that $3 million only purchases a 10 percent share, then the company is worth $30 million; if the $3 million purchases 40 percent, then the company is worth $7.5 million.

Venture capitalists often calculate what they believe a company will be worth at the time of exit, say three to five years from now. That terminal value is then heavily discounted to reflect the risk, the fact that their investment is illiquid and that they have contributed to the success of the business. The discount can be as high as 75 percent.

Most entrepreneurs have a bit of trouble recognizing the justification for such a heavy discount. Their rationale is if the investor puts in $1 million now for a 10 percent ownership, when the company goes public in 18 months for $500 million, that 10 percent will be worth $50 million, a very nice rate of return. An investment of $1 million now will be worth $50 million in 18 months.

The VC looks at it in a different way. The company won't go public until three years from now and will only be worth $300 million. Then the VC discounts that $300 million by 75 percent. So the company is only worth $75 million, and 10 percent of $75 million is only $7.5 million. So the VC has to wait a year and a half longer to have an equity stake worth much less than the entrepreneur's scenario.

The VC can also use a net present value calculation, which means the company's worth in three years is brought to today's value by discounting the company's cash flows or net income for that time period. It's discounted for a number of reasons; the further out in years the income is received, the heavier the discount, because a dollar earned today is worth more than a dollar earned five years from now. It's also discounted based on the risk; the more risk involved, the higher the discount.

And finally, the VC can calculate what percentage of the company is required now, given the amount of the investment and the value of the company in the future, to generate a required rate of return.

Entrepreneurs, being naturally enthusiastic people, tend to get carried away with their projections and assume there will be no obstacles to the company becoming a roaring success. Venture capitalists, being naturally skeptical people, will take these same projections and discount (lower) them based on the degree of risk they see that the projections will not turn into reality. The more skeptical venture capitalists are, the greater the percentage of the company they will want for a given level of investment.

Reaching an agreement on the price of the company's stock depends on how this natural gap can be bridged. A valid question for the entrepreneur to pose is "If this investment is so terribly risky that you need 80 percent of my company, why do you want to get involved at all?" The investor's counterargument is then "My investment will cause your company to be larger and more valuable. Wouldn't you rather own 20 percent of a large, successful company than 100 percent of what you have now?"

A LITTLE ANALYSIS IS BETTER THAN NONE AT ALL

Occasionally entrepreneurs propose deals based on absolutely no financial analysis; instead they use this questionable logic: "I need $5 million. I don't want the investor to have control of my business, but I need to give them a nice chunk. How about 30 percent?" Despite the imperfections in the process of trying to project future cash flows in a growing business, it is better to at least try to tie your valuation of the company back to the projections instead of using this nonvaluation method of business valuation.

ADVICE FROM VENTURE CAPITALISTS

Gerry Langeler, OVP Venture Partners, www.ovp.com

"Entrepreneurs need to stop worrying about valuation. The market will decide that, they won't. There is no way to determine it other than in comparison with other deals that VCs are willing to fund at the time. While .VentureOne, www.ventureone.com, and the like can provide some recent metrics, the real issue is, what is someone willing to pay for what percentage of your stock? Until you have two people bidding to fund you, you have no leverage on valuation. Our method is rather simple: We look at the stage of development. True seed (no business plan yet) is low single-digit millions premoney. Business plan but no validation (i.e., no beta version) is mid-single digits. With some customer feedback you might reach high single digits. Customers who have tried it and are ready to buy might move the valuations into the low 10s.

"It is all very subjective and at the end of the day each side has to feel the deal is a good deal or walk away. There seems to be a direct correlation between entrepreneurs who worry valuation and dilution to death and those who either (a) don't get funded or (b) optimize for short-term dilution versus long-term value and never build a major enterprise."

Dennis Spice, Open Prairie Ventures, www.opven.com

Should entrepreneurs do their own valuation? "I can see this argument both ways. Unfortunately, it sets the wrong tone to put a valuation number in the business plan that is uninformed. I think what's refreshing, if you don't know how to value your company, is to put something in that says "valuation to be determined later." Leave it flexible. Leave room for negotiations. This says to me, these guys at least understand this is a hard thing to determine. We could work together to come up with something reasonable. I think our partners end up being more flexible than if you come in and say, 'Valuation is $48 million. Period.' How did you come up with that? Well, we just decided it was $48 million, they say.

"If entrepreneurs can be flexible, it helps. Some folks already made a valuation decision when they come to us. Some of this comes from angel investors getting involved. A strong angel says the company value is a certain amount; this forces the entrepreneur to put the figure in the executive summary."

Bill McAleer, Partner, Voyager Capital, Seattle, www.voyagercap.com

What is your biggest challenge when valuing an Internet start-up company? "We always have to deal with the value expectations of the entrepreneur, in light of what is happening in a given market space. Is the entrepreneur going to get the kind of value he expects based on what he has observed is going on in the marketplace? There is frequently a misalignment in value expectation between the venture capitalist and the entrepreneur.

"Valuation depends to some extent on how quickly the business and the market are going to develop. Some go faster, some slower. Many companies think that as long as they have a product, they will receive a high valuation. There are still the issues of how fast the sales process for the product will go and how much structure needs to be built into the marketing and sales function. If the company relies on direct sales, we have to look at how long it will take and how expensive it will be to build out the company's marketing plan.

"With Internet companies, the rate of growth is more variable and therefore less predictable. Some types of technologies, communications being one, in some cases have longer sales cycles that are easier to estimate. With Internet companies, they can grow surprisingly faster than expected, but they can also disappoint."

Tom Turney, Managing Principal, NewCap Partners, Inc., www.newcap.com

"Availability is more important than price!"

Peter Edwards, Partner, Altira Group LLC, www.altiragroup.com

"Sit back and visualize all the ingredients that must be present, and all the events that must occur, in order for you to be successful. Assess the relative contributions that must be made by the management team, the company's technical employees and staff, and the company's investors and financial advisors. If you are both earnest and honest, you will know in your heart when you are giving fair value and when you are getting it. Let that sense of fairness guide you, and it will serve you well."

Bob Marsh, General Partner, Red Rock Ventures, www.redrockventures.com

"Valuation in an early-stage deal (our focus) has more to do with venture funding market conditions than anything calculable from forecasts, market sizes, etc. We look for a company attacking a large ($1B+) *available* market and then simply peg the company against comparable deals we've seen or have done recently at the same stage of development (i.e., if it's three founders and a Power Point presentation but nothing else, it's a very different situation than a company with a couple of VP-level management people involved, product close to beta, etc.)

"Net-net, it's more like a house appraisal than a financial calculation."

Mike Shields, Partner, Magnet Capital LP, www.Magnetcapital.com
"Fully understand the mathematical formulas being used for valuation."

Getting Advice

Although it is possible to read books on the subject of valuing a company and setting the price for an investment, being able to employ these analytical tools well only comes through the experience of having been through the process many times. If you are negotiating with professional venture capitalists, you are at a distinct disadvantage, because they have put deals together many times, and know how to structure them in their favor. In such situations you need people on your team who have seen many deals put together. Among the options available to you:

- Certified public accountants who work on corporate finance transactions
- Business valuation consultants
- Investment bankers who specialize in smaller or mid-market companies
- Attorneys who are experienced with venture capital transactions.

Don't assume these professionals are completely out of your price range. They may be willing to defer part of their advisory fees until the deal is closed, especially if you have reasonable prospects of getting investors interested in your company or are in discussions with investors at the present time.

DEAL TALES: HELP! HELP! WE NEED YOUR ADVICE (AS LONG AS YOU TELL US WHAT WE WANT TO HEAR)

The young, excitable CEO of an exciting young company called and said he needed to retain a financial advisor to help plan the growth of his rapidly growing business. The company had gone from start-up stage to nearly $10 million in revenues in just two years. Not having a finance background, the CEO said he needed the advice of "experts." He had been toying with the idea of taking the company public, because someone had told him that any Internet-related company was valued at 10 times revenues in the public stock markets. (This "someone" person is highly knowledgeable.) In other words, the CEO thought his company was worth nearly a $100 million. He was eager to get going on creating a business plan for his company and asked for a proposal including our ideas about what the company might be worth.

We sent a proposal that pointed out that his prospects of obtaining capital, whether from private investors or the public equity markets, depended on whether his company had a sustainable competitive advantage that could lead to further growth similar to what he had experienced in the past two years. Merely putting the label "Internet" on the businesses does not ensure vast riches. In fact, the niche he was in was fairly difficult to attract investors to; doing so would require being reasonable about the valuation of the company. We waited for this anxious fellow to get back to us. A week went by. Then two. Finally we e-mailed him to see if he received the proposal. "I got it" was his terse reply, and that was the last we heard from him. Moral: Bearers of good news can charge whatever they want. Those who bring bad news must work at a substantial discount.

ADVICE FROM THE EXPERTS ON ESTIMATING YOUR COMPANY'S VALUE

Steven B. Turner, Managing Partner, and Laurence Herman, Director, CapitalKey Advisors, Inc., www.CapitalKey.com, a middle-market investment bank and data company

"A common problem our venture-stage clients face is how to value their company. This is actually a problem both the entrepreneur and the venture capitalist struggle with. It just isn't clear to either party how to place a substantiated valuation on a relatively early-stage business without a meaningful history of financial performance. For these reasons, the tools that sponsors of traditional private equity firms (which invest in more established companies) use to value a business—discounted cash-flow analysis, purchase price multiples, comparable public company valuations, internal rates of return—are not useful to the venture capitalist.

"So with all this uncertainty, how do all the venture capital transactions get done? It turns out there are no formulas for calculating valuation, but there are rules of thumb for valuing a venture-stage business.

"Generally, the average premoney valuation for an Internet company's first venture round financing is between $3 and $12 million. At that stage, the business is more than an idea, with some initial implementation, such as a half-built web site and initial alliances. The valuation of a business, however, goes up exponentially as the entrepreneur clears each hurdle of development. The venture capitalist, who must be intrigued by the idea if he chooses to invest at all, realizes that as the entrepreneur gains traction in the business model, the risk to investors drops, making a higher value easier to swallow. This simple concept—that the longer you can wait, the better valuation you'll get—should never be overlooked.

"Other factors can also dramatically increase the valuation of the company. If the management team includes a well-respected manager in the industry, the valuation may increase by a factor of two to three from that initial starting point. If the executive is a leading executive in the industry, with a name and credentials that fly off the page of the business plan, the credibility he or she brings can increase the valuation by a factor of 5 to 10. A strong roster of angel investors or well-known coinvestors also give the venture capitalist comfort and enhance the company's valuation.

"Some ideas, however, have such a limited upside that no matter who is running the company, or how far along their development curve they are, the range of possible valuations has a ceiling. Generally, venture capitalists have very aggressive expected returns. Ideally they'd invest $10 million for 40 percent of the company and watch it develop into a $2 billion public company in 18 months. While they realize not every investment is a home run, they can at least rationalize these optimistic returns if the idea they're investing in is scalable. A business model with broad applicability (which using the Internet or software applications can provide) can justify a high valuation at an early stage. A conventional business model, with a limited market, however, will, for obvious reasons, have limited value."

"Valuation can be driven by need. In reality, however, the management team's self-assessed valuation changes somewhat with how badly they need the money or how much money they want to raise. This is not surprising considering the inexact science of valuation. For example, one of our clients wanted to raise anywhere from $5 to $10 million. This client realized that the longer he waits to finance, the better his valuation is likely to be. Nevertheless, this particular client wanted a $10 million financing to accelerate his growth and get a head start on his competition. For that overriding reason, he was willing to lower his valuation and in doing so give up a greater stake in the company to raise more money in one shot. An entrepreneur may also find the money-raising process so time-consuming and burdensome that he'd gladly sacrifice some equity now to be able to forgo another financing. The entrepreneur's time is money, as the saying goes, and the longer the company can go without revisiting the financing process, the more attention its management team can spend building the business.

"Another company might have approached the financing differently. If the company needed that first $4 million to survive and move forward (just as a fish will die from lack of oxygen if it doesn't keep moving, a start-up company will lose its competitive edge if it doesn't get funding; money is the oxygen of a growing business), they might be willing to part with more equity (financing at a lower valuation) to get it. But if they could take or leave the next $6 million and felt confident that they could raise more money in a subsequent financing, they'd likely raise their valuation for a larger financing. A bridge loan, perhaps pegged to the next round valuation to defer nasty valuation negotiations, can restore leverage to the company.

"Add some precision to your valuation. When dealing with an interested angel investor, the entrepreneur may have more control to dictate the terms of the financing. But venture capitalists have hundreds of unread business plans on their desks and superior information about the market for venture-stage deals. So before you walk into a meeting with an unsubstantiated valuation, it's best you arm yourself with some comparables to back up your information. Comparables are other companies in your similar stage and in your industry that have received venture financing.

"The trick to proposing a valuation to a venture capitalist is to balance your own enthusiasm with market reality. You never want to underestimate your value, but it's a fine line between appearing aggressive and confident and looking like a greedy jerk. If you propose a valuation that's out of the ballpark, you'll lose credibility. Use the Internet to search for information on the other companies in your space or a similar space. Their valuations, or the amount of money they raised and the percentage stake sold in their financings, can back up your valuations.

"Despite all your efforts, the bottom line is your business idea has to strike a chord with institutional venture capitalists. They're not going to invest in your idea because they know your uncle and want to help you out, like some angel investors. Venture capitalists will draw from past experience, estimate their expected returns from investment, and assess whether the investment will satisfy their own investors. Similarly, the valuation they'll invest at is as much a function of feel as any scientific method. So do your homework, consider your valuation carefully . . . and cross your fingers."

ADVICE FROM VENTURE CAPITALISTS ON ESTIMATING YOUR COMPANY'S VALUE

Paul W. Schaffer, Executive Vice President, Cardinal-Fox Capital, Managing Partner of Fox Capital Fund I, L.P., and Champaign-Urbana Venture Fund, LLC, www.foxfund.com and www.cuventure.com

"Often too much time is spent arguing about valuations. The ultimate value of an entity is what can be obtained when the investment is exited. Especially in early-stage investments, entrepreneurs defend the value of their company without fully understanding what it takes to get that idea to a profitable conclusion.

"Entrepreneurs should focus more on developing a strategy to market their product than worrying about an arbitrary assignment of the value of the company. There is a lot of money out there chasing a lot of deals. Entrepreneurs need to focus on taking 'smart' money from investors who can help them advance the ball. In the final analysis, entrepreneurs and early-stage investors are generally financially better off when they are diluted by 'smart' money that can exponentially increase the value of the company."

Larry Kubal, Managing Director, Labrador Ventures, www.labrador.com

How can an entrepreneur learn the basics of valuation? "The marketplace drives valuation, and the early-stage VC marketplace is not efficient with perfect information. The VC, involved in a constant stream of deals, can compare one opportunity to the next. Moreover, the VC can add the historical perspective by comparing a current deal to ventures that he or she has funded in the past.

"The entrepreneur does not have this sort of valuation context. To develop some context for their specific venture, an entrepreneur should consult their personal network as much as possible. 'Comparables' are exceedingly difficult to find in venture deals since much of the valuation in the early stage is not just based on the idea and business model but also on the management team. Ultimately, the value will be set by someone with an interest to invest. When asked by a VC what your valuation expectations are, the entrepreneur can use the well-worn and time-tested response of 'We will let the market decide.'"

Has the entrepreneur's perspective changed about what a fair valuation should be? "In a macrosense, it is difficult to know whether an entrepreneur's perspective has changed about what a fair valuation should be. Valuations and valuation expectations fluctuate in the market. Most movement is due to either the eagerness or the reluctance of the VC community as a whole to invest. I think that the atmosphere since April of 2000 has been noticeably subdued. Many VCs have turned inward and are spending an increasingly higher percentage of their time and energy working with their existing portfolio companies. This greater reticence to invest in new start-ups has dampened many entrepreneurs' expectations.

"At Labrador Ventures, the valuations at which we have invested have not changed dramatically from the peaks of optimism to the troughs of pessimism in the marketplace. I think that the types of entrepreneurs we favor realize that valuation is only one of many factors to consider in the selection of a funding source. In addition, mature entrepreneurs are always balancing off opportunity costs versus valuation. Raising capital at higher valuation does not create value as much as building the company. Most successful entrepreneurs are focused on building a major enterprise and not on raising capital at the highest valuation possible."

How do the wild fluctuations in the performance of IPOs affect the valuation method or criteria you employ? "While IPOs and their valuations do have considerable visibility and therefore impact the psyche of the marketplace, I believe that they have little long-term impact on seed- and early-stage valuations. There can be a short-term, knee-jerk reaction to a shock in the public market valuations resulting in an investment paralysis. However, longer term, this reaction is always countermanded by the sheer weight of capital that has been committed to VC funds and the pressure on VCs to put it to work.

"Furthermore, about 85 percent of profitable exits from venture-backed companies are through acquisition and not via IPOs. In addition, the seed-, early-stage venture financing is the part of the venture business farthest from the IPO process. Accordingly, the IPO valuation ripple effect is significantly attenuated by the time it reaches startups seeking capital."

Superior Management, a Large Market, and Unique Products Create Value

One of the most often asked questions by entrepreneurs relates to how venture capitalists calculate the equity share they demand in exchange for the funds they invest. How do they arrive at 20 percent or 50 percent? We asked venture capitalists to rate a number of factors they use to value the investment, with a rating of 5 being the most important and 1 being the least important.

Quality of Management	**4.5**
Size of the market	3.8
Product qualities	3.7
(uniqueness, brand strength,	
patent protection)	
Rate of market growth	3.5
Competition	3.5
Barriers to entry	3.4
Company's stage of development	3.2
Industry the company is in	3.0

Seven out of 10 venture capitalists rated Quality of Management as a 5, and nearly nine out of 10 gave it a 4 or 5. There were a few mavericks among those surveyed, however: 7 percent gave management quality an importance rating of only 1 or 2.

No other factor came close in importance. The next most important, Size of the Market, was given a rating of 5 by only 30 percent of the respondents, followed by Product Qualities, which received a 5 from about one out of four respondents.

Note that all of the factors received an average score of 3 or higher. Thus all of the factors were viewed as significant, and entrepreneurs should take care to clearly articulate each of them to investors.

TO INVESTORS, MANAGEMENT IS EVERYTHING

It may not be fair but there it is. Quality of management is the most critical factor in venture capitalists' decision to invest; lack of quality management is the reason given most often when VCs decline to invest; and quality management is the most important factor when venture capitalists value a company.

CHAPTER

18

Due Diligence: A Two-Way Street

M ost investors give entrepreneurs a fairly long list of information
they need to help them make a decision about whether to invest.
This can be an agonizingly slow part of the transaction for an entrepreneur anxious to obtain funding. It can also involve a lot of the
management team's time, as they prepare the information requested by
the investor.

Despite the disruption in normal business routine that can be
caused by having to prepare all of this information for potential investors, it is important for entrepreneurs to be as forthcoming and
open as possible, to avoid creating the impression that they are hiding
something.

Venture capitalists have an extraordinary ability to check out the
management team's background and experience, successes and failures,
evaluate the true size and potential growth of the market, and get independent views from the technical/scientific community regarding the vi-

ability of proposed technologies. A venture fund may have $100 million of capital, but it will seem as if it has 150 million contacts and sources of information. This is why it is so foolish of entrepreneurs to overstate their past accomplishments or provide bloated estimates of the size of their industry or market space. Investors are better at geometry than entrepreneurs are; they are highly skilled at measuring space.

What do people you've worked with in the past think of you? How would your creditors/vendors evaluate your financial management? If your product/service is already being marketed, what do customers say about it? What do the seed investors in your company think about your management skill? Have you had any personal problems in the past that investors could find out about?

Is all of this information gathering necessary, or is it really a form of snooping? Are these guys VCs or are they going to sell the pictures to the *National Enquirer*?

The answer has three parts:

1. Entrepreneurs come in all different backgrounds, lifestyles, and mental states. Many have had colorful, up-and-down histories. Some investors even say that one of the powerful motivations to become an entrepreneur could be characterized as almost a form of revenge; the entrepreneur may have experienced pain or failure in the past and now is fueled by a desire to show the people who may have contributed to the pain or failure that they were wrong and the entrepreneur was right. The tricky thing is determining whether past failures are isolated and have become this great source of inspiration, or whether they are part of a broader pattern of failure.

2. There's no entrance exam to be admitted into entrepreneurship. You just get an idea and build from there. Investors have to predict whether a given management team can consistently perform at a high level for at least the three to five years the investors are involved. The ability to make this prediction requires input from as many sources as possible. Because of the incredible difficulty of creating and growing a business, investors have to evaluate personalities as well as skills of the people involved, to make sure this management team has the inner resources of strength and de-

termination as well as the acquired management or technical skills.

3. Venture capitalists have to report to their limited partners, the financial institutions that put the money in their fund to begin with. The detailed information gathering supports the venture capitalists as being good stewards of the money, as careful as you can be in the turbulent world of funding start-up companies in brand-new market spaces.

ADVICE FROM A VENTURE CAPITALIST

Patrick Sheehan, Partner, 3i Group, www.3i.com

What is the objective of due diligence from the investors' standpoint? "The objective of it is to provide adequate clarity of all the identified issues, so a decision can be reached with a reasonable degree of faith or comfort. Some things are easy to summarize quickly, some are difficult. Due diligence takes on a life of it own, and clearly it is bad news all around if it is not a managed process. The art is in managing the process and closing it down; where it goes wrong is when VC companies discover new issues. They are reopening the boxes rather than trying to close them. The skill is in process management, knowing what you are trying to achieve in a very specific sense."

During the due diligence process, entrepreneurs should make full disclosures. Think of ways of presenting the company's potential in the best light, particularly providing your own suggested outside experts for venture capitalists to contact who will back up your assertions.

Perform your own due diligence on the investors. This is one instance where turnabout is more than fair play: It's the best play the entrepreneur has.

Now it's your turn. It is vitally important that entrepreneurs recognize their right to ask questions of the investors. Due diligence is a mutual exchange of information. Ask about other deals they have made, for business references, for the names of CEOs of other companies they have invested in. Talk to the CEOs of those companies about the experience they have had with the investor group. Ask for financial statements or a balance sheet. Ask for a letter from the venture capitalist's bank that documents that the funds are available. If the investor is seriously contemplating a business combination, not just discussing the possibility of one, there should be no problem getting this information.

Use contacts in the business community to find out more about the group and its reputation. Ask your trusty advisory group to do some checking of its own. A simple but very useful question for you to ask the investor is: Where did you make your money? or Where does your funding come from? If an investor refuses to give you the information you request, it should be a red flag that this may not be the ideal investor for you. And if you find out the investor has never been involved in a venture capital–type transaction before, it is reasonable to wonder whether he or she will be able to endure the inevitable ups and downs of small-company ownership.

You need to know whether the investor's expectations concerning the company's performance are reasonable. You do not want the partnership to become strained the first time the company has any kind of setback. This is why understanding the personalities of prospective investors is so important.

Most venture capital companies post a lot of the above information on their web site. They will tell you how much money is in their current fund, if there have been previous funds, what companies they've invested in, who is on their board of directors, and who their accountants and attorneys are.

The aspect of the capital search process that seems to terrify entrepreneurs the most is trying to evaluate the intentions of the person on the other side of the negotiating table. How do you know that the person or firm you are dealing with will act in an ethical manner and work with you to build a successful company? Or is the person's real intention just to gradually take your company from you and turn you into a low-paid employee?

Enough horror stories have circulated about "evil" investors that some entrepreneurs are adamantly opposed to the whole idea of seeking venture capital for their businesses. By exercising caution and by carefully investigating prospective financial partners, entrepreneurs should be able to learn the difference between venture and vulture capital.

Information Companies Are Asked to Provide Investors

Here is a sample, but not exhaustive, Due Diligence Check List. (Some items may not apply to a purely start-up situation.)

Corporate Records

Articles of incorporation, including the original articles, any amendments, plans of merger or other corporate reorganization

By-laws of the corporation

Minutes of corporate meetings from inception of the corporation (including any meetings in which there was a change in corporate control)

Number of shares of each class of stock authorized and number of shares issued and outstanding

Number of shareholders, their names and addresses, and description of classes of stock

Copies of any and all materials filed with the SEC or state securities commissioners

Name and address of the transfer agent for the corporation for the past five years

List of any litigation involving the corporation during the past five years

Name and state of incorporation of any holding companies or subsidiaries of the corporation

Financial Records

Audited financials of the corporation if available for the past five years or, unaudited financials

Any offering memoranda or prospectuses used in the sale of the company's securities

Accounts payable ledger and aging reports

Accounts receivable ledger and aging reports

Inventory of production supplies, work in progress, and finished goods

Inventory of furniture, fixtures, and equipment

Depreciation schedules

Note payable and note receivable documentation

Analysis of prepaid expenses and Analysis of accrued expenses

Copies of corporate tax returns, payroll tax returns, and sales and use tax returns for past three years

People or Entities Involved with the Corporation

Name and address of legal counsel and all accountants for the corporation for the past five years

Names, addresses, and resumes of all officers and directors of the corporation

Names and addresses of business references for principals of the corporation

Names of the largest customers

Names of the largest suppliers

Contractual Obligations

Amounts and number of any options or warrants outstanding; copies of any employee stock option plans

Copies of all bank financing and security documents and lines of credit together with most recent balances of statements showing amount due

Copies of all employment agreements with the key officers of the corporation

Copies of any shareholder agreements with or among any of the shareholders of the corporation

Copies of any other long-term liabilities, leases, or commitments

Outstanding contracts with customers

Outstanding contracts with suppliers

Copies of leases

Intellectual Property

Copies of all patents, trademarks, or other intellectual property relating to the products of the corporation, together with copies of any assignments or security interests granted regarding this property

ALL SEGMENTS OF YOUR BUSINESS MODEL WILL BE SCRUTINIZED

Your product benefits will be assessed. If you are still in research and development mode, an outside independent consultant may be called in to confirm the product's status and determine what additional time or resources may be required to bring the product to market. The market size and demographics will be analyzed, as will your marketing strategies and costs.

Much of this should have been covered in your business plan. The more documentation you have available for the VC, the easier and less stressful the due diligence process will be.

Each member of the management team will be reviewed regarding educational background, personal references, business experience, and credit evaluations.

Scams to Avoid: Are Those Buzzards We See Up There?

Entrepreneurs are optimists: They want to believe that somewhere out there is the perfect investor for their company, a benefactor who will provide several million dollars and then fade into the mist. Sort of a fairy godmother, with a checkbook instead of a magic wand. This personality predisposition can lead entrepreneurs into the clutches of sleaze weasels.

PSEUDOINVESTORS

An "investor" calls—or you call an ad in the paper—and after a brief discussion the person says yes, he would like to review your business plan. You send it, perhaps you even get the person to sign a confidentiality agreement. A few days later the "investor" calls and says he's very interested and asks a lot of questions. You meet with the person, probably at a restaurant or some other public place, not in the person's office. Why? He doesn't really have an office but doesn't want you to know that. After the meeting, you receive a fax or letter that outlines the terms for his investment. These terms are close to what you want. You sign the document and return it to the "investor." You then receive—and this is the scummy part—a document that puts the terms in legalese and also contains a clause that says you will pay the "investor" a sum of money—a couple thousand dollars or so, perhaps even as much as $10,000, nonrefundable—to compensate him for his time in performing due diligence. You have to sign this document and return it with your check for the requested amount in order for the "investor" to proceed. *No credible investor is going to ask you for up-front money. This is just a ruse to get your money; the "investor" never had any intention of investing.*

BROKERS IN INVESTOR'S CLOTHING

Most finders or intermediaries are aboveboard and honest, but there are exceptions. The "investor" calls you and says that he heard that you had a great idea and were looking for investors. He gives some reasonable explanation of how he heard of you and says he might be interested; could you send him your executive summary? He doesn't hesitate to sign a nondisclosure agreement. You meet with him and again, he asks questions, maybe even a couple of well thought out ones. In a day or so he calls and sets up another meeting. At that meeting he says that he's sorry he can't invest, he just put all his money in a new web site, but he loves your concept and knows several buddies who would be tickled to invest. The catch is you have to pay him a finder's fee. He wasn't an investor all along, just a broker fishing for a client—you.

VULTURE VENTURE CAPITALISTS

These are the entrepreneur's worst nightmare. The "investor" really is an investor—he has money, just not many ethics. After careful review of your business plan, meetings with you, and due diligence, he decides to invest. The terms—the amount of money he invests and the equity he receives—are close to what you want. After carefully reading the legal documents that his attorney has prepared, you notice that there is a performance clause, usually a profit or income amount, which will be difficult to meet, or there may be a debt-to-equity ratio that must be maintained. You must pledge your ownership in the company as collateral and guarantee that you will meet the performance requirements or the debt-to-equity ratio. If you don't meet the requirement, you forfeit your shares to him. Because you have faith in yourself, you know that will never happen. But guess what? You can't meet the requirement because your new investor has the ability to affect that very performance requirement. He has to cosign checks and purposely delays; or he's the one who has to make deposits and he doesn't; or something similar. The whole investment has been a setup to take the company. There's nothing you can do; it's too late to have your attorney change the agreement. You lose.

DILIGENT DILETTANTES

Some angel investors are in the business of looking at companies but not investing in them. They love the thrill of being courted by entrepreneurs. They will ask numerous questions, visit the entrepreneur countless times, phone several times a week—but they never have any true intention of investing in the company. Diligent dilettantes will tell you that they are just looking for the "perfect" situation, but that doesn't exist, of course. The time you spend with such dilettantes is time taken away from pursuing serious investors or, more important, running the company. These people can be difficult to spot because they talk an excellent game about being true angels. But one clue is when you cannot move the investor toward any kind of decision. Most real angel investors have so many deals come their way that they have to be able to say yes or no within a reasonable length of time.

KNOWLEDGE VAMPIRES

These are even more obnoxious individuals for entrepreneurs. Not only do they waste your time, but they are looking at your deal only in order to learn more about your industry or market space. They want the benefit of your hard-won knowledge without having to expend much effort acquiring it.

Entrepreneurs have to realize that the market knowledge they have accumulated is valuable. Entrepreneurs must be wary when an individual they do not know approaches their company as a potential investor. Angels or venture capitalists whose reputation can be verified are the best way to go.

LOANS FOR LOSERS

An individual calls (writes, e-mails, faxes) and provides a title that sounds as if the person is an officer in a bank or lending institution. The person then says that he or she is looking for new lending opportunities. If you fill out the loan documents and send them in with a fee processing payment (usually between $500 to $1,000), the person will guarantee that your company will get the loan, regardless of credit history. You send in the fee and never hear from the person again.

The offshore version: The "loan officer" says he or she represents off-shore money that needs to be invested quickly. If you send a good-faith deposit of $5,000 (upward to $50,000) to show that you're credible and to open an account with the offshore bank, you will receive a deposit in that new account of whatever amount of money you'd like, up to $1 million or more. Of course, the instructions are for a cashier's check for the $5,000 to be sent to the "loan officer" along with a deposit slip of a bank account at that bank. And guess what? You never get the bank account opened or hear from the "loan officer" again.

Another version has the deposed widow (sister, daughter, niece) of a foreign country's high-placed official calling. She wants to leave that country but needs an American bank account to secretly transfer a hidden stash of cash. She can't get it out of the country legally so she needs you to open the bank account. Of course you have to open the account with at least $10,000 to show your good faith. Then she'll transfer several million dollars into the account. You get a 10 percent "management" fee, plus you can use the account balance to guarantee a credit line for your company. Naturally if you deposit the $10,000, don't expect it to stick around.

A Last Word on Scams

When he heard we were covering scams, an entrepreneur sent us this cautionary tale:

"Only [last] Saturday did I have to turn down a 'venture capital group' with a $500 million fund (or so they said). When I asked for three or four references, e.g., the names and phone numbers of the CEO or CFO of three or four companies in which they had invested so I could learn 'how great it is to work with you!' the alleged VC company partner become irate, indignant . . . and finally admitted they: (1) had not made any investments as yet, because (2) they did not have the $500 million fund yet. They wanted our business plan to help attract investors for their fund!

"The lesson I learned was: conduct your due diligence vigorously. Remember, if they had invested in me, I would have been their best salesman and reference, and I would find time to talk to anyone about them 24/7! Also remember that *no* respectable VC firm asks for money from the entrepreneur."

ADVICE FROM AN ENTREPRENEUR

"We have an Internet-based e-learning business that is in its early stage. Last fall we mailed a one-page executive summary to some of the VCs that attended the local venture capital conference. One of those VCs was a group called CV Worldwide (not their real name) whose president was George J. MBA, CFP.

"We heard back from Mr. J and sent him our full executive summary. He faxed us a confidentiality agreement and a 'Consulting Agreement' proposing for CV Worldwide to provide its services to help us obtain funding. We thought because Mr. J was listed in the venture capital conference list of attendees, we should meet with him to see if we wanted to take the next step of forking over a $1,200 up front fee. We met with the VP of Sales, Mr. L, at their location in the Midwest.

"At that meeting, Mr. L painted a very rosy picture of their success in helping entrepreneurs to obtain funding, actually stating that because they had such a vast contact base, funding could be completed in four to six weeks. Being somewhat naive about this process, we signed the agreement, gave them a copy of our full business plan, and paid them the $1,200 (which had a money-back guarantee).

"After four weeks of not hearing anything from them, we called Mr. L. He stated that he had bundled our business plan along with several others and sent them to his vast network of contacts. He stated that he felt that we wouldn't have any problem obtaining funding.

"After not hearing from him for a couple more weeks, we called him and again was assured that funding would not be a problem. We even received a letter stating that they had a web site for their clients at www.CV-world-wide.com (this is not the actual web site URL) so their clients could keep up with the status of their funding. Needless to say, the site never worked.

"As more and more time went by, we kept asking Mr. L about our funding and kept getting the same answer. Then we received a letter from Mr. M stating that CV Worldwide was turning over its accounts to a finance company in Chicago. At that point, we tried to contact Mr. M without success. We mailed a certified letter to the finance company and to Mr. M requesting a refund of the $1,200. The finance company called us to let us know that they had no record of receiving anything from Mr. M regarding our company and that Mr. M had closed up shop and was missing. The finance company said that several people had contacted them regarding Mr. M's letter but that they had no legal relationship with Mr. M and couldn't refund any monies paid to CV Worldwide.

"So, we learned a hard lesson."

Nada, Nope, Never

No legitimate venture capital company will ever require the entrepreneur to pay any kind of fees to them to review the entrepreneur's business plan, perform due diligence, or consider investing.

Just because a company has the words "capital" or "venture(s)" in its name does not mean that it is a venture capital firm. (And no—the company above was not named Capital Ventures Worldwide).

CHAPTER
19

Give a Little, Get a Lot: Negotiating

—

Negotiating is a personal process that is not as easy to provide guidance about as, say, writing the business plan to present to venture capitalists; there is not necessarily a set pattern to follow. Some entrepreneurs are "naturals" at negotiating; others find the whole thing distressing. It's really like embarking on a long journey with places along the way where you stop, reflect on what you have seen so far, and make the decision to keep going or return safely home, back where you started.

On this road, you ask yourself these four questions:

1. Will this transaction help my company in both the short and the long run?
2. Are these the type of people I want to do business with?
3. Will they add more to my business than money?
4. Is this transaction fair?

QUESTION 1: WILL THIS TRANSACTION HELP MY COMPANY IN BOTH THE SHORT AND THE LONG RUN?

It's easy to get caught up in the short-run need for capital. After all, capital is the lifeblood of any business, an absolute necessity. But short-run thinking can be short-sighted thinking, because the financial partners you choose are likely to be involved with you for a number of years, and once they are in, it is difficult to get rid of them against their wishes.

QUESTION 2: ARE THESE THE TYPE OF PEOPLE I WANT TO DO BUSINESS WITH?

This is a more subjective question than the first one but of equal importance. Nothing takes the joy out of the experience of owning your own business as quickly as does being in partnership with people you can't stand. Are these ethical people with a good reputation? How have they treated their other "partners" in other companies in which they have invested? You are going to be working closely with your financial partners, and it is critical that you share common goals and objectives for the business and agree on fundamental business practices.

If you sense friction early on in the negotiations, you may experience heat after the deal closes.

ADVICE FROM A VENTURE CAPITALIST

Nick Efstratis, Partner, Wasatch Venture Fund, www.wasatchvc.com

"First off, get everything out on the table. In other words, make sure the venture firm doesn't feel that there are unknowns yet to be discovered about the company, its founders, its financial situation, etc. And vice versa. The entrepreneur should make sure that all of their questions about the venture fund are answered. Remember, the VCs that an entrepreneur chooses are his or her allies, consultants, strategists, and perhaps most important, his or her greatest source for raising additional funds. Openness and trust make for a much better relationship and should speed up and simplify any negotiations."

QUESTION 3: WILL THEY ADD MORE TO MY BUSINESS THAN MONEY?

Many owners of emerging businesses seeking capital tend to overlook the contribution a venture capitalist can make to the business apart from the capital provided. Most small businesses have a relatively thin management team, with definite gaps in experience or capability. A financial partner who is an expert in your industry could certainly be of assistance in helping you with your business strategy, in developing marketing channels, and with sales contacts. Professional venture capitalists sometimes take offense with entrepreneurs who just want money and do not welcome their participation in the business.

QUESTION 4: IS THIS TRANSACTION FAIR?

From the entrepreneur's standpoint, fairness means an equitable sharing of the profits or value created in the enterprise. Astute investors do not want to enter into a transaction in which the owners/managers do not receive an adequate split of the rewards of the business' success, because an unmotivated management team is probably not going to be able to build a large, profitable company.

However, greed being the incredibly powerful force that it is, the logic of having a motivated management group is not going to prevent some investors from trying to craft a deal that is totally in their favor.

Fairness is, again, subjective, and clearly in the eye of the beholder. But you, the entrepreneur, want to be the beholder, not the beholden, when the transaction is completed. So, what steps can you do to ensure fairness?

- Study other transactions with companies similar to yours and find out what kinds of terms were proposed. Familiarize yourself with the terminology of deal making, so you do not come off as unprepared or inexperienced when you are discussing terms with the investor.

- Get some people on *your* side of the negotiating table. The negotiating process is no time to be the rugged individualist. You need a team of advisors, at least behind the scenes advisors, to help you determine whether the deal should go forward or not. Many entrepreneurs have, in effect, an informal advisory board made up of attorneys, CPAs, CEOs of other companies, and similarly experienced people who have seen other financing transactions and can help them avoid the pitfalls.

NEVER LISTEN TO SOMEONE WHO SAYS INVESTORS HAVE TO HAVE CONTROL

You should never assume that you must give up control of your company to venture capitalists in order to secure financing for a start-up. Some of the larger venture capital firms, in fact, prefer to have a minority share because they believe that a management group with a higher equity stake is more likely to put their full energies into building the company.

FINE PRINT CAN BE HAZARDOUS TO YOUR WEALTH

One of the most perilous parts of structuring a venture capital investment involves the performance criteria set for the existing owners/managers. These parameters are set to protect the investors in the event the company underperforms relative to what was projected. The fine print of the agreement could specify that the investors receive more shares, giving them control, for example, or may say they have the right to bring in their own management team, or even sell the company out from under the original owners in order to recoup their investment. You, the entrepreneur, should assume that actual results *will* vary from what had been forecast, and you must be very cautious when agreeing to the performance criteria that will be used to trigger any of these changes.

We heard of one wealthy individual investor who never objected to puffed-up projections and therefore outrageous valuations but set the management performance criteria based on those projections, knowing full well that management could not achieve the results and he could take over the company. He let the entrepreneurs hang themselves by their own spreadsheets.

End Result of Negotiations: Employment Opportunities for Lawyers, Lots of Paper, Then a Deal

When the partners of a venture capital firm or an angel investor decides to invest in a company, the next step is to draft a document called a term sheet that summarizes the most important parts of the transaction's proposed structure. It really is just a summary; all of the terms are elaborated on later in the closing documents for the transaction. The closing documents include the actual stock purchase agreement and a shareholder's agreement.

In layman's terms, what terms are covered in a term sheet?

Dollar amount of the capital being invested

Type of security—common stock, preferred stock, and convertible debentures are some of the choices

Number of shares the investor proposes to purchase

Purchase price per share

Target date for closing of the transaction

Capitalization of the company after the transaction takes place: who will own what amount of shares, in other words. (The founders might own 55 percent, the investor would own 35 percent, and 10 percent might be reserved for employees of the company and would be distributed as the company and the management team grow.)

Other terms would cover:

How dividends will be distributed to investors and founders

How the proceeds would be distributed to investors and founders in the event the company is sold

Provisions to protect investors from having their ownership share diluted by the next round and subsequent rounds of financing

The all-important voting rights section: how the ownership of shares are translated into the rights to vote on key issues before the board of directors, and how many seats on the board founders and investors are allowed

Key decisions that would require the consent of the investors, such as the founders selling their majority interest in the company

Investors' rights to receive periodic reports

The term sheet does not bind the investors to complete the transaction with the company, and the terms are subject to completion of due diligence. The value of this document, besides demonstrating to the company that the investors are truly interested, is that the more the two parties commit to the term sheet, the fewer disagreements or misunderstandings there are later on.

The closing documents do bind the entrepreneur and the investor together, however, so all participants in the transaction benefit if all the key issues surrounding the management and decision-making authority of the company are spelled out and agreed to.

There are a myriad of ways to structure investment in private companies. The fact the investors do not own 51 percent of the stock does not necessarily mean they don't "control" the company. All sorts of requirements can be put in place through the closing documents to give the investors effective control of the important decisions of the business. Control means controlling strategy and direction, not just holding shares.

As a company grows through its life cycle from seed to exit, the amount of control the founders have almost always ebbs. The only time entrepreneurs have full control of the company is when it exists only as an idea in their head. The more the company is worth, the less entrepreneurs tend to be in control, even though their wealth grows right along with the company's value.

ADVICE FROM A VENTURE CAPITALIST ON HOW TO NEGOTIATE

Mike Witherill, Partner, EstreetCapital.com, a venture capital firm in Phoenix, AZ

"While many entrepreneurs are savvy about technology trends, market positioning, and management, most are surprisingly naïve about a key aspect of the funding process: negotiations. The following tips will help entrepreneurs be more effective during negotiations.

"Be prepared. Many entrepreneurs do not understand what warrants, antidilution clauses, and conversion provisions are, let alone their implications. My advice is for entrepreneurs to hire expert professional advisors and learn from them. While they will provide the entrepreneur with knowledge and strategy suggestions, keep in mind that ultimately the entrepreneur has the final responsibility for all decisions.

"Be realistic about valuation. We have heard entrepreneurs say 'My company was valued at $ during the last round of funding,' In fact, it is irrelevant what a company was worth in the past. Market conditions change and a company's value will be determined by overall market and industry factors that entrepreneurs have no control over. It is unproductive to focus on this issue.

"Keep the big picture in mind. During negotiations, it is easy to focus intensely on certain key numbers like valuation or the percent equity stake the venture capitalist will receive. While entrepreneurs want to make sure that they are in the same ballpark as the venture capitalist, spending hours negotiating about small differences is not productive. If the company is as successful as the entrepreneur and the venture capitalist believe, everyone will do well.

"Choose comparables carefully. When eStreetCapital determines the value of a company, we consider both private and public comparable companies, discounted cash-flow analysis, and our own experience. Occasionally entrepreneurs get caught up in focusing on one public company comparable that has a high market cap, but whose revenue or business models are different enough to invalidate a comparison. By definition, the market value of a company is what somebody will pay for it, not what the founder would like it to be worth.

"Treat negotiations as a partnership agreement, not an adversarial process. Many entrepreneurs worry that venture capitalists will take too much of their company. Venture capital is expensive money because it invests in extremely risky early-stage companies. Even with all of our due diligence efforts to qualify an investment opportunity, only about half of our investments are ever fully realized. If entrepreneurs want to build their companies gradually, there are plenty of other financing options. At eStreet, we see ourselves as partners with our portfolio companies and we work diligently to help them succeed.

"Be aware of general negotiation principles. While some of the points mentioned here are specific to the venture capital funding process, know that understanding classic negotiation theory will be invaluable to any entrepreneur. For example, being forthright, not pulling any last-minute changes, and building on areas of common agreement work well in the venture capital environment. When all parties follow these principles, the process can be very simple. eStreetCapital financed Opnix in 13 days because of a compelling market opportunity, propri-

etary technology, and a superb technical management team represented by an excellent negotiating team."

Creativity Is an Essential Component of Dealmaking

One company we worked with had an incredibly energetic management team that bootstrapped the enterprise right to the brink of greatness over the course of three years. They needed that last $2 million of capital, though, to ignite a growth phase that would take revenues from $4 million to $35 million in 18 months. An investor group was ready and willing to put in the $2 million, but it was made up of a partnership from London that required the group to have numerical control of the stock—at least 60 percent—in order to do a deal all the way on the West Coast of the United States. The entrepreneurs gagged over the prospect of surrendering control of their "baby" right before the good times started to roll. The problem was, using our simple valuation formula, there was no way to support a valuation of the company where a $2 million investment was worth less than 50 percent of the company. The founders rightly argued that the company could be worth $50 million within 18 months, so the investors would have earned $30 million on $2 million in a year and a half. Not bad work, if you can get it.

Simple Valuation Formula

Valuation Before Investment but After 3 Years of Struggle	$1.5 million
Investment Needed to Make All Dreams Come True	$2.0 million
Valuation After Classy British Investors Come In	$3.5 million

$$\frac{\$2 \text{ million}}{\$3.5 \text{ million}} = 57\% \text{ Ownership for the Investors}$$

The founder of this company came up with a great solution. "Sure," he said, "you can have 57 percent, so you are comfortable with the amount of control you have, but we want the right to buy you back down to 30 percent in 18 months, if the financial projections are realized and the company has the cash to do the buyback. We'll give you a 45 percent return on the stock when we repurchase it."

"Done deal," said the fellows from London.

ADVICE FROM AN ENTREPRENEUR WHO HAS SUCCESSFULLY RAISED CAPITAL

Jeff Kohler, CEO of Reason, Inc. a VC-funded company that develops Web-based applications for the management of wireless products and services. The company's services include an online help desk for corporations and an e-commerce site for retailers of wireless products. Founded in 1998, Reason is based in Aurora, Colorado. Reason recently completed its second round of financing at $5.5 million.

Tell us about the initial meeting with a venture fund. "The first meeting with a venture capitalist is typically a pleasant one, believe it or not. In fact, we've had many 'first meetings' with many venture capitalists as well as many second, third, fourth, fifth, and sixth meetings with venture capitalists. This is typical—rarely does a company find one VC and have a few meetings, then sew up the financing. It is a long process of finding the right fit between company and investor.

"The presentations and business plans we have prepared for VCs—shown and discussed at many, many meetings—have gone through more than a dozen major revisions in the span of just the six months leading to our most recent round of financing. The one thing that remained consistent through all these changes was our focus on explaining the pain in our industry (wireless communication), how Reason will relieve it, and why we are the best people to do the job. As a general rule, I believe VCs invest in the people, the industry, and the solution."

Take us through the steps you took to find investors. "The VC process goes something like this: You get in touch with a potential VC via a referral, typically, and then give a couple minutes' overview on the phone of who you are and what you are doing. If that remotely meets their criteria, they will usually set up a meeting for you to meet them and present your case. After that meeting, if they are intrigued, they will ask for another meeting to explore the plan in more detail. After that, there are almost always more meetings—often up to five more—to refine their knowledge of the industry and your solution.

"Once the VCs have a significant comfort level with where you are going and feel there is a good fit, they may ask you to present to all of the partners in a firm. (This is in addition to all the meetings noted above.) In our experience, the final decision is a group one made by the partners.

"On average, you will spend 45 minutes to an hour with a VC at the first meeting. In our case, my partner and I (the cofounders of our business) set up all the meetings and did the presentations. In follow-up meetings, it was sometimes necessary to bring in our technology expert. The presentations we prepared were in Power Point, with slides designed to follow the typical path of discussion.

"We found that the first meeting with a VC starts with a discussion of who you are, what your experience is, and why you are qualified to tackle the project at hand. You may highlight some board members, prominent angel investors, or other alliances that back up your experience and show that you have already made inroads on your business model and plan. I have never come across a VC who was interested in providing 'seed' funding for your business. They want to see that you've been able to raise money already, that other people have bought into your plan, and, best of all, that you have paying customers active or inked (no betas).

"This initial conversation leads to a discussion on the identification and solution to a problem in an industry. Specifically, VCs want you to spell out what your unique selling proposition (USP) is and attempt to show why you have an 'unfair advantage' in the industry. These 'unfair advantages' may include your unique experience, alliances with large customers that allow you to get to market quicker than anyone else, or proprietary technology.

"I think there is an urban myth out there that VCs are big risk takers. They represent investment dollars from a variety of funds, so it's reasonable to assume they need to balance risk and reward. They don't see the same level of risk that the founders, friends and family investors, or your angel investors see. Those are people who probably gave you money when there was little or nothing to show for it. In our case, the first $2 million came on nothing but us and an idea on a PPT (Power Point) software presentation. VCs typically come in when a lot of the dirty work is done and you're close to building a large, thriving business. Your presentation must reflect that you are at this point."

Were there any surprises in the process? "It's remarkable to me how relatively little time is spent going over the full business plan or your financials. In fact, I would guess that no VC ever read the 30-page business plan we spent two months developing. It was when we got the plan summarized to seven pages that I believe VCs may have at least perused it.

"Initially, financial discussions were limited to a quick glance at revenue projections over the next couple of years. Big VCs like big numbers, while smaller VCs are comfortable with smaller numbers. Showing top-tier VCs that you may generate up to $10 million in sales over the next three years isn't going to garner much interest, as they are looking for industry leaders with the opportunity for IPO or acquisition in the short term a distinct possibility.

"Timing is everything when top-tier VC investing is involved. I once had a VC glance at our financial projections and respond, 'We typically just cut the revenue in half, and that gives us an idea of where you might be.' So one of the funnier things to say to a VC is that your projections 'are very conservative.' You might think they are, but chances are they're not. It's not that you shouldn't have your financials in order, however. Get a solid, top-line look at major revenue and expense lines and do your pro-formas. You never know who your audience will be and what their backgrounds are. Not speaking intelligently to the subject when asked can kill a deal quickly."

How did you cope with rejection? "Maybe it's a West Coast VC nuance, but we laugh about how we have never been told no so nicely, so many times, by these VCs. If you're like us, you will hear things such as 'We really like you guys, we like where you are going, but we don't have the bandwidth right now to support what you are doing,' or 'We think you're on to something. Keep us posted as you progress and perhaps we'll look at your next round.'

"You can't blame them, though, with so many great ideas and so many smart people out there, but so few partners in a VC firm that can travel and sit on your board. They really do need to be choosy. The fact is that they might really like your idea and think it has merit but there's just something else on their desks with a little more upside or something more akin to their area of expertise.

"Most VCs, whether they fund your firm or not, do like to help a company out with a network of people and resources. They are happy to provide contacts. This is an important asset, and important to keep in mind when finding VCs. A VC firm specializing in biotech is probably not going to look at a business-to-consumer deal, for example, as they just won't have the same network of people and resources."

How many investors did you end up contacting? "The window of opportunity for VC funding is short. It's important to contact as many firms as possible through referrals, while always keeping in mind that any particular VC's interest in your company could lead to funding. VCs have a way of stringing you along for weeks or months until the final partners' meeting. If the partners vote your deal down, you need to have other VCs in the pipeline.

"And in the meantime, keep moving your business along quickly by developing your infrastructure and lining up customers. A live, paying customer is worth more than anything you can put in a business plan or PPT presentation. And if you're like us, the harder you work, the luckier you will get, and your money will come in from one or more of your sources sometime."

CHAPTER

20

Closing the Deal and Living Happily Ever After

Failure to understand the time required to be successful in finding capital is probably the single biggest mistake business owners make in the capital search process. Perhaps because the search seems like a disagreeable task, they wait until the capital needle is on empty before they begin looking. Any venture capital firm or professional investor goes through a series of analysis, research, and documentation steps, or due diligence, before any funds are transferred. In most cases, it is impossible to hurry these steps along; the time they take to complete are at the discretion of the investor or lender, not the entrepreneur. From a negotiating standpoint, the more critical your need for funds, the weaker your position.

How Quickly Can a Company Obtain Funding?

When asked how quickly the venture capital company had *ever* invested in a company, from the time they received the business plan

249

until the deal closed, more than four out of five reported they were able to close a deal in less than 60 days, with 41 percent saying they had closed a deal in under 30 days. The average for all respondents was roughly 40 days.

DEAL TALES: PICK A COMPANY, ANY COMPANY

Occasionally entrepreneurs take way too seriously this notion that a strong management team is the key to getting capital. We know of an entrepreneurial group that was in the business of starting companies—not starting and building them, just starting them. They came up with half a dozen good ideas and wrote business plans for each of them, listing the same management and advisory group for each venture. The roster on the team was impressive—technical experts, marketing whizzes, experienced Wall Street guys, even people with high-level political connections. But they had no intention of actually executing all these plans. They were just going to go with whichever one received funding first. This is like asking investors to select from a take-out menu. Surely, Mr. Rich Person, there's something that looks appetizing to you. So much for the idea of being committed and dedicated to your company succeeding. The whole point of the process here was to reel in an investor, not build a company.

DEAL TALES: SEND OUT EXECUTIVE SUMMARY, WAIT TWO DAYS, THEN PANIC

An entrepreneur we knew raised the term "overanxious" to new heights. After completing his business plan, he sent the executive summary out via e-mail to about 25 venture capitalists. He seemed to have trouble with the concept that while e-mail speeds up the transmittal of information, it does not guarantee an instant response. We received the following phone calls from this entrepreneur after he sent the letters.

Day 2: "I haven't heard anything back yet. Is that unusual?"

Day 3: "Still haven't heard from any of them. This is starting to become frustrating."

Day 4: "Got one e-mail decline back. What's with these other VC firms? They're so slow."

Day 5: "Do you think there's something wrong with my executive summary?"

Day 6: "I really think we need to rewrite that summary. We're not getting through to the VCs."

Day 7: I told my secretary to tell him I was out of the office all day.

Day 8: "Got three nos today. Tried to get the partners on the phone and find out why. Got the runaround. I thought we'd have made much more progress by now than this."

Day 9: "I'm going to revise the business plan over the weekend. We must have screwed up in how we presented the company. The business model must be all wrong or something."

Day 10: "It's me again. You're probably sick of talking to me, aren't you? I can't believe how long this is taking."

Finding money takes time and an almost heroic degree of patience. There is no way around these unpleasant facts.

DEAL TALE: DON'T WORRY, WE'VE GOT CANDLES

An entrepreneur named Bob was desperate to get venture capital. He had taken the company as far as it could go on the company's own funds, and things were looking bleak. A meeting at Bob's company office was scheduled with a venture capitalist, who was a good fit. While touring the facility with the VC, the utility company came and shut off the electricity for nonpayment of the bill. "I told you we needed the money," Bob said.

The worst time to look for money is when you've absolutely got to have it.

ADVICE FROM A VENTURE CAPITALIST

Rob Mitchell, Centura Capital, Charlotte, NC

"Most entrepreneurs underestimate the time that is needed to close a transaction. As a subordinated debt investor, we need 60 days to close, although we usually try to close in less time. Preferred stock investors usually need more time in order to investigate the viability and sustainability of the company's product or technology. Making contact when there is only two weeks of cash left won't work. Entrepreneurs also underestimate the complexities of outside capital. The closing process raises many business issues, many of which had never been considered. For example, an investor may require the creation of a board of directors that has the power to alter strategy or even fire the CEO. They may also establish limits on the sale of stock or increases in salary. Their involvement will require the company to formalize policies and procedures, such as compensation plans and accounting policies, rather than continue the less formal methods of before.

"These are painful, but necessary steps to make a company more professional and more able to execute its business plan."

How Long Should an Entrepreneur Expect the Funding Process to Take?

The more important factor, however, is not how quickly the venture capitalist has ever closed but the *average* time it takes to close a deal.

Surveying venture capitalists on this subject, the results are as follows:

Time to Closing	Venture Capitalists' Response
Under 30 days	1%
30–60 days	18%
60–90 days	45%
90–120 days	26%
120 days +	10%

The average for all respondents was just over 80 days, or nearly three months—double the quickest time period. Another way of viewing this information is to recognize that, typically, only 19 percent of venture capital companies close a deal in two months or less. The wide variation in average time to close is important for entrepreneurs to understand as well: roughly 20 percent take less than two months, more than one-third take in excess of three months. Several venture capitalists stated that there was no difference between the quickest they had ever closed and their average length of time required for closing.

Most entrepreneurs seeking capital do not allow enough time for the funding process in their planning. Remember this fact.

ADVICE FROM A VENTURE CAPITALIST ON CLOSING

Matt Harris, CEO, Village Ventures, www.villageventures.com

"Keep momentum high, don't assume that you should stop running your business to focus on raising money. On the contrary, you need to keep delivering results during the financing process to keep the VC eager to work hard on your deal."

Entrepreneurs Are on the Accelerated Plan

Twenty-two percent of entrepreneurs believe it should take less than 30 days to close, while only 1 percent of the venture capitalists actually close in less than 30 days. Nearly half of the entrepreneurs believe it should take 60 days or less to close, while only 19 percent of the venture capitalists close in that time period. However, about two-thirds of the entrepreneurs assume it will take 90 days or less, which is close to the average actual closing time. The entrepreneurs had a wide range of expectations when it came to closing, from seven days to over a year.

The results of our survey of entrepreneurs are as follows:

Time to Closing	Entrepreneurs' Response
Under 30 days	22%
30–60 days	25%
60–90 days	20%
90–120 days	15%
120 days +	18%

DEAL TALE: WAITING FOR RIP VAN WINKLE

One year in April we sent a business plan to a large, well-known venture capital firm for review. The client really needed funding quickly and was very eager to get going. The following December—nearly eight months later—we got this letter: "I just had a chance to read the first few pages of your business plan. I hope to finish it and get back to you sometime early next year." Luckily, the client was a young man. The lesson learned? Patience is not only a virtue but a necessity when looking for capital.

Moving the Transaction Along

The slow pace of negotiations is the bane of the entrepreneur's existence. You need the money now, not five years from now. One way to speed the process up at least a little bit is to set concrete goals for completion of each phase of the transaction and get all parties—and all parties' attorneys—to agree to the time frame. Before the phrase "I'll get back to you," escapes the venture capitalist's lips, say, "So, I can expect to hear back from you on your due diligence list by this Friday, correct?"

You can save time by being prepared regarding what to expect in terms of due diligence requests. Have your business plan ready before contacting any investors. Some companies prepare a large binder with the usual due diligence information already in it, neatly tabbed and divided, ready to hand over to the investor after the confidentiality issues are settled. Another valuable time-saving technique is to choose an attorney who gets things done on time.

Exit Strategies

SAY GOOD NIGHT, GRACIE (AND GOOD LUCK WITH THE IPO)

While venture capitalists would prefer to be your partner, they don't want to be your partner forever. Much of the payoff of their investment is in the final transaction or the exit strategy.

ADVICE FROM A VENTURE CAPITALIST

Shanda Bahles, General Partner, El Dorado Ventures,
www.eldorado.com

"Focus on building a business that can stand alone, and if someone
makes you an offer you can't refuse, take it!"

An IPO seems to spark the imagination. But the most frequent type of
exit is actually the merger or acquisition. According to the NVCA, over
the last 25 years, the number of venture capital–backed companies that
have gone public totals only around 3,000.

GOING PUBLIC

Initial public offerings—IPOs—have garnered the most publicity because of the volatility of the market and because of the implication that
an IPO will generate the greatest returns to both the shareholders and
the founders.

BECOMING AN ACQUISITION TARGET

Merging with another company, or being bought out by a major company, doesn't sound as glamorous as an IPO, but it is just as effective in
creating wealth for the shareholders of the bought company.

BUYING THE VCs OUT

A management buyout of current investors isn't as popular as the first
two alternatives. It usually involves debt financing through traditional
loan sources. The venture capitalists usually don't receive quite the return they would if the company had gone public or if there had been a
merger.

LIMPING ALONG AND CLOSING SHOP

Nobody wants to consider the alternatives of limping along or closing
shop. But remember, not every venture investment is a home run. There

is the possibility that the company will never achieve star status. Lately a number of venture-funded dot.coms have had to face major layoffs and closures.

ADVICE FROM A VENTURE CAPITALIST

Chris Starr, Associate, Eastern Technology Fund,
www.easterntechnologyfund.com

What advice would you give to an entrepreneur in determining an exit strategy? "I would advise entrepreneurs to consider all of the possible exit strategies. Conventional exit strategies generally fall into two categories: (1) initial public offerings or (2) mergers/acquisitions. There are actually six strategies for exiting a company, each depending on a company's stage development or lack thereof.

"*Going public.* Going public is often the best way to exit a company, which explains its popularity. Simply put, the public market will usually pay more for a company than any other source. The high valuations obtained in the public marketplace are a function of the liquidity achieved by spreading the investment among many hands.

"*Sale to another company.* Negotiating a sale to another company is another popular method of exiting a company. This method offers flexibility because sale structures can be tailored to the needs of the entrepreneur, investors, and buyers/merger partners. Possible methods of sale include: sale of company stock for cash, sale of stock for notes, sale of stock for stock, sale of assets for cash, sale of assets for notes, sale of assets for stock, earn-outs, or any combination thereof.

"*Sale back to company.* This exit is less popular but certainly possible. Because venture capitalists and private equity investors operate on the foundation that all investments are for sale at the right price, entrepreneurs may be able to negotiate a buyout from an investor. Usually the company must use cash flows, a bank loan, or some other debt financing to provide the investor with a suitable return.

"*Sale to a new investor.* Sometimes a company may desire to take on a new investor. Sometimes the new investor is in the form of a new venture capital/private equity investor. More often the investor is a corporate partner with a synergistic investment rationale.

"*Liquidation.* At some point, some companies are worth more for their liquidation value than as an operating concern. In such situations, liquidation is often preferable over reorganization/bankruptcy and may salvage relationships with investors and creditors.

"*Reorganization/bankruptcy.* This is not a desirable exit but one that is frequently resorted to. This strategy usually results in a very bad situation for investors. Entrepreneurs who wish to maintain their relationships with their investors should avoid this situation at all costs.

"In summary, I recommend evaluating all options, then selecting the option with the most value. In all situations, work with the best professionals you can find to provide the legal, accounting, and investment banking functions."

CHAPTER
21

Putting It All Together

Ten Steps in a Transaction

STEP 1: FINDING VENTURE CAPITALISTS WHO ARE WILLING, CAPABLE, AND A GOOD FIT

At this very first stage of a transaction, you must establish that the venture capitalist has the financial capability to do the deal and is seriously interested in proceeding with a transaction.

You also must determine whether the venture capitalist is a good fit with your business. This means a venture capitalist who is knowledgeable about your industry and invests in similar type companies, at the stage in a business' life cycle that your company presently is in.

259

STEP 2: INTRODUCING YOUR COMPANY

Your goal at this stage is to give VCs enough information about your business to motivate them to want to proceed with more in-depth discussions, leading to negotiation of an offer to invest. This is the time when you convince them of the profit potential of your business. The business plan you have written is the logical information to start with, although some people prefer to give a shorter "executive summary," or simply arrange for an in-person meeting. The meeting usually is more productive, however, if the prospective investors have had some time to study the business and formulate questions to ask. The reason some entrepreneurs do not wish to give out the business plan initially is our next topic.

STEP 3: MAINTAINING CONFIDENTIALITY

Most companies have confidential aspects to them—trade secrets, strategic plans—that they do not want revealed to just "anyone." It can be harmful to have certain types of information fall into the hands of competitors; there may be sensitive financial matters that the owners of the company do not want generally known.

On the other hand, investors need to know as much as possible—they'd prefer to know everything—in order to evaluate the risks and merits of the company. In order to reach some kind of common ground, most companies rely on having investors sign a nondisclosure agreement, also called a confidentiality agreement, before giving them significant strategic and financial information. Your attorney can help you develop this letter.

Again, a word of caution: Most professional venture capital firms as a matter of policy refuse to sign these agreements for fear of being sued, because they may look at a number of very similar companies each year. With these groups, insisting on having the agreement signed will mean they will decline to talk further with you. Angel investors, however, are usually willing to sign a nondisclosure agreement.

STEP 4: THE MEETING(S)

It is hoped that the VCs agree to meet with you because you and your business plan have done a good job of describing the potential of your business for growth and profitability. Now you have to convince them that your management team is capable of accomplishing the goals set forth in the plan. Among the things you have to show them are:

- You completely understand all aspects of your business plan; you were involved in its preparation.

- You are honest and have integrity. You are a worthwhile person to "partner up" with.

- You have vision—the ability to see coming trends in your market and take advantage of them.

- You can inspire others in your company to great performance.

- You have an understanding of the financial aspects of running a business and will be a good steward of the investors' money.

- You are totally committed to the venture and do not have any obligations that will prevent you from spending the long hours it takes to build a large enterprise.

- You are willing to make a full disclosure to the investors of both the positive and the negative factors about your company, its strengths and weaknesses, the opportunities and the risks.

STEP 5: GETTING DOWN TO TERMS (AND GETTING YOUR ATTORNEY INVOLVED)

If all goes well in the meetings with the venture capitalists, things will progress to the point that one side or the other will want to suggest the basic structure of the deal, which is often referred to as preparing a term sheet. The term sheet can be a very brief, bullet-point statement of how much money the investors would put in, what equity share they would receive, the time frame for completing their analysis of the company and getting the formal documents ready in preparation for closing the transaction, and other basic terms. Before you suggest terms in writing, it is best to obtain the advice of an attorney about how to word the language of the document and other ideas he or she may have concerning what terms should be included in the letter. Your attorney will also help make sure that you remain in compliance with all applicable federal and state securities laws every step of the way.

The objective of the term sheet is to get both sides to agree on the basic structure of the transaction and to make certain there are no major misunderstandings before everyone spends a great deal more time on the deal.

You have many choices regarding what form the investment will take.

Common stock ownership represents the ultimate controlling interest in the company and usually includes voting rights. In a liquidation of the company, the common stockholders receive distributions only after all the other debt and equity holders have been satisfied.

Preferred stock is a class of equity that grants certain additional rights—such as dividends or prior claim in the event the company is sold or liquidated—over those held by common shareholders.

Notes are unsecured debt with maturities that are short to intermediate in length, one to five years. They may be guaranteed by an officer or an owner of the company.

Bonds are longer-term debt, often secured by hard assets, such as equipment. They may also be unsecured, however.

Debt with warrants (rights to buy equity at a later date for a fixed price) is a popular form of investment because it allows the investor the current return of a debt instrument along with the opportunity of purchasing equity in the company. If the company does well and the stock becomes valuable, the warrants enhance the investor's total return. The possible capital appreciation from the warrants is called an "equity kicker."

Convertible debentures are medium-to long-term unsecured debt instruments that allow the investor the option of turning the debt into stock in the company.

STEP 6: DUE DILIGENCE

The term sheet will normally state that acceptance of the deal by the venture capitalists is subject to completion of due diligence. This is the investigative phase of the transaction, in which investors look into your company, its records, its history, and its financial condition in great depth. You, in turn ask the questions of the investors necessary for you to determine if they would make good partners for your company.

STEP 7: FILLING IN THE DETAILS

As the transaction moves toward a close, the documentation that is passed back and forth from the VCs to the entrepreneur becomes more specific and detailed. The next formal document after the term sheet is sometimes called the letter of intent. This states the financial terms in more detail and usually spells out other aspects of the deal, such as employment agreements and compensation for the management team, proposed date for the deal to close, composition of the company's board of directors after the investment is made, buy-sell agreements in the event one or the other party wants out of the company, expenditure authority, and rules for payments of dividends. At this stage, the letter normally still does not bind either party; the close of the deal still is subject to due diligence.

A letter of intent often is modified several times by both parties before it is signed. Again, you should work with your attorney on drafting your response to a letter of intent from the investors. (Note: In spite of the number of times we mention how indispensable a capable corporate lawyer is in investment transactions, we are not sponsored by the American Bar Association.)

Once the letter of intent is finalized, the next step is to prepare the final closing documents, including the purchase or subscription agreement.

STEP 8: PURCHASE/SUBSCRIPTION AGREEMENT

The closing documents bind both parties to completing the transaction. Among the documents is the stock purchase agreement (in the case of an equity transaction). This document contains legal language that ensures the transaction is in compliance with securities laws.

STEP 9: TO CLOSE OR NOT TO CLOSE

Now you are at the point of no return: If you sign the documents and accept the funds, you are in business with new partners—they own part of your company, in effect, part of you, if the company was your "baby."

There are emotional aspects to selling part of your company. You may feel remorse at the prospect of giving up part of the independence you were seeking when you started the company in the first place. But you have to weigh that against the unavoidable fact that it is very difficult to grow a large company without outside capital.

STEP 10: FEAR AND LOATHING AT THE CLOSING

All capital seekers find themselves in the position of worrying about whether an investor is going to actually write a check. Never count on investors' commitments until you receive the funds. This is particularly true with angel investors who have difficulty saying no with finality. They prefer to say "I like what I see but I'm still thinking." That could easily mean that they have already decided to decline, but the entrepreneur—anxious for the deal to close—interprets it positively. Professional venture capitalists have so much practice saying no that they usually have no trouble telling you they are no longer interested. There have been cases, however, when they go completely through the due diligence phase, even hiring consultants to study the market or the technology, get all parts of the deal negotiated—then abruptly decline.

Sometimes entrepreneurs stop looking for investors because they erroneously think they have a commitment from one or from a group. It's always better to have two offers from investors, and have to decline one of them, than to find you have none at all.

The Real Life Story: Putting It All Together— Following a Technology Company from Its Inception, Its Funding, to Being Acquired

In the mid-1990s, an enterprising young engineer named Daniel Fu founded Poseidon Technology. (The name was later changed to HotRail.) This company develops advanced, integrated technologies for high-speed switching, interconnect, and scalable processing for Internet systems. HotRail's technology is designed to significantly increase the performance of next-generation networking systems by eliminating data-flow bottlenecks, while providing for cost-effective, reliable, and highly scalable systems.

Poseidon was selling about $1 million worth of product and was close to break-even—Daniel had basically bootstrapped the company to this point—when in 1995, at his father's suggestion, he contacted Dr. Bob Larson, a general partner of the venture capital firm Woodside Fund, located in Woodside, California. Daniel asked Bob to be an advisor and serve on the board of Poseidon. In exchange, Daniel offered Bob 10 percent founder's stock, which was contributed to Woodside Fund.

Woodside Fund's latest partnership, Woodside Fund IV, invests between $5 and $10 million in early-stage ventures in Internet and electronic commerce, computer software, telecommunications, and networking, located in northern and central California. The fund serves as the lead or colead investor in most of its portfolio companies.

After analyzing the market and the position of Daniel's technology, Bob advised him to think about developing a new-generation product. The current product had lost its technological edge, and sales were flat. Bob encouraged Daniel to consider recent advances in semiconductor technology and processor capability and to focus on the needs of the market.

Daniel came up with an innovation he called "point-to-point" symmetric multiprocessing. Bob worked quickly and closely with Daniel and a patent attorney to obtain the necessary intellectual protections.

The next milestone was achieved when Bob helped Poseidon secure a strategic partnership for joint marketing. Bob and Woodside Fund general partner Vincent Occhipinti then introduced Daniel to Rick R. Shriner, a seasoned executive in the semiconductor area with experience at Motorola, Intel, and Apple. Rick agreed to join Poseidon as CEO.

With the leadership in place, the new team put together a business plan and sought venture capital funding. Woodside Fund brought in the ideal colead for the first round—Gordon Campbell of TechFund. Mr. Campbell had originated the concept of the fabless semiconductor company (a company that develops semiconductor products and manufactures them at someone else's foundry) while CEO of Chips 'N Technologies.

TechFund and Woodside Fund led a $7.5 million first round in which Chase Capital Partners, Charter Ventures, and others also participated. The company hired nearly 50 top engineers to carry out the chip design efforts, along with marketing personnel. Strategic relationships were developed with other chip and server vendors, including DEC, Compaq, IBM, Siemens, and Samsung. Bob and Vince assisted company management in all these critical moves.

Woodside Fund then participated in the second round, investing funds from Woodside Fund IV, as well as in the third and final round of funding. HotRail exited Woodside's portfolio through acquisition by Conexant, in a transaction valued at nearly $400 million.

DISCUSSION OF THE PARTNERSHIP

Participants

Daniel Fu, founder of HotRail (initially named Poseidon Technology), and now VP Technology for Conexant

Rick Shriner, CEO of HotRail (still on after merger with Conexant)

Vincent M. Occhipinti, Woodside Fund's founder and managing director

How difficult was it to obtain venture capital?

Daniel Fu: "I knew Bob Larson, managing director at Woodside Fund, before we started looking for funding. Bob joined our board of directors and was helping us develop the company. Getting funding was different in 1994/95—back then I thought that you had to have a breakthrough product before you sought funding. We were selling a product and we were bootstrapping the business. Because I was both the technical person and the salesperson I was getting very valuable feedback from our customers. That feedback combined with Bob's encouragement to develop the next generation chip set, and his technical support enabled us to develop a real breakthrough product. The next step was we developed a strong partnership with AMD, a major customer. When we reached this milestone, Bob said it was appropriate for Woodside Fund to lead a financing. So because we had an ongoing relationship with Woodside

Fund, getting funding was relatively easy."

Rick Shriner: "Most important is having developed a relationship with the VC firm or firms. This takes care of the first issue, which is: Do the key players feel right to the VC partner? The key difficulty is building the relationship and getting to know the partner while always reserving a bit more to tell them later. Getting seed money and Series A starts with who you are and your background and then they deal with the creditability of the idea. The Series A for a good team and credible idea is only of moderate difficulty. You need to be sure you can delineate the value proposition and basic positioning of the company and, a well thought out plan to get started is critical. The Series B and follow-on financings are much more difficult as the partners watch, listen, and judge how well you are working to your plan. They look at whether you are overcoming obstacles or not and how you have been dealing with the myriad of problems like hiring strong technical resources in Silicon Valley."

What did you learn from the experience, if you had to do it all over again?

Daniel Fu: "1. It's best to include at least two VC investors—the balance is helpful, and the knowledge base and experience is wider.

"2. There are a lot of third-rate investors. You need to be careful—go with the most reputable VC firms like Woodside Fund, and check references."

Rick Shriner: "What you learn is to watch the money closely, worry a great deal about relationships and company positioning, with a keen eye on economic factors that can influence whether you are worth additional investment or not. An example for HotRail was working out of the server ChipSet arena and into the communications Internet IC category. Positioning great technology into a high-value proposition pays off for the VCs, and they will fund you and back you with increased investment with relative ease of funding when it is right.

"One final thought is that board meetings are of critical importance. They take place every five to eight weeks, and it is imperative that you show significant progress at each meeting and you treat each meeting as if you are asking for more money even though that is months away."

How quickly was the venture fund able to make a decision to invest in your company?

Daniel Fu: "It was fast because we had ongoing relationship with Woodside Fund—that shortened the normal process to just a few weeks."

Rick Shriner: "Get ready to stretch your money and be patient. Whatever date you think the funding will take place or needs to occur, you can be sure it will take four to eight weeks longer to herd all the cats to the same tank even if the fish look attractive. Make sure you have a commercial bank signed on as they will 'bridge' you to till the money comes in. They require less warrants than VCs. The commitment for a decision to move forward is actually pretty fast. Once you meet with them and there is an interest, you hear within one to three weeks and the due diligence process gets intense. When they indicate interest but don't dig at the due diligence, you can bet that they have two to three other priorities that are getting attention and you are the fallback. They have to get their money placed to satisfy their investors, and it is competitive out there. The best situation is when you have multiple VCs and you are very confident of your positioning you can usually get one or two of them to commit early with good levels of investment and then you can carefully work the others into line. Still, expect that it will take longer than you want it to. There is another sidelight to all of this. You have to keep the technical teams' heads down and working and not worrying about the funding. You need to keep them informed but only to the level of them understanding that you are working on it and are confident that it will be there in time. Note, not *on* time but *in* time. An important difference. If you use full disclosure with them you find them analyzing the numbers, the potential funders, suggesting many alternatives, and in general not doing their work. Everyone has a critical role in a start-up and there is not room for volunteering considerable time on other issues."

How did the venture capital firm add value to your business apart from the money?

Daniel Fu: "Woodside Fund added tremendous value from the beginning. They introduced Rick Shriner who became CEO—which was extremely valuable. Woodside Fund knew Rick well because they had worked with him in the past. Rick was CEO right through the merger with Conexant.

"Woodside Fund helped us shape the company's strategy and helped us develop our funding strategy. Bob Larson was a very important part of the team dynamic in that he was very good at helping us work out issues and disagreements—he was respectful, patient, and always a gentleman.

"Also, when we were at a very critical stage—we were running out of money—Woodside Fund, in addition to providing ongoing financial support with other members of the syndicate, introduced us to an investor (who is now a Woodside Fund limited partner) and encouraged them to invest an additional $5 million, which they did."

Rick Shriner: "The biggest help to an experienced team is connections to other VCs, industry pundits, potential customers, other start-ups that are likely synergistic with your technology, technical and management hiring. They can get you through the door, or to a candidate, but you still have to have a story and positioning to close them. For the less experienced team, which is often more commonly found, they can find 'Gray-Haired Talent,' and they can provide initial training in some aspect that you may be unfamiliar with or get you to the right sources to solve your problem. Remember that they want you to succeed and will move mountains if required to help get you what will in the end benefit them."

Vincent M. Occhipinti: "Woodside Fund was impressed with the enthusiasm and technological genius of Daniel Fu and his familiarity with the industry. What Daniel needed was mentoring and coaching to develop the next-generation technology. We felt that Woodside Fund could be his partner in forming the company by providing guidance in the development of the company's strategy and helping to secure a strategic partnership for HotRail.

"To Daniel's credit, he was receptive to bringing in complementary skills. We introduced Daniel to Rick Shriner, who became the CEO. Rick had been an executive at Intel, Apple, and we got to know him when he was CEO of one of our portfolio companies.

"We then made a list of what other investors would be well suited to participate. We brought in Gordon Campbell of TechFund. He was one of the founders of the concept of the 'fabless semi-conductor.' We felt he could make a significant contribution to the team and he became a valued partner in the first round of funding, which totaled $7.2 million.

"It is expected that start-ups will have more than one challenge on the road to success. HotRail had a number of challenges—including financial and technological hurdles. We feel our advice, support, and patience helped HotRail's management succeed. We really believe that a strong management team carries as much importance as our involvement in the success of a start-up, since they are the ones who must execute."

How was the venture capital company to work with in good times, and then in difficult times, at your company?

Daniel Fu: "What's important is that we could count on Woodside Fund in the most difficult times—both Bob Larson and Vincent Occhipinti contributed to our development."

Rick Shriner: "In the good times they are reactive and ready to help but only as you need it. They do provide plenty of suggestions but pretty much monitor and let you roll. In difficult times they are there and more interactive. They will ask more questions and listen intently, and expect that you will seek them out with plans, thoughts, and requests. Remember, a venture often has more than one partner with other investments. They will have assessed your situation, decided how far they will go, and generally not tell you all that. They expect that you will fight even harder than they will to keep going.

"When we had major funding problems at HotRail due to technology geared around AMD, who was getting deeper in trouble, and a semiconductor industry that was in the tank (1997–98), Woodside in particular stayed close and brought us Ontario Teacher's Pension Plan Fund to review our situation. We in turn supported Woodside's need for investment in their LLP, and they supported us strongly. In the end we got the funding and ultimately everyone won. This brings up the key synergistic relationship between the start-up and the VC. When you are supportive in both directions you stand a better chance of survival and ultimate payoff than otherwise. Remember that funding buys time. Time is what every start-up needs to discover where the real value is for their technology. I don't think anyone starts and finishes on the same plan. You go through many transitions, and it is the team's ability to adapt and change that ultimately determines the level of the finish or victory."

Could you describe your working relationship with Woodside? How often did you talk to the partner in the firm?

Daniel Fu: "It's a very close relationship. I would talk to Bob every other week unless something big was going on. He was always accessible when we wanted to talk."

Rick Shriner: "This was how I did it but, frankly, I think it works. First rule for the CEO is call the investors often, before they call you. On your board, pick two or three key partners and make it a point to keep them up to speed either weekly or biweekly. Talk with them three or four times between board meetings. Talk about status, challenges, personnel concerns, money, money, money, and most of all develop a relationship of trust. Remember whose money you are spending. Don't ask the partners to call each other. Call them and when necessary e-mail all of them or get them together on a conference call. Don't intentionally or unintentionally leave one of them out unless they can't be reached or said okay. Know what you are saying and why before you call them or sit down with them. They sense quickly that you have a direction and 9 out of 10 times will go with your recommendation as long as you demonstrate you have thought it through. Remember that you are the leader and they are the advisor and want to play that role. In the case of Woodside, I was on the phone with Bob Larson often. With Bob, I felt I had that level of trust that I could let him hear the good and the bad and how I saw it or felt about it. He could then provide back his sage advice based on having been there without me worrying that I said too much. It just worked and the chemistry was good."

You elected to have your company acquired as an exit rather than going public. Why was this a better choice for your company and its investors?

Daniel Fu: "HotRail did not approach the investment bankers to sell the company at first. We did sign up an investment banking firm for an IPO. However, some strategic partners approached HotRail about acquiring us. Conexant was one of the potential acquirers. The management team presented the opportunity to our board. That led to multiple rounds of negotiations with multiple potential acquiring companies. Conexant emerged as the winner."

Rick Shriner: "There were a lot of things that went into the decision. The primary one was that the technology that we had developed was fundamental and entailed a lot of IP which meant the risks of getting to a profitable customer base and the IPO were still quite high. At the same time it was newly repositioned into the 'hot' communications IC marketplace, which raised the company value substantially for the right acquirer. In the end, when Conexant realized where we could help them, they bid a sufficiently high number of shares of Conexant to swing the vote by the current VC investors to okay being acquired. It was also clear that in our space most of the technology was being purchased by the larger companies as they rapidly positioned themselves against their competition. The real question was not to be acquired or not, but when? We had been talked to in the summer of 1999 and chose to push it away and build value in the company. This turned out to be the right answer. Possibly, we could also have held off till late 2000, but the stock market, the election, semiconductor industry economics could have reduced our value while still moving forward. In the end, you check your gut and decide."

Vincent M. Occhipinti: "Prior to April 2000, we were predisposed to working toward an IPO exit within one year. However, with the market caps declining significantly after April 2000—and there were still significant technology risks—when we were presented with very attractive opportunities to exit with a high valuation, we decided the merger was the best alternative. The returns to investors were outstanding and everyone benefited—management, founder, investors, employees. With a valuation in the $400 million range, most investors made a minimum of five to 10 times return on their investment in less that three years' time."

How long was the venture capital firm your partner before you sold the company?

Daniel Fu: "The relationship began in 1995 when Bob Larson and I started working together. Vince and Bob knew our CEO, Rick Shriner, starting in 1995 when Rick was a CEO of one of Woodside Fund's portfolio companies."

Rick Shriner: "Woodside had been a near partner or close partner of HotRail for approximately four years. Their substantial investment tracked to about three years."

Any words of encouragement to your fellow entrepreneurs who are looking for capital now?

Daniel Fu: "If you feel that you can make a contribution to an industry, or if you have a dream, write down your ideas and talk to a good venture capitalist—seek advice and possibly funding."

Rick Shriner: "Get your story and positioning right. Test it with experts that you can find and talk with. Find ways to meet the VCs. Expect to have to work 10 to 15 of them to find one to two that fit and like your story. Be patient and build your relationship before pushing for the close. After getting the money, remember where it came from and nurture the relationship."

Final Thoughts:
You Can Get There from Here

Ways to Improve Your Chances of Obtaining Capital

- Put together a strong, experienced management team with people who have been successful in the past.

- Research the investment criteria of the venture capitalists to ensure that what you offer is what they are looking for.

- Use every method you can think of to reach potential investors. Don't rely simply on referrals, or on contacting them yourself, or on an intermediary to find the capital for you.

- Hone your market research and analysis skills. Systematically gather information on your competitors, so that you can make a credible case for why your product/service offering will be better.

- Put together a clear, concise, realistic business plan that gets the reader excited about the opportunity your company presents. The plan must not only cover what you are going to do but *how* you are going to do it.

- Let other experienced businesspeople read and critique your plan, testing it for clarity and reasonableness. Never send a first draft to the venture capitalists. Proofread it a number of times.
- Keep trying, don't give up. Continually widen your network of contacts to give you more avenues of approach to investors.
- *And don't forget to put your name and phone number in the business plan, so the investor can call you!*

Skills and Traits of Successful Fund Raisers

- Networking ability, in order to find a large enough pool of prospective investors
- Communications skill, to be able to tell investors a compelling story about your company's potential
- The judgment necessary to recognize a fair deal and turn down an unfair one
- The tenacity it takes to put up with rejection and dead ends, and begin again with enthusiasm and dedication
- The patience to allow the funding sources to complete their due diligence
- A flair for the creative give-and-take of negotiating

Let's profile the techniques used by an entrepreneur who has been successful at raising capital and compare him or her to the person who does not meet with success:

Successful Entrepreneur	Unsuccessful Entrepreneur
Targets partners whose investment parameters fit his company well	Uses scattershot approach
Gregarious networker always building contacts	Hires a finder and hopes for the best
Prepares thorough presentation on company	Tries to "wing it" in meetings with investors
Allows at least six months to complete process	Starts when money is needed "yesterday"

Flexible and creative in negotiations	Rigidly sticks to a given deal structure
Openly discusses positives and risks of business	Tries to keep investors in the dark
Willing to keep partners involved	Seeks complete autonomy

This is not to say that every person who does all the steps in the first column will automatically receive funding and the person who acts like the one in the second column will not; the idea is to do everything you can to improve your odds of being funded, and you swing the odds decidedly in your favor by using the tactics in the first column.

Conclusion

If you have read each chapter of this book, you have heard the words of hundreds of people deeply involved in the private equity markets—those who have the precious capital and those who desperately need it. These voices offered very different perspectives and opinions on the process of raising venture capital and the state of the venture capital industry. The voice that summed it up for all of us was the venture capitalist in Chapter 2 who said, "It's a great time to be an entrepreneur!"

It certainly is. Private funding of early-stage companies is at last beginning to move toward functioning as an efficient market, providing entrepreneurs with increased access to more money and more "brain power" than ever before. Innovative approaches such as angel networks and business incubators are popping up in communities throughout the United States.

In a way, though, this marketplace has not changed that much at all. It still seems to take more time and effort to find money than it should, from the perspective of most entrepreneurs. And we can view raising capital successfully as having some of the same components as entrepreneurship itself. You must have the ability to take risks, and you must work with and trust in the abilities and honorable intentions of other people.

And just as with starting a company, the outcome is unpredictable. The best efforts at raising capital may bear no fruit, with the serious consequences of lost market opportunities for the entrepreneur, even the potential of going out of business altogether. Others find that perfect financial partner after just a few days or weeks of networking.

Some of the maxims we have been taught have turned out to be myths:

- The venture capitalist you meet with has just as much chance of being an engineer as a financier.
- Venture capitalists do not limit themselves to talking only to entrepreneurs who have been referred to them by someone they know. It's not such a good old boy network after all.
- Valuing an early-stage company does not require 25 pages of spreadsheets. It is a meeting of the minds between a reasonable entrepreneur and a reasonable investor, helped along by some relatively simple formulas.
- Angel investors are not in the game just for the money but for the satisfaction they receive from helping companies succeed.

In fact, investors have a zeal for the task of building companies that certainly equals that of the entrepreneurs themselves. The return on energy invested seems as valuable as the return on capital invested.

We have also seen that just as the Internet changed free enterprise throughout the world, it may well change the financing of private companies in just as sweeping a fashion.

What stands out most, however, is how very different investors are. There is no such thing, really, as "the VCs" or "the angels." When we take a close look at them, they form a broad, extremely colorful spectrum, just like the entrepreneurs. There really is an investor to fit every company, to meet an entrepreneur's every advisory or mentoring need. The challenge remains to find them.

The other side of the argument is that there are not really very many absolute truths entrepreneurs can rely on to prepare themselves for seeking capital or to guarantee success. Investors did not completely agree on what constitutes a winning business plan, for example. Our debunked myth about not necessarily needing a referral to get in front of investors was still a set-in-stone maxim for a significant number of VCs. Be referred to us or forget it, they said.

When you study all of the opinions in this book, you are also left with the conclusion that much work needs to be done to make the private equity market truly meet the needs of the entrepreneur.

The inability of venture capital firms to keep up with the volume of entrepreneurs contacting them has, unintentionally in many cases, created an impression that they are rude. They advertise themselves as being in the business of providing financial and intellectual capital to entrepreneurs but often ignore potential "customers" when they try to contact a significant decision maker in the firm.

Entrepreneurs need to improve their professionalism as well. They waste an incredible amount of the time at venture capital firms simply by contacting the wrong firms because they do not take the time to find out whether their company fits the investment parameters of that firm. Since most firms now have web sites, there really is no excuse for not knowing what firms' interests are before you contact them.

We recently received a handwritten letter asking us whether we wanted to invest in a real estate project in New Mexico. We have no idea what the entrepreneur was thinking when he licked that stamp. He said he wanted to grow herbs that might cure cancer. Maybe he thought we were into biotech investing. Or farming?

Despite the increased focus of the news media on the challenges of raising capital, there is still a lack of general knowledge about the nuts and bolts of this process and not enough blueprints of success for entrepreneurs to follow. Venture capitalists need to increase their efforts to get this information out to entrepreneurs through the media.

Angel networks provide the highly useful service of allowing entrepreneurs into the "arena," letting them meet a number of investors at once. Why are there not more of these around the country?

We still face geographic inefficiencies in venture capital: Capital flows as if from inexhaustible underground springs in Silicon Valley but dribbles along like a defective playground drinking fountain in parts of the Southwest and the Midwest. Given all this, though, the private capital markets in the United States today can be characterized as offering:

- More money
- More highly qualified people to advise and mentor entrepreneurs
- More tools to help entrepreneurs find investors
- More mechanisms to bring investors and entrepreneurs together

So let's revisit our conclusion: It's a great time to be an entrepreneur! And it is entirely likely that the best is yet to come.

23

Words of Encouragement
and Advice

Words of Encouragement from Entrepreneurs Who Found Venture Capital

"The key for us was selling the company, not the product. Investors have to understand the vision and how it will be achieved. They want to know how you are going to attract the talent it takes to build a Tier 1 company. They want to know that you've completely thought through what your long-term financing requirements will be. They want to know how you will scale the company from startup to long-term success. Clever product ideas come and go. Solid companies will last forever.

"If you don't have the experience to flesh out your plans and to sell at this level, find experienced help to do it. You won't be successful building a company, let alone getting funding, without it. If you don't have the network of sales, marketing, finance, and other professionals to draw on to get started, you aren't ready to play the game. Start networking now to build your formal and informal

support infrastructure. It will take time, but you will need the time to hone your plan and your skills. The opportunities for launching a new business aren't going away soon."

Brian Hoover, President, TouchScape Corporation,
www.touchscape.com

"Investors fall into four categories: (1) Yourself, your friends, and your family; (2) angels, vendors and professional advisors; (3) corporations investing for the future; (4) investment advisors, a.k.a. venture capitalists. The first three groups invest 'their own money' for fun and profit, and the fourth group invests their clients' money for commissions and fees on a performance basis. If you really believe in what you propose, you will invest your own money and give your friends and family a chance to get in on a good thing first. If not, try to sell your lack of confidence to the others! They are always impressed when the first investors come from group 1 and 2. The logic is that you will work hard to make the venture work and will not quit!"

Owen P. Doonan III, Chairman, THE-Group,
The Handicapable Executive Group, Duxbury, MA

"Like any market for buyers and sellers, understand what the other side is trying to do and make sure you understand what you are trying to do. We are the beneficiaries of a very successful time with much larger amounts of flexible financial resources than only a few short years ago. Investors have incredible pressure to place these resources to work as soon as possible while not compromising the investment objectives. If investors cannot understand the opportunity quickly, they will move to the next opportunity as they have no time to spend on defining the opportunity. It's the entrepreneur's job to do this. A concise description along with quality support data on the market and financials that is easy to read will get the investor's attention. Also, the more flexibility the entrepreneur has (i.e., type of investment, exit strategies, growth objectives, etc.), the larger the investor audience. Finally, do your homework on the marketplace related to investment value for your opportunity and be reasonable with the dilution of ownership, thinking from the investor's point of view. Otherwise, time is wasted on both sides."

Bill Dawson, entrepreneur

"Three things: hard work, hard work, hard work."

Roberto Guerrieri, CEO, UGIVE.COM

"Building a company has been the best experience of my life! Talk to as many VCs as you can before making your final decision. You learn something new from each and every VC you speak with. VCs hold a huge wealth of information that they are willing to share with you. Get as much of it as you can! Don't rush or panic with the first term sheet on hand. Don't take 'not interested' personally. Many times VCs don't invest in you because of their lack of interest or knowledge in that specific area. Try to find someone who can introduce you to a VC. It makes a big difference if you can say that someone referred you. Don't be scared or intimated by them. They are usually extremely nice and friendly. The VC you are going to choose will be your long-time partner, so make sure you enjoy each other's company. Never give up, work hard, and have FUN!"

Taraneh Derak, CEO/President, Yubé, Inc., www.yube.com

"Don't give up and remember that you never know where you might find the money. In my case, I actually found someone in the industry I was going after willing to fund the company."

Gary A. Pudles, President, AnswerNet, Inc.
www.AnswerNetNetwork.com

"Understand your business, your customers, why your product/solution is valuable, how it is differentiated, how you will make a profit, how you will enable your business to scale, how your business will remain differentiated in the future."

Austin Erlick, entrepreneur

"If you have an idea for a business that truly creates significant value, you will be able to find funding. The tricks are: a) to develop a sound business plan. b) to concentrate on finding the right match, i.e., the right VC for your business taking into account things like their: geographic focus, average size of investment, investment philosophy/objectives focus in terms of company stage, other portfolio companies, etc. In this sense, finding funding is very much of a marketing exercise, i.e., figuring out the right 'consumer' for your concept. c) to persevere."

Steve Tsai, CEO, ActBig, Inc., www.actbig.com

Words of Encouragement from Venture Capitalists

"We live in a time of highly justified entrepreneurial exuberance. There is more capital available for technology start-ups than at any other time in history. Busi-

ness opportunities to build major life-changing enterprises abound, based on fundamental shifts in technology. The type of creativity where one can 'think outside the box' and devise practical business solutions will be rewarded with incredible wealth creation. Entrepreneurs who work the hardest and are most persistent will have the most luck in raising capital and building successful companies."

Larry Kubal, Managing Director, Labrador Ventures, www.labrador.com

"Raising money is hard work and usually takes twice as long than you think it will. Be organized and thoughtful through the process, and surround yourself with the best people you can as your core founding team. Leverage every contact you can to get access to the venture community."

Jim Marshall, General Partner, Selby Venture Partners,
www.selbyventures.com

"Look at every no answer as an opportunity for free consulting from some of the brightest minds in industry. Suck the brains of the VCs who turn you down, and you'll both dramatically improve your chances of getting a yes from the next VC and improve your chances for real success!"

Gerry Langeler, OVP Venture Partners, www.ovp.com

"Raising capital is the least interesting part of business. Even VCs don't like raising capital. It's hard. If you concentrate on writing a crisp executive summary, there's a lot of capital available. It's a matter of using their network to find investors. If a person has a crisp executive summary and is active in networking, they can be confident they will be funded by someone. Now, they have to remain flexible, though. Great ideas, with a crisp summary, can get money."

Dennis Spice, Managing Partner, Open Prairie Ventures, www.opven.com

"We scan hundreds of business plans every month, and if the first page doesn't clearly describe what the company does and why it is interesting, I don't read further. If a business can't communicate to potential investors, why should I assume it communicates any better with customers?

"I recommend strongly that entrepreneurs place themselves in venture capitalists' shoes. Feed us the information that we'll need to be comfortable in approving an investment. Think of it as if you were a marketing executive arming a sales force to launch a new product—provide a compelling story and strong support such that making a decision is easy."

Steve Payne, General Partner, The Ignite Group, www.ignitegroup.com

"This may sound trite but persistence is the key—never give up—don't take no for an answer. Leave 100 voice-mails on a venture capitalist's voice-mail machine—they will call you back just to get rid of you. There is enough money out there, so someone has to spend it. Come up with some creative reason why you, as an individual, are better than all the other entrepreneurs out there. Humor can be an advantage."

Chris Young, Partner, New England Partners, www.nepartners.com

"Two words: polite persistence. Because of the number of opportunities that we are confronted with, it is very difficult to get our attention. If you persist through e-mail, voice, and any other means you can think of, you have a better chance of getting your plan read and it also gives us an indication that you will get the job done, whatever the job may be."

Bernhardt Zeisig, Partner, VIMAC, Venture Investment
Management Company LLC, www.vimac.com

"Make sure you recruit a strong management team to run the company. If it is a start-up, you must have people who have successfully done it before. If you do not fit these qualifications then find a CEO that does."

Michael Mahoney, CFO, Wind Point Partners,
www.Windpointpartners.com

"Know your business plan forward and backward—because you will be grilled on it. Even if you're not financially oriented, make sure you have someone with an understanding of the finances present to explain assumptions and financial projections.

"Market, people, competition (existing and potential), competitive advantage and barriers, financing—are all critical things that VCs want to know about.

"Anticipate that the VC knows little or nothing about your company.

"Power Point slide show is great, but whatever the case, have some presentation prepared—tell a story. Plan to keep the meeting to no more than an hour."

Kevin Gabelein, Managing Director, Fluke Venture Partners,
www.flukeventures.com

"Assemble the most credible, talented, dedicated, and honorable team that you can, and find a venture funding source that will add the most value to your business. Trust your gut instincts, as early-stage venture investing and investments are much more of an art than a science. Be persistent and confident in your approach without being rude, cocky, or offensive. If your idea has merit, it will get funded."

Keith Bank, Managing Director, KB Partners, LLC, www.kbpartners.com

"Find the right way to get to people, using networks and resourcefulness, and not blindly sending out your business plan."

Larry Phillips, Managing Director, Primedia Ventures,
www.primediaventures.com

"An entrepreneur seeking funding has one of the hardest jobs. You must have perseverance and determination. Your ultimate goal must be to get the venture capitalist to see your view of the world. It is crucial for the entrepreneur to get in front of the decision makers. Don't give up and do not let the word no stop you from pursuing your dream—pursue it with even more resolve. Asking others to fund your company requires a special kind of courage. Be proud that your courage takes you to a higher plane of existence."

Dennis J. Dougherty, General Partner,
Intersouth Partners, www.intersouth.com

Index

Printed in the United States
34110LVS00002BC/13-15